LIBRARY
OF
MESMERISM
AND
PSYCHOLOGY.

IN TWO VOLUMES.

COMPRISING

Philosophy of Mesmerism,   Electrical Psychology,
On Fascination,   The Macrocosm.
        Science of the Soul.

" All are the parts of one stupendous whole,
Whose Body Nature is, and God the Soul."

VOL. II.

NEW YORK:
PUBLISHED BY SAMUEL R. WELLS,
No. 389 BROADWAY.

Kessinger Publishing's
Rare Mystical Reprints

THOUSANDS OF SCARCE BOOKS
ON THESE AND OTHER SUBJECTS:

Freemasonry * Akashic * Alchemy * Alternative Health * Ancient Civilizations * Anthroposophy * Astrology * Astronomy * Aura * Bible Study * Cabalah * Cartomancy * Chakras * Clairvoyance * Comparative Religions * Divination * Druids * Eastern Thought * Egyptology * Esoterism * Essenes * Etheric * ESP * Gnosticism * Great White Brotherhood * Hermetics * Kabalah * Karma * Knights Templar * Kundalini * Magic * Meditation * Mediumship * Mesmerism * Metaphysics * Mithraism * Mystery Schools * Mysticism * Mythology * Numerology * Occultism * Palmistry * Pantheism * Parapsychology * Philosophy * Prosperity * Psychokinesis * Psychology * Pyramids * Qabalah * Reincarnation * Rosicrucian * Sacred Geometry * Secret Rituals * Secret Societies * Spiritism * Symbolism * Tarot * Telepathy * Theosophy * Transcendentalism * Upanishads * Vedanta * Wisdom * Yoga * *Plus Much More!*

DOWNLOAD A FREE CATALOG
AND
SEARCH OUR TITLES AT:

www.kessinger.net

THE PHILOSOPHY

OF

ELECTRICAL PSYCHOLOGY:

IN A COURSE OF

TWELVE LECTURES.

BY JOHN BOVEE DODS.

STEREOTYPE EDITION.

NEW YORK:
SAMUEL R. WELLS, 389 BROADWAY.
1871.

Entered, according to act of Congress, in the year 1850, by

C. P. DODS,

in the Clerk's Office of the District Court for the Southern District of New York

DEDICATION

TO G. C. MARCHANT, M.D

My Dear Sir—For twenty years past I have been intimately acquainted with you, and I enjoy the pleasing reflection that we have, during that entire period, remained warm, personal friends. Fully sensible of your sterling integrity and honor as a man and a distinguished American citizen, and sensible that the science of Electrical Psychology will prove to be most deeply interesting to your discerning and gifted mind, and that you will love, honor, and cherish it as you do the other sciences of the day with which you have become familiar; and having so often and deeply felt your friendship in acts of kindness, I claim the favor, as an expression of my confidence in your goodness, and also in your medical skill, to dedicate this work to you. You will perceive that I have intentionally written it in a fanciful style, so as to make it pleasing to readers in general; and surely you, as a critic, will overlook this, as I have also endeavored to please the scholar by throwing out before him a fair and liberal specimen of original thought. As such it is most respectfully inscribed to you by your sincere friend,

J. B. DODS.

CONTENTS.

	PAGES
DEDICATION,	3
INTRODUCTION,	9-13

LECTURE I.

ELECTRICAL PSYCHOLOGY—ITS DEFINITION, AND IMPORTANCE IN CURING DISEASES, ... 15-32

Invitation by members of United States Senate to lecture on the Science of Electrical Psychology—Man should use his reason—His space is small, yet his power extends to other worlds—The greatness and majesty of Nature—Her mysterious operations—Man a progressive being—Author's reference to his Mesmeric Lectures—Has for twenty years argued electricity to be the connecting link between mind and matter—Letter from Hon. Richard D. Davis, with editorial remarks on the mysterious nature of the experiments—Hiram Bostwick, Esq., cured of palsy—Two girls cured of deafness—Lady restored to speech and sight—Editorial advice to physicians to learn this Science—Resolutions of Dr. Dods' class of forty-five persons in favor of this Science—A lady cured who had not walked for eighteen years—Distinction between Mesmerism and Electrical Psychology.

LECTURE II.

BEAUTY OF INDEPENDENT THOUGHT AND FEARLESS EXPRESSION, ... 33-48

Electrical Psychology has claims to philosophy—Its strangeness awakens the deepest feelings of contempt among skeptics—Those who scoff and sneer have received their ideas by inheritance, without labor, as they did their estate—Such, though learned, are the greatest enemies of science—The march of intellect—Improvements of the day—The chariot of science commenced its career at the morning of creation, with but few on board, and will continue to roll on without end—Its passengers here are mortals; in eternity, immortals—The variety and richness of the intellectual and moral field—Use of the school and college—Divines should not fear science—It cannot destroy the Bible—Creation successive—Its vastness—All sciences have been opposed, and their discoverers persecuted — Harvey — Galileo — Newton — Fulton — Gall — Spurzheim — Combe — The Fowlers, of New York — Men should seek for true fame, and not a momentary popularity—True fame defined—A specimen of it in the example of Christ.

LECTURE III.

CONNECTING LINK BETWEEN MIND AND MATTER, AND CIRCULATION OF THE BLOOD, ... 49–64

Let not opposition surprise—The characters from whom it comes are pointed out—Immutability of truth—It cannot be affected by the belief or unbelief of men—Electrical theory of the universe—Electricity eternal—The agent employed by the Creator to move globes and carry on the operations of nature—It is a universal agent, and the cause of light, heat, vegetation, twilight, evaporation, storms, earthquakes, and hurricanes—Man an epitome of the universe—All substances in him—Mind has both voluntary and involuntary powers—Brain is the fountain of the nervous system—Mind the cause of all motion, and can touch nothing but electricity—From mind to dead matter is seven links—Mind holds its royal throne in the brain, and executes its commands through electricity, its prime minister—Circulation of the blood—Its philosophy is new—Heart, with its ventricles and auricles—Why nerves attend the arteries and not the veins—How the brain is supplied with electricity—Why arterial blood is cherry-red, and venous blood purple.

LECTURE IV.

PHILOSOPHY OF DISEASE AND NERVOUS FORCE, 65–81

Circulation of the blood concluded—Circulating system is two systems—Arterial blood is *positive*, venous blood is *negative*—The notion refuted that the heart circulates the blood and exerts a force of 100,000 pounds—The heart is moved by the involuntary force of the cerebellum—The blood is moved by the *positive* and *negative* forces of electricity taken in at the lungs by inspiration—Philosophy of disease—One cause only for all diseases—Diseases do not originate in the blood, but in the electricity of the nerves—They begin in the finest invisible substance in the body and end in the grossest—All convulsions in nature begin and end thus—Blood not rendered impure by foreign substances carried into it, but by being thrown out of balance in its circulation—Diseases caused by mental or physical impressions—Disease settles upon the weakest organ or part of the body—Nervous fluid thrown out of balance is disease, and when equalized is health—Half of the nervous fluid is under the voluntary control of the mind—The other half is not

LECTURE V.

CURE OF DISEASE AND BEING ACCLIMATED, . . 82–91

Philosophy of disease—Mental and physical impressions—Rationale of its cure—Man riding—Head aches—Meets a robber—Headache cured—The healing principle is in us, not in medicine—Equalize circulation by nervous force—Emetics do not

PAGE

possess the vomiting principle—Vomiting is produced by nervous force—Examples and proof—Diseases cured by mental impressions, even though caused by physical impression—Medicines produce physical results—Example of a peach-tree—Physicians should state to the patients what medicines they administer—How to preserve health—Bathings—No disease cured by an opposite—Philosophy of becoming acclimated—Mineral and vegetable kingdoms—Man a vegetable of second growth—All vegetables and animals adapted to their climates—Foreign substances should not be eaten—Change of our flesh and bones—Clothing adapted to climate—God has not erred in disposing the vegetable substances over the globe—Truth immutable.

LECTURE VI.
EXISTENCE OF DEITY PROVED FROM MOTION, . 99–118

Reason fearless of consequences—The power of electricity—Its awful manifestations—Nothing compared with Deity—Spirit supposed to be immaterial, but is not—Supposed to be the result of mechanism, but is not—Dr. Priestly—Atheists—The resurrection—Spirit is a substance—Electricity is universal—Mind is the opposite of dead matter—Body and nature compared—Each organ has but one function—The chain of elementary substances considered, from the heaviest up to the lightest—Only one substance has motion, this is mind—The unseen is the reality, the visible is not—The tree is an outshoot from the invisible life of the seed—All powers are in the unseen substances—Earthquakes—Man and nature alike—Involuntary powers of mind—Involuntary powers of God—His voluntary powers create—His involuntary govern through established laws—God's voluntary powers cannot be thwarted, his involuntary can—First human pair—Difference between being born and created—The acorn and the oak, which was first—Geology—Creation and government of the globe—Premature deaths argued—Two brains—Voluntary and involuntary powers—The office of each proved by preparing food and eating it.

LECTURE VII.
SUBJECT OF CREATION CONSIDERED, ... 119–147

All motion originates in mind—Thought is not mind—Creation is a vast subject—Man's right to reason on any subject—Worlds made out of electricity—Nothing cannot be made into something—Apostle Paul—Bible sense of *create*—Something must be eternal—God, space, and duration considered—Philosophical necessity—Electricity is the body of God—Each animated body is an outshoot from mind—God's mind is not omnipresent, his body is—Mind is form—The serpent—The lobster—All feeling in mind—Amputations—How mind moves the body—

One hundred elements—Mode of creation—Gradually from the invisible to the visible forms—Boyle—Bishop Watson—Requires electricity, out of which the globe was made, to govern it—One hundred cords fastened on one hundred elements in electricity—Positive and negative forces—Ultimates and primates—Gold and phosphate of lime—Sun is electricity—Philosophy of twilight—The globe not yet finished—Newton—Comets—Elliptical orbits—Volcanoes—Philosophy of variation of the compass—The globe yet in its embryo—When finished—What future generations will say of us.

LECTURE VIII.

DOCTRINE OF IMPRESSIONS, ... 136-151

Creation and Electrical Psychology—All substances in man—It requires electricity, out of which he was made, to govern him—Philosophy of digestion—Chyle, serum, blood, flesh, tendons, bones—Positive and negative forces—Blood the universal solvent of the body as water is of the globe—The brain—Stomach—One hundred elements—Law of equilibrium—Nature like man is thrown out of balance and becomes sick—Hurricane and tornado—Rheumatisms and broken bones preceding a storm—Thunder storms—Cause of hail—Earthquakes—Earth may have a bowel complaint—Volcanoes—Eruptions—Nature is cured by her own impressions, and so is man—Sleeping in unhealthy climates—Keep positive to surrounding impressions—Citizens of Charleston, S.C.—Country fever—Dr. Mason Good—Fear—Cholera—Salem witchcraft—Pleading guilty—Danger of executing persons on their own confessions—Judges and jurors.

LECTURE IX.

CONNECTION BETWEEN THE VOLUNTARY AND INVOLUNTARY NERVES, ... 152-161

Electricity the connecting link between mind and inert matter—Goose pimples on the arm—Insulated stool—Nerves are magnetic—Electrometer—Why mind removes warts, king's-evil, or tumors—Dr. Warren, of Boston—Electro-nervous fluid heals—Why it heals—The voluntary and involuntary powers—Throne of the mind—Each person has two distinct brains through which the mind acts—Connection between the voluntary and involuntary nerves—How one may affect the other—Death occasioned by the want of sleep—Death is the sleep of the involuntary powers—Suspended animation in alligators, toads, serpents, raccoons, etc.—Suspended animation in some human beings for several days—Its philosophy or cause—Danger of premature interments—A man in New Jersey, his case stated—The circulating and nervous systems compared—The mind's throne in the medulla oblongata—Philosophy of natural sleep—Conclusion—Poetry on Hope.

healthy climates—Keep positive to surrounding impressions—Citizens of Charleston, S. C.—Country fever—Dr. Mason Good—Fear—Cholera—Salem witchcraft—Pleading guilty—Danger of executing persons on their own confessions—Judges and jurors.

LECTURE IX.

CONNECTION BETWEEN THE VOLUNTARY AND INVOLUNTARY NERVES, ... 164-130

Electricity the connecting link between mind and inert matter—Goose pimples on the arm—Insulated stool—Nerves are magnetic—Electrometer—Why mind removes warts, king's evil, or tumors—Dr. Warren, of Boston—Electro-nervous fluid heals—Why it heals—The voluntary and involuntary powers—Throne of the mind—Each person has two distinct brains through which the mind acts—Connection between the voluntary and involuntary nerves—How one may affect the other—Death occasioned by the want of sleep—Death is the sleep of the involuntary powers—Suspended animation in alligators, toads, serpents, raccoons, etc.—Suspended animation in some human beings for several days—Its philosophy or cause—Danger of premature interments—A man in New Jersey, his case stated—The circulating and nervous systems compared—The mind's throne in the medulla oblongata—Philosophy of natural sleep—Conclusion.

LECTURE X.

ELECTRO-CURAPATHY IS THE BEST MEDICAL SYSTEM IN BEING, AS IT INVOLVES THE EXCELLENCES OF ALL OTHER SYSTEMS, ... 181-198

Electrical Psychology is in its infancy—The power it is destined to exert over disease in coming ages—It is the most sublime system of philosophy in existence—Excels astronomy and geology, which are great—Its importance not realized—It uses safe remedies—Discards poisons—It takes its medicines from the fields of nature where the patient lives—Animals do the same—The different medical systems noticed—They should all be combined in one system of Curapathy—Hydropathy considered—Aeriapathy considered—Electricity, galvanism, and magnetism are useful—Called Electropathy—Terrapathy considered, or earth cures—Earths should be applied to the system in various forms, particularly in inflammations—Man needs but little medicine—Attention to food as to quantity and quality is about all he needs—Why Terrapathy cures is argued—Difficult to solve—Can physicians tell why any medicine cures?—Instinct of the rattlesnake to cure himself when bitten—A negro, on being bitten, ate the same plant and was cured—Most of the valuable medicines were discovered by old country women, old hunters, and Indians, and not by doctors—With much opposition they were forced to adopt them—Their opposition to Peruvian bark, the virtues of which were discovered by monks—The clergy opposed it—A state of health and disease considered—Negative and positive forces considered—Positive electricity belongs to the air, negative to the earth—There are positive and negative diseases—How cured—Herbs are the eldest born children of mother earth—They always hang upon her breast—Clay poultices—The body buried in soils—Instances where Terrapathy has cured—The Master and the blind man—The clay and spittle—Absorbent power of earths—Sting of a bee cured—Grease spots, how removed from silks or woolens—The scent of a skunk removed from clothes by earth—The cause of this considered, and the supremacy of Electro-Psychological Curapathy shown over all medical systems in being.

LECTURE XI.

THE SECRET REVEALED, SO THAT ALL MAY KNOW HOW TO EXPERIMENT WITHOUT AN INSTRUCTOR, ... 199–232

As this science involves all medical systems, and embraces other agents besides, so it should be understood by all—Doctors should understand it—It often saves life when medicines fail—It can be thoroughly learned and practically understood in ten hours—Dr. Dods will teach it if preferred—He is located in New York—Will attend to imparting instruction and lecturing abroad, if invited—Ignorant persons have gone abroad pretending to teach it for ten dollars, for two dollars, and some for twenty-five cents—Some have changed its name to that of Electro-Biology—To prevent imposition the secret is revealed—How can those teach its philosophy and its application to disease who are ignorant of the human system?—More is here taught than by any lecturers—God has stamped simplicity on his works—Each organ of the body performs but one function—There is but one nerve through which ideas are transmitted to the mind—Ideas are successive, not simultaneous—We can not attend to two public speakers at once—The mind has a spiritual brain and spiritual organs—The nerve through which impressions are communicated to the mind is located in the organ of Individuality—All the organs are double—This nerve has infinite branches to all the voluntary parts of the body to communicate motion—A pebble thrown into Lake Superior—Its illustration—Philosophy of sympathy—Personal identity—The brain is the earthly house—To control a person, a communication must first be established;-either by or without contact—The philosophy of communication in general—Positive and negative forces of male and female electricity—Every one has his electric circle—One in twenty-five is naturally in the psychological state—The various modes of taking communication—But one way after all—Directions given—The grips—The

CONTENTS.

PAGES

Ulnar, or Cubital Nerve—The Median Nerve—Both are compound nerves—The Median Nerve is the best for communication—Its branches connect with the five senses—Various directions given how to experiment—Effects produced upon the subject—The coin described, and how to use it—The number of sittings—Other substances may be used—The science divided into five plans—Mesmerism is No. 1—The gripe No. 2—The coin No. 3—The experiments No. 4—And its application to curing the diseases of those not in the state is No. 5—Each of these plans explained—Directions how to mesmerize fully given—How to awake him by an impression—Can not experiment without a communication—All philosophy requires *cause,* *medium,* and *effect*—God could not affect the globe, nor its inhabitants, if he were isolated—Why the experiments are conducive to health—Philosophy of a surgical operation without pain while the patient is awake and rational—Connection between the mind and nerves of sensation—Case of Henry Clay in an exciting speech in Congress—He felt not the insertion of a pin into his flesh—Dr. Channing's remarks on no pain being felt by the martyrs—None is felt from a wound in the heat of battle—Inference.

LECTURE XII.

GENETOLOGY, OR HUMAN BEAUTY PHILOSOPHICALLY CONSIDERED, ... 233

Human beauty founded on the doctrine of impressions—Our species gradually improved—Born into existence with such forms as we desire—Beauty loved, desired, and praised by all—The mother by mental impressions variously affects the fœtus—Has produced abortion—Was frightened at a cub and produced an idiot who acted like a bear—A lady frightened by a parrot—Her child born a mediocre—A son born with compressed temples, caused by the mother seeing a lamb's head crushed—A child born with one arm and leg—Effects produced by longings—Color of wine transferred to the fœtus—Strawberry, blackberry, etc., transferred—Objections of medical writers are groundless—It is no new truth—Old as human records—Laban deceived Jacob—Rachael and Leah—Jacob's cattle speckled—He used speckled rods—Its philosophy—Aqua regia dissolves gold—Galvanizing metals—Making a bank plate—Identity of letters, marks, and engravings preserved on metals—Application of this to the subject—Menses are the raw material to form the child—How it is formed—How to produce it in her own image—How to make it resemble her husband, or any one else—Influence of her love or hatred on the fœtus—Effects of jealousy—Every object she sees has a tendency to produce a favorable or unfavorable result on the child—Mind has spiritual organism—Philosophy of effects produced upon the fœtus—The mother's responsibility—Importance of governing her passions, feelings, and emotions—Importance of Phrenology—How the highest specimens of human beauty may be produced—A talented lady considered—Pictures, countenances, forms, landscapes—Under what impressions to conceive—Her room, its furniture—Her mind, how employed in contemplating the beautiful in nature and art—Her food, and how to proceed till the time of delivery—All great men produced by talented mothers—Talent depends more on the mother than father—But few are now qualified to produce beauty—Improvement gradual till the work shall be universally consummated—Those in the psychological state considered, and the husband's influence on such—Importance of educating woman in all the sciences, and in political economy and history, equal to man—The responsibility of her station in rearing her child—The inconsistency of committing her child to the care of ignorant or base servants—The pulpit—Its moral power—It neglects this great subject and must be aroused to nobler action—The gospel of Christ—The millennium—Agricultural associations are improving both vegetables and animals—Rewards offered for the most beautiful specimens—But nothing done to improve and beautify the human form—We will begin it—Future generations will consummate it—Poetry on hope.

INTRODUCTION.

The author received the following invitation from the undersigned honorable gentlemen, members of the United States Senate, to lecture in Washington city, District of Columbia:

"WASHINGTON, Feb. 12th, 1850.
"To Dr. Dods:
"Dear Sir—Having received highly favorable accounts of the addresses delivered by you, in different sections of the Union, on 'Electrical Psychology,' a department of science said to treat of the philosophy of disease, and the reciprocal action of *mind* and *matter* upon each other, we would be gratified if you would deliver a lecture on the subject in this city, at the earliest time consistent with your convenience. With a view to the accommodation of members of Congress and the community generally, the Hall of Representatives, if it can be procured, would be a suitable place for the delivery of your discourse.

"Yours, truly,
"Geo. W. Jones,   Tho. J. Rusk,
"John P. Hale,   Sam Houston,
"H. Clay,   H. S. Foote.
    Dan. Webster."

To the above the following answer was returned:

"To the Hon. Tho. J. Rusk, Sam Houston, H. S. Foote, Geo. W. Jones, John P. Hale, Henry Clay, and Daniel Webster, all of the United States Senate:

"Gentlemen:
"In reply to yours of Feb. 12th, I would respectfully say, that I feel myself highly honored to receive an invitation from you, to lecture upon the philosophy of Electrical Psychology in the United States Capitol. With this invitation I comply, and it affords me much pleasure to do so. Owing, however, to circumstances and previous engagements, my earliest and only time during my present visit in Washington, will be on Saturday evening, Feb. 16th. I will therefore appoint that time as most suitable to my convenience, and commence my lecture at half-past seven o'clock.

"With sentiments of high consideration, I am
"Yours, truly,
"J. B. Dods."

The science of Electrical Psychology I have taught to more than a thousand individuals, and in all cases I have uniformly charged gentlemen *ten* dollars for tuition, and ladies *five*. I have also made it a uniform practice to lay them indiscriminately under written obligations, pledging most solemnly their sacred honor, as ladies and gentlemen, that they would never teach it to any persons but of good moral character, nor, in any instance, for a less price than above stated, and that they would lay all those whom they taught under the same written obligations and pledges. But it so happens, that unprincipled individuals, regardless of their pledges of sacred honor, have, in numerous instances, violated them, and taught, or at least pretended to teach, this science to others for any price they could obtain. There are, however, many honorable exceptions to this course of conduct among my students, and I am proud to bear this testimony to their faithfulness.

The substance of the first NINE of these LECTURES was delivered, by request, in Washington city, last February, and immediately published. The sale of the work has exceeded my expectations, and, in this Fourth Edition, I have fully revealed the secret, so that the reader, by the faithful perusal of my Lectures XI. and XII., will be as well qualified to experiment as those unprincipled pretenders, above noticed, who go about as teachers. They have even made their pupils believe, that nothing was necessary for them to know only the *nerve or gripe to get a communication and to speak in a positive manner and full tone of voice to the subject!* But you will perceive, on reading this work, that they have not taught you the A, B, C of this science. Its philosophy has cost me seven years of intense study, and it can not be revealed in a moment, not taught but by a workman. Honor and justice, under all these circumstances, require me to publish the mode of experimenting, so that those who shall teach it hereafter, will be compelled to study and prepare themselves for the work, as qualified instructors, because something more than the SECRET, which Lecture XI. reveals, will now be required.

J B DODS.

NEW YORK, September 26th, 1850.

ELECTRICAL PSYCHOLOGY.

LECTURE I

LADIES AND GENTLEMEN:

I HAVE received an invitation from several EMINENT MEMBERS of the United States Senate, to deliver a Lecture on the Science of Electrical Psychology—the philosophy of disease—the connecting link between *mind* and *matter*—their reciprocal action upon each other, and the grand operations of nature that this science may involve. In compliance with this invitation, I now stand before you for this purpose, and will endeavor faithfully to discharge my duty. In order to do my subject justice, I shall be under the necessity of making a very liberal draft on your time and patience. Sensible that I stand here by the invitation of those distinguished orators, statesmen, and generals, whose eloquence, in defence of LIBERTY, has been felt by thrones—whose wisdom has given laws that are respected by all nations on earth, and make millions of freemen happy—and whose heroism has breasted the battle storm in defence of human rights—it may well be expected that I should, in some measure at least, feel the embarrassment that the occasion itself must naturally inspire.

As the Creator of the universe has endowed man with reason, and assigned him a noble and intelligent rank in the scale of intellectual and moral being—and as he has commanded him to use this faculty—so I may with justice remark, that he who *cannot reason* is a fool; he who *dare not reason*, is a coward; he who *will not reason*, is a bigot; but he who *can* and *dare reason*, is a MAN.

The realms of nature lie open in boundless prospect above, beneath, and around us. As inhabitants of this globe, we occupy but a small spot—the centre, as it were, of the immense universe that swarms with a countless variety of animated beings, and contains endless sources of mental and moral delights. Order, harmony, and beauty are so perfectly woven together and blended throughout NATURE, as to form the magnificent ROBE she wears, and with which she not only charms and even dazzles the eyes of the beholder, but conceals the overwhelming power and majesty of her PERSON. As she moves, the most grand and awful impressions mark her footsteps on the globe's surface or centre—in air or ocean. She smiles in the gentleness of the calm, and frowns in the fury of the storm.

But whether silence reigns, earthquakes rumble, or thunders roll, she keeps her mighty course unaffected by the revolutions of ages.

At the same time that there is confessedly something most grand in the operations of nature, and even while the most gifted minds are reveling with delight amidst her magnificence, and feasting upon her splendors, there is still something humiliating in the thought, that incomprehensibility continues to hold its dark and sullen empire over the causes of many of her most sublime manifestations. For a period of twice three thousand years, she has concealed beneath the shadow of her hand, not only the cause of worlds rolling in their ceaseless course through the illimitable fields of space, but also the rise and fall of vegetation, and the phenomena of life and death.

Man is intellectually a progressive being. Though confined to a narrow circumference of space, and chained to this earth, which is but a small part of the unbounded universe, yet as his mind wears the stamp of original greatness, he is nevertheless capable of extending his researches far beyond the boundaries of this globe. His mind is capable of a ceaseless development of its powers. From the faint glimmerings of infantile reason, he passes on to that intellectual strength and grandeur when he can take a survey of the planets, the dimensions of the sun, trace the comet in its erratic course, analyze the works of God, and comprehend the vast and complicated operations of his own mind. How sublime is the contemplation, that he can invade the territory of other worlds, bring their within field-view of the ken of his telescope, and see them play their aerial gambols under the superintendence of attraction and repulsion.

But before I proceed any further, it becomes necessary that I clearly state the subject of my present course of Lectures, so that we may enter upon it understandingly, and, if possible, with a clear conception of its nature and importance to the human race. The subject, upon which I am entering, is that to which I have given the name of Electrical Psychology, as the one which is, in my estimation, the most appropriate. PSYCHOLOGY is a compound of two Greek words, viz., *psuche*, which means *soul*, and *logos*, which means *word*, *discourse*, or *wisdom*. Hence by PSYCHOLOGY we are to understand the SCIENCE OF THE SOUL. And as all impressions are made upon the soul through the medium of electricity, as the only agent by which it holds communication with the external world, so you readily perceive not only the propriety but the entire aptitude of the name ELECTRICAL PSYCHOLOGY.

Twenty years ago, I discovered electricity to be the connecting link between mind and inert matter, and on this discovery the philosophy of the present science is based. Ever since 1830, I have contended, that electricity is not only the connecting link between MIND and *inert* MATTER, but is the grand agent employed by the Creator to move and govern the universe. These views, in opposition to the doctrine of inherent attraction in matter, I advocated in Taunton, Massachusetts, in two Lectures I delivered before the Lyceum in 1832. The substance of these is embodied in six Lectures I delivered at the MARLBORO CHAPEL, in Boston, January 1843, by request of members of both branches of the Massachusetts Legislature then in session in that city; and they have been most extensively published in this country, and republished in England. In that work they are applied to the philosophy of Mesmerism. I make these remarks so that ladies and gentlemen present on this occasion may know, that my views of the ELECTRICAL THEORY of the universe, and the CONNECTING LINK between mind and inert matter, are not the breathings of a momentary impulse, but of long and matured deliberation.

Electrical Psychology takes a most extensive range, and embraces a field rich in variety of thought. It is so startling to human credulity, that its truth cannot be believed, only by passing it through the ordeal of the severest scrutiny by oft-repeated experiments. As to the character and force of these experiments, I cannot better express them than in the following editorial notice from the "Saratoga Republican."

The editor of the Saratoga Republican having received a letter from the Hon. Richard D. Davis, formerly a member of Congress, in relation to this science, writes as follows:

"Dr. Dods, who professes to have discovered a new science, to which he applies the name of Electrical Psychology, is at present giving a series of remarkable experiments, in our village, by way of illustrating its truth and undoubted reality. By it he professes to be able to perform the most startling and cunning experiments, upon persons fully awake, and in the most perfect possession of all their faculties. Controlling their motions—standing up, they find it impossible to sit down; if in a sitting posture, they are unable to rise till the operator allows them to do so. He claims to have the power to take away the powers of hearing, speech, sight, and the memory, etc., whenever he pleases, and to return again these faculties instantly; that he can change the personal identity of certain individuals, making them imagine for the time being that they are persons of color, that they belong to the opposite sex, or that they are some renowned general, orator, statesman, or what-not. He professes to be able to change the appearance and taste of water in rapid succession to that of lemonade, honey, vinegar, molasses, wormwood, coffee, milk, brandy; the latter producing all the intoxicating effects of alcohol. He brings before his subjects the threatening thunder-cloud. They see the lightnings flash and hear the thunders roll; the storm bursts over their heads, and they flee to a place of shelter, under a table, bench, or any thing that offers protection. All this while the individuals experimented upon are perfectly awake and in possession of their reasoning faculties.

"We are well aware, that the first impression upon the mind of the reader will be, that all this is absurd, ridiculous, and utterly impossible. This would be the natural conclusion of every one who had never witnessed any of these surprising phenomena; but the reality of all this is maintained by some of the most respectable and talented men in the country. We have permission to refer to several individuals of the highest standing and character, who are believers in this science, and have been pupils of Dr. Dods. We have before us a letter written by Hon. RICHARD D. DAVIS, from which we make the following extract. Mr. Davis says:

"The science which Dr. Dods teaches, is to my mind alike novel, instructive, and useful—full of speculation fit for the loftiest intellect, and replete with rich instructions for every condition of human life. So far as I am able to judge, I can safely say, that no person of ordinary capacity and intelligence can take the usual course of lessons from the doctor, who will not at its end sincerely acknowledge himself more than tenfold repaid for its cost of time, trouble, and expense; and the more the ability and information of the individual may be, the more ready will be the acknowledgment. I am unwilling to express more than half the gratification and instruction which I have received, and if my recommendation can prevail with any one to become his pupil, it is most cheerfully and earnestly given."

What I have now read in your hearing, will give you some idea of the nature of the experiments, and also what claims Electrical Psychology has, in the opinion of distinguished men, in relation to its pretensions to science and usefulness. But there is no question, that ladies and gentlemen, after admitting that these experiments are truly wonderful, and to them incomprehensible, will yet ask, of what use are they to the human race? The great usefulness and transcendent importance of this science to the human race consist in it curative powers over those diseases that medicine can not remove. As facts come home to men's bosoms, and rebuke the skeptic in a voice of thunder, so I cannot give a better answer to the question, nor render you a better service, than to read a few extracts from the city papers of Auburn, New York, where I last lectured and experimented. It is as follows:

"HIRAM BOSTWICK, Esq., so long and so well known in this city [Auburn] and county, during more than two years before he saw Dr. Dods, did not take a natural step. For a year and a half last past, could only slowly drag his feet along, as though they were attached to wooden legs, and, at that, did not attempt to drag himself about the streets. Besides an attack last spring (which was the fifth stroke of palsy he had received), he could not even distinguish light from darkness, with his right eye. In a word, he was dead to happiness and usefulness. He met Dr. Dods, and in less than a week he was taking walks of a mile in length. With his right eye he distinguishes persons, and is constantly improving, while he is daily promenading our streets with the perfect control and use of every muscle, and is quite as happy as any man we meet."

I will read again from another Auburn paper. It is as follows:

"Do the dumb speak and the deaf hear? In Auburn, in October, 1849, they do. This forenoon, two girls went to the City Hall, neither of whom could hear a conversation in an ordinary tone. They were operated upon some five or six minutes each, upon the principles of Electrical Psychology as taught by Dr Dods, and when they left, one of them could distinctly hear an ordinary conversation, and the other could as distinctly hear a whisper."

"Yesterday noon, a lady from Massachusetts called upon Dr. Dods, at the Western Exchange. Her eyelids were so drawn down over her eyes that she could not see, and she could not talk. In twenty minutes she could both see and converse. If any one discredits this statement, let him ask Gen. Wood, the gentlemanly proprietor of the Exchange. When this blind and dumb lady came, her female attendant stated to Gen. Wood, that her friend had not opened her eyes for three years, and for the last year had not uttered a syllable. The afflicted lady made the same statement, after the doctor had restored her wonted powers of speech. During the three years, she was for one of them confined in a dark room, to avoid the supposed injurious effects of light. She could not raise the upper lids of the eyes.

"Such was her situation when she called upon Dr. Dods at the Exchange yesterday; and in half an hour she left again, drinking in with delight the prospect about her, and from which for years she had been entirely shut out, and while at the same time she poured forth her joy in words which it may be well imagined were those of the purest ecstasy. Her friends tried to prevail upon her, when she reached the carriage at the door, to shield her eyes, lest the sudden change from darkness to glare should have a deleterious influence upon those sensitive and delicate organs; but a gaze about the city was too rich a treat to be lost, and she availed herself of the opportunity to enjoy it.

"As this lady had been so long and so severely afflicted, had availed herself of the knowledge and skill afforded by the medical profession, and was at the time traveling in search of health, I thought the case worthy of mention.

"Do not understand me to be one who, even if in his power, would do any thing to depreciate the high estimation in which the medical profession is so justly held. Not at all. I regard it as one of the noblest of all pursuits, and believe that its practitioners, as a class, are not excelled, if equaled, by any other in kindness, self-denial, and humanity. But I will say, that every physician ought to understand Dr. Dods' system of Electrical Psychology. There is no room to doubt that it will not only give him a knowledge of laws and phenomena of the human economy he does not now know or comprehend, but will enable him to afford relief and restoration in cases where before it was out of his power.

"Granting this to be so—and the appeal here is to facts which cannot lie—what is the duty of the honest physician? Is it to sneer at a system or science which, with a respectable face, makes even these pretensions?—which professes to unfold laws and powers of mind and body which they do not understand, and backed up by actual, tangible results, which utterly dumbfound the whole of them? Is *sneering* his duty, when his hands hold the scales in which are deposited life and death? Is it not rather his duty to investigate the matter—to probe it to the bottom—to know all that can be known about it?

"The community will answer these questions, because they are deeply interested in the answer. In this city, cures will be performed within one year, by the pupils of Dr. Dods, in cases where the present medical system has been exhausted in vain. This will test the question. And by this test, every physician who sneers at Electrical Psychology will be compelled to abide. From it he *cannot*, and *will not* escape. I will refer now to only one beauty of the electro-psychological treatment of pain and disease. Its pharmacy is always perfect—it is of God."

From the extracts which I have now read in your hearing, from the Auburn papers, you will at once perceive the power and glory that hover around this science, and the importance which is claimed in its behalf as one of the greatest blessings ever vouchsafed to the human race. So that you may see the high estimation in which this science is held by the citizens of Auburn, generally, where these cures were performed, I will trouble my audience but once more, and ask their indulgence while I read the resolutions they unanimously passed in behalf of Electrical Psychology as a great and important science, which resolutions were published in the Auburn papers. I will also read the prefaced remarks of the editor They are as follows:

"ELECTRICAL PSYCHOLOGY.—Dr. Dods closed his Lectures, in Auburn, on Saturday evening. It will be seen by our columns this afternoon, that the gentlemen composing his CLASS, availed themselves of the occasion to express their views of Electrical Psychology, and of the manner in which the DOCTOR sustained his relations as their Instructor in his system. It is enough to say that the CLASS numbered gentlemen of undoubted intelligence."

"*Proceedings adopted by the Auburn Psychological Class.*

" At a meeting of the CLASS of forty-five persons, who had taken private lessons of Dr. J. B. DODS in the science of Electrical Psychology, held at the City Hall, in the city of Auburn, on the 27th day of October, 1849, John P. Hulbert was called to the chair, and Dr. S. N. Smith appointed secretary.

" On motion, a committee of three was appointed by the chairman to draft and report to the meeting resolutions expressive of the views and feelings of Dr. Dods' pupils, in the city of Auburn, in respect to the lessons and lectures given them by him."

" On motion, the chairman and secretary were added to the committee.

" The committee reported the following resolutions, which were unanimously adopted by the meeting.

" Resolved, That the science of ELECTRICAL PSYCHOLOGY, as taught to this class, by Dr. J. B. DODS, in a series of private instructions and lectures, we believe to be founded in IMMUTABLE TRUTH, and that it will accomplish for the human race an inappreciable amount of good.

"Resolved, That we believe ELECTRICAL PSYCHOLOGY has been, and will be eminently useful in alleviating the pains of the suffering, and in the cure of diseases; that it is as comprehensive as it is beautiful and beneficent; and that it is not only eminently calculated to enlarge and elevate the mind, but to impress upon it more exalted ideas of the infinite wisdom and goodness of the DEITY.

"Resolved, That we tender to Dr. DODS our thanks for the courteous and gentlemanly manner in which he has discharged his duties to us as his pupils. That he has, in all respects, redeemed every pledge or assurance that he gave us when we became his pupils, and that in parting from him we give him our warmest wishes for his prosperity and happiness.

"On motion, resolved, That the proceedings of this meeting be signed by the chairman and secretary, and delivered to Dr. DODS, and that they be published in the newspapers of the city.

"JOHN P. HULBERT, Chairman.
"S. N. SMITH, Secretary."

The subject of these Lectures is now fairly open fore us. I have explained what I mean by the term ELECTRICAL PSYCHOLOGY, and why I saw fit to give the science this name. The wonderful and startling phenomena that hover around it, like so many invisible angels, and which are made manifest in the experiments produced, I have also candidly stated. They consist in the fact, that one human being can, through a certain nervous influence, obtain and exercise a power over another, so as to perfectly control his voluntary motions and muscular force; and also produce various impressions on his mind, however extravagant, ludicrous, or wild—and that too while he is in a perfectly wakeful state. I have stated, that it is one of the most powerful remedial agents to alleviate the pains of the suffering, and to cure those diseases that set the power of medicine, and the skill of the ablest practitioner, at defiance. And from the published newspaper articles, letters, and resolutions of most highly reputable, and even distinguished men, which I have just read in your hearing, you can form an opinion of the effects produced, of the cures performed, of the high estimation in which this science is held by those who have acquainted themselves with its secret powers, and of their high estimate of its incalculable importance to the human race, and the future amount of good it is ultimately destined to achieve.

I have only read to you the testimony of the citizens of Auburn, but could produce the testimony of thousands more, from the various portions of the United States where I have lectured—of the importance of this science in the cure of diseases; and those, too, of a more startling character than any I have named. I can produce the testimony of hundreds, that this science has, in fifty minutes, restored to Lucy Ann Allen, of Lynchburg, Virginia, the use of her limbs; who had not walked a step in eighteen years, nor had she even been able to raise herself up from her pillow so as to sit in her bed for more than fourteen years. Such is the nature and intrinsic grandeur of this SCIENCE; such are the experiments and facts connected with it; such are its results that stamp it with the high impress of its sterling importance to mankind; and such are its lofty end and aim; and as such it must stand when the pillars of strength and beauty that support our Capitol shall fall and be crumbled to dust.

Some have the impression, that Electrical Psychology is, after all, but Mesmerism. In answer to such I will say, that there is a very marked difference between the two sciences, and this difference is easily pointed out. MESMERISM is the doctrine of *sympathy;* ELECTRICAL PSYCHOLOGY is the doctrine of IMPRESSIONS. In Mesmerism there is a sympathy so perfect between the magnetizer and subject, that what he sees, the subject sees—what he hears, the subject hears—what he feels, the subject feels—what he tastes, the subject tastes—and what he smells, the subject also smells; and lastly, what the magnetizer wills, is likewise the will of his subject. But the person in the electro-psychological state has no such sympathies with his operator. His *sight, hearing, feeling, taste*, and *smell* are entirely independent of the operator, and he continually exerts his will against him, and resists him with all his muscular force. The person who is aroused from the mesmeric slumber, has no remembrance of what transpired in it; while the person in the electro-psychological state, is a witness of his own actions, and knows all that transpired. The person in the mesmeric state can hear no voice but that of his magnetizer, or the voices of those with whom he is put in communication. But the person in the electro-psychological state, can hear and converse with all as usual.

If these distinctions are not sufficiently marked to settle the points of difference, then I will mention two more. I have found persons entirely and naturally in the electro-psychological state, who never could be mesmerized at all, nor in the least affected, under repeated trials. The other point is, that no person is naturally in the mesmeric state, but thousands are naturally in the electro-psychological state, and live and die in it. MESMERISM and SOMNAMBULISM are *identical;* they are one and the same state. And as no person is naturally in the somnambulic state, so no one is naturally in the mesmeric state. Though the experiments of both these states are performed by the same nervous fluid, yet this does not render the two sciences identical, any more than that they are rendered identical with fits, or insanity, which are caused by the same nervous force. These observations being sufficient for my purpose, are respectfully submitted to you for your candid consideration.

LECTURE II.

LADIES AND GENTLEMEN:

As the subject of Electrical Psychology is now fairly introduced, its phenomena stated, and its importance to the human race clearly pointed out, we are now prepared to enter the diversified fields of nature; to glance at the operations of mental and material existences; and to proceed understandingly to the consideration of its claims to PHILOSOPHY, as the foundation on which it rests, and the power by which its existence must be sustained. But as I am fully sensible that such strange facts as I have stated are most trying to human credulity—sensible that they are calculated to awaken the deepest feelings of contempt in the bosoms of the skeptical, and to draw forth the sneers of mankind—so I must be indulged to speak, in the first place, of the march of science, the beauty of the independent expression of our thoughts, and to notice the fate of the opponents of science in all ages of the world.

Entering, as I do, upon a theme entirely new, I am by no means insensible of the embarrassments that surround me. Were I called to address you upon any other subject than that of ELECTRICAL PSYCHOLOGY, I should stand before you with other feelings than those that now pervade my breast. It is by no means an enviable task to step aside from the long beaten path of science into the unexplored and trackless regions of solitude and silence. By so doing, and daring to think for myself, I am well aware that I assume no very enviable position as it regards popularity. Independent thought and fearless expression have ever drawn forth the scoffs and sneers of that portion of our race who have adopted, without investigation, the scientific opinions of others. I refer to those only who have received their ideas from others by inheritance, as they did their real estate. For the one they never labored, and for the other they never thought.

Such persons, though professing to be learned, and perchance even claiming to be the guardians of science, are nevertheless its greatest enemies; and by exerting their influence in favor of old opinions, however absurd, and against any innovations, however true, useful, or grand, are checking the mighty march of mind. They are clogs of more than leaden weight hanging upon the chariot wheels of science that are rolling through our world. It commenced its career at the breaking morn of creation, with but few passengers on board, and has continued its course with increasing speed and growing glory down to the present moment. It now travels with the brilliancy and rapidity of the lightning's blaze, and even compels the very lightnings to speak in a familiar voice to man! Yes; they even write, not only their forky gambols on the bosom of the dark cloud, but they write on paper, and transmit human thought as swift as thought can move.

The chariot of science is destined to continue its majestic course, in duration coeval with our globe! Still more! it is destined to outlive the dark and sullen catastrophe of worlds! The chariot of science, with ever increasing power, magnificence, and glory, is destined to pass the boundaries of the mouldering tomb—to snatch immortality from the iron grasp of death, and roll on in living grandeur through the eternal world, gathering new accessions of intellectual beauty and unending delight. Its passengers here are mortal men. There they will be angel, archangel, cherubim, seraphim, and the glorified millions of our race! The mind of man wears the impression of divinity, the stamp of original greatness; and is destined to ripen in mental vigor as the wasteless ages of ETERNITY roll. Hence the very principles of our nature as an impression from the hand of God, forbid us to stand still. Their command is ONWARD.

If no human being had dared to hazard the expression of an original thought, then nothing in the realms of science would have been disclosed by speech, nor penned in books. A dreary, barren waste, wrapped in solitude and night, would have reigned for human contemplation. But instead of this frightful picture of desolation, we see those fruitful fields of mental and moral beauty, so rich in the scenery of thought, and in endless variety, present themselves to our view. A secret rapture of thrilling delight fills the heart as we glance over this lovely scene, on which human research has thrown a splendor surpassing that of the noontide blaze.

Had not some master spirits dared to freely speak and write their thoughts, then those pretended friends of science, who now oppose every thing that may appear to them both new and strange, would have been destitute of that knowledge they obtained from books; and not daring to think for themselves, they would have remained in mental night. It is by daring to step aside from the beaten track of books, and bringing forth from the dark arcana of nature into the light of day some new truth, that we add our mite to the common stock of knowledge already accumulated. He who denies us this grand right of our nature is a scientific bigot, and has yet to learn, that even the school and college were only established to discipline the mind for action. There the student, through books and instructors, is only made to see how other men have dared to think, and speak, and write, and thus his mind, being made to feel its innate freedom, power, and greatness, becomes inspired with a self-determination to do the same. This makes the MAN, and answers the lofty end of human existence. On the other hand, he who goes through life, leaning entirely upon books and the opinions of others, without thinking for himself, renders his present existence a blank, inasmuch as he lays his head in the dust, without its having bequeathed one original thought to the world, for the benefit of after generations.

The truths that God has established inherent in nature, are not only infinitely diversified, but are at the same time immutable and eternal. No possible addition can be made to their number, nor is it in the power of man to create or annihilate a single truth in the EMPIRE of NATURE. They exist independent of his *belief* or *unbelief*; and all he can do is to search them out, and bring them forth from darkness into the light of day. And he who has the magnanimity to do this, so far from being opposed and persecuted, should be sustained and encouraged as the benefactor of his race.

The Creator of the universe is the Author and Proprietor of the great volumes of nature and revelation. Hence divines, at least those who are men of letters, should not start at any new scientific revelations, and exclaim, "If this be true we must give up our Bibles!" As men of science, they have nothing to fear from new discoveries in the shoreless ocean of truth. The volumes of NATURE and REVELATION both claim the same perfect Author, who had every thing open and naked to his omniscient inspection, and exercised infinite wisdom in producing and establishing the order and harmony of the universe.

Though this globe, and perhaps the whole of our planetary system, was finished six thousand years ago, yet we have no reason to suppose that this was the first effort of his creating energy. We are floating in an immensity of space that knows no bounds, like the mote in the sunbeam. This is peopled with rolling worlds, in number beyond an angel's computation. And the residue, which has not yet become the abodes of light, life, order, and beauty, is filled up with matter still in its uncreated state. Hence the work of creation has been going on from eternity, and will continue to progress, so long as the throne of the self-existent Jehovah endures, without ever arriving at an end in the sublime career of creation! New brother creations are every moment rolling from his omnific hand, and that creating fiat will never, never cease.

These ideas of the wonder-working Jehovah, from whose all-forming hand worlds and systems of worlds are continually rolling, and have been, for millions on millions of ages, force upon us those amazing conceptions of the oppressive grandeur of his works under which the mind labors and struggles in its contemplations, but is borne down, and lost and bewildered in the immensity of the theme. ORDER, VARIETY, AND BEAUTY, in endless succession meet us on every hand.

All this has been accomplished by the Infinite Mind, through electrical action, and bespeaks the vastness and sublimity of the subject. It is the science of the living mind, its silent, mysterious workings, and energetic powers. It is a science that involves the majestic movement of rolling worlds, the falling leaf, and claims the GREAT LAW of the universe as its own. The vastness, as well as the transcendent importance of the subject, clearly evince that it is worthy to be embraced by every independent, noble, and generous mind. You will pardon me, Ladies and Gentlemen, for having, by a momentary digression from the present chain of my subject, anticipated a few ideas in relation to the creation and its vastness. These more properly belong to a future Lecture, when I shall come to show what connection this science has with the universe—with rolling worlds—yes, with a falling leaf. The fall of a single leaf is a catastrophe as dreadful to the thousands of inhabitants of its surface as the destruction of this globe would be to us. And the blotting out of our globe from the catalogue of worlds, would no more be missed amid the immensity of creation than the fall of a leaf compared to the sublime magnificence of the countless forests on this globe. From this digression I return to my subject.

That Electrical Psychology should meet with opposition from men of a peculiar constitution of mind, and a certain degree of scientific attainments, is nothing strange. Nor is it at all miraculous, that a few who are deemed men of talents, should oppose, and even deride it as a humbug. But as GENIUS is supremely higher than TALENTS, so I boldly and safely make the declaration that no man of GENIUS has ever opposed Electrical Psychology; nor in any age of the world has GENIUS ever been enlisted in opposing the dawning light of any of the sciences that have arisen on earth from the morning of creation to the present day. But as before remarked, that this science should meet with opposition from that class of scientific men, who always stand watching the direction in which the breeze of popularity may chance to blow with the strongest force, and who are anxious, through these means, to bring themselves into notice, and thus gain a momentary fame from the passing crowd, is nothing strange. It only proves the fact that ELECTRICAL PSYCHOLOGY is, in the infancy of its being, destined to share the fate of all great and useful sciences, that now stand unshaken in the republic of letters. All, in their infancy, received from such men a like opposition, and upon their founders they freely breathed out their derision, scorn, and sneers.

Harvey discovered the CIRCULATION of the blood, and disclosed it to the world. He was opposed and derided, and much of that *talent, learning,* and *cunning* we have referred to, was enlisted against him. They sought to paralyze the towering wing of his genius; to blast his reputation; to wither the fairest flowers of his domestic love, hope, and joy; and to hurl his brilliant discovery from the light of day to the darkness of night. But Harvey's name stands immortal on the records of true fame, and the blood still continues to frolic in crimson streams through its living channels, while his learned opposers are forgotten. Galileo discovered the rotation of this globe on its axis. So great was the opposition of the learned powers combined against him, that they arraigned him and his theory at the august and awful bar of humbug. There they fairly tried him and his discovery under the splendid and majestic witnesses of *derision*, *sneer*, and *scorn;* and the court very gravely decided, that his discovery was a heresy, and that he must openly acknowledge it to be so to the world. To this sentence he submitted—acknowledged his theory to be a heresy, but remarked, that he nevertheless believed it true. Galileo lives in the bright page of history. That sentence did not arrest the globe in its mighty course. It still continues to roll on its axis as he discovered and proclaimed, while the learned opposers of his theory, who courted popular favor at the expense of honor, are sunk into merited oblivion.

Newton's genius, when he was but a boy, intuitively drove him to study *gravitation* by piling up small heaps of sand, and to notice more strictly this power in the falling apple. It drove him to study *adhesion* by watching the union of the particled water at the side of some favorite stream; and to perfect this science he is next at the centre of the globe. From gathering pebbles in boyish sport on the ocean's shore, he is next among the stars, and at length proclaims to the world his system of PHILOSOPHY and ASTRONOMY. He was derided and mocked as a silly-headed fool, and his whole magnificent system was spurned with sneering contempt and pronounced a humbug by the old school of philosophers and astronomers. But substances continue to respect the law of *gravitation*, and rolling worlds to obey the law of *attraction* and *repulsion*. NEWTON lives in the brightest blaze of fame; for his name is written in starry coronals on the deep bosom of night, and from thence is reflected to the centre of the globe; while the opposers of his magnificent discovery are sunk to the shades of unremembered nothingness. The clouds and mists of their own evanescent fame have become their winding sheet.

Fulton was derided, and even men of science pointed at him the finger of indignant scorn, because he declared that steam—a light and bland vapor, which could be blown away by human breath—could move an engine of tremendous power, and propel vessels of thousands of tons burthen against wind and waves and tides. They declared it to be the greatest of humbugs, and the most silly idea that ever entered a silly brain;

or else the trick of a knave to make men invest capital in order to effect their ruin. His friends, even though not over-sanguine of success, yet defended him as a man of honor. But FULTON " stood firm amidst the varying tides of party like the rock far from land, that lifts its majestic head above the waves, and remains unshaken by the storms that agitate the ocean." So stern was the opposition, that some of the committed skeptics, who sailed from New York to Albany in the steamboat that first tried the experiment, declared, that it was *impossible* they had been conveyed a distance of one hundred and fifty miles by steam power! and that it must, after all, have been some power aside from steam, by which they had been enabled to reach Albany! The impression of FULTON's GENIUS is seen on all the machinery moved in our happy country by this subtile power. It is seen in railroad and steamboat communications, that bring the distant portions of the United States in conjunction. It is seen in the majestic STEAMSHIPS of England, that bring her and the transatlantic world into neigborhood with us, by a power that triumphs over all the stormy elements of nature. FULTON, as a man of GENIUS, is remembered as one of the great men of the universe, while his opposers are silent and forgotten.

Thus far, I have spoken of the physical and mechanical sciences only, involving the chemical properties of material substances, and the general operations of nature. I now come to those that relate to the improvement of the mind. I come still nearer home. The SCIENCE of PHRENOLOGY, so beautiful, elevating, and useful in its nature, and having so strong a bearing upon the character and destiny of man, as an intellectual, social, and moral being, and even involving the dearest interest of our race—has been, and by some still is, most shamefully abused. GALL, its discoverer, was persecuted; and SPURZHEIM, COMBE, and FOWLER have received unmerited abuse. The two Fowlers, of New York, have for years withstood the storm of opposition. Thus far, they have most successfully met and repulsed the assaults of men—won the victory—gathered new accessions of strength, and still hold the field. They are business men, who never slumber at the post of duty. They have made new discoveries and improvements; gathered an immense variety of cabinet specimens of skulls and busts, from the idiot up to the most brilliant intellect—from the cold-blooded murderer up to the melting soul of a benevolent and philanthropic Howard. They have made a righteous development of true character in the phrenological examinations of thousands of human heads; have directed the anxious parent how to train up the child of his affections; have pointed out to the sighing lover how to choose a congenial spirit of companionship for life; and have poured the light of mental and moral improvement in silvery streams on the GRAND EMPIRE

OF MIND. Yet such a science as this has been called a *humbug!* and such men as these have been assailed. Their bones are worthy to repose with the great men of the universe, and their names shall live on the bright scroll of fame down to the last vibrating pendulum of time—shall live when the opposers of phrenological science shall have sunk from human remembrance.

Such has been the fate of all sciences in the infancy of their existence. The moment they were born into life, the battle-axe was raised against them, and each in succession has fought its way up to manhood. The victory in favor of truth has always been sure, and millions of sycophants in the contest have perished.

How lamentable is the consideration, that there are those in this day of light, who, regardless of the warning voice of past generations, coming up from ten thousand graves, still shut their ears and close their eyes—and even sacrifice principle, to keep popular with those on whom they depend for a momentary fame. But they are not the men whose names will stand imperishable in the annals of history, to be handed down to future generations. They are destined to perish from human remembrance, and not a trace of them be left on earth.

I would not be understood as dissuading you from the pursuit of true fame. I do not despise its noble glory; but am fully sensible, that of all characters ever formed and sustained by human beings, that of true fame stands unrivaled and supreme on the page of history.

Though man is mortal, and his present existence ephemeral, yet during the short span of three-score years and ten, to what a transcendent height in the cultivation of his powers is he capable of soaring! True, his station is humble, yet he who, with an unstained hand, has honorably grasped the meed of righteous fame, has clothed himself with power, has wreathed his brow with undying laurels, and invested himself with the true majesty of his nature. Fame has been alternately assigned to the hero, the statesman, the philosopher, astronomer, theologian. But fame is not confined to any rank or pursuit in life. It can only exist in the breathings of righteousness. The philosopher and astronomer, though chained down to earth by the law of gravitation, and tabernacled with the worm, may feel within a stirring greatness that allies them to higher intelligences in future worlds, and that bids them bear their brow aloft. They may station themselves on a mental elevation above the world, and lift their towering heads to the stars. From this pinnacle of glory, they may range in loftiest thought the universe of God and even struggle to grasp the unbounded empire over which Jehovah reigns, with all its moving worlds, and yet, if this be all, true fame does not lie here. It is not the birthright of the philosopher or astronomer, unless they are in possession of something more than intellectual power.

True fame is not the birthright of the hero. The blaze of glory that has for ages encircled his head, and with its brilliancy so long dazzled the world, is beginning to grow dim. The laurels that decorate his sullen brow have been gathered at the cannon's mouth, from a soil enriched with human gore, and watered by the tears of bereavement. That fancied pinnacle of glory on which he proudly stands, has been gained by conquest and slaughter. His way to it lay over thousands of his fellow-creatures, whose warm hearts had ceased to throb; and the music that followed his march, was the widow's moan and the orphan's wail. True fame does not lie here. It sounds not in the cannon's roar, the clashing steel, the rattling drum, nor in the frightful crash of resounding arms! It is not heard in martial thunder. It is not seen in villages on fire, nor in Moscow's conflagration—that ocean of flame! True fame breathes not in the deep-heaving sigh of despairing love, nor draws its immortality from dying groans on fields of war. It has a higher origin—a nobler birth—a more elevated aim. True fame consists in the LOFTY ASPIRATIONS AFTER INTELLECTUAL AND MORAL TRUTH; and when these are found and cherished, that so deep will be the convictions of duty, sustained by sterling honor, that no popularity—no bribes of wealth and splendor—no fear of frowns, nor even the hazard of life exposed to wasting tortures shall deter that man from expressing and maintaining such truth. He who does this, possesses true and righteous fame.

Should the scoffers of rising science challenge me to produce such an example of true fame ever being set on earth, I would point them to one perfect specimen on the sacred page. I would point them to the SON OF MAN, in the majesty of whose virtues, honor, and firmness in proclaiming truth, language is impoverished, all human description fails, and the living light of eloquence is darkened forever

LECTURE III.

Ladies and Gentlemen:

Perhaps I have dwelt sufficiently long upon the preliminaries of my subject. I have done so to bring distinctly before you its nature, and clearly state its incalculable importance to the human family. I have done so to remind you of the opposition, sneers, and scorns that the noblest sciences have encountered in the infancy of their being, and in all ages of the world. I have reminded you that this has been done, not by men of GENIUS, whose names are registered on the scroll of true fame, and have come down to future generations, but it has been done by that particular class of the learned who have so large a share of the love of approbation as to study public opinion, and follow it, right or wrong, and thus beg a momentary fame from the passing crowd, which is destined to expire in darkness, and vanish from human remembrance, before the breaking light of truth. I have dwelt thus long upon these points, so that opposition to this science may not surprise you, nor the real character of the opponent be mistaken.

Having removed every obstacle that might embarrass my course, and having plenty of sea-room, I am now ready to embark in defence of one of the greatest of causes. I stand before you to lecture upon the wonderful and mysterious science of Electrical Psychology. I stand here to exhibit by tangible experiments those wonderful phenomena that cluster around it, and philosophically to defend its paramount claims to immutable truth. The successful discharge of this incumbent duty, forces upon us the necessity of ranging the universe, and summoning the vast works of earth and heaven to the bar of reason, in order to investigate their *effects*, and trace them back to their correspondent causes. You are the empanneled jury to try this cause, and I rejoice that I have the honor to argue so interesting a point before the CONGREGATED TALENT AND WISDOM OF MY COUNTRY. However skeptical men may be in relation to any thing new, yet so far as stern reality is in its nature concerned, we have this pleasing consideration, that the *unbelief* of men cannot frown truth into falsehood, nor can the *belief* of men smile falsehood into truth. Hence the *belief* or *unbelief* of mortals cannot in the least affect those truths that God has established inherent in nature, and with which his unbounded universe swarms.

I stand here to defend the electrical theory of the universe against the assaults of men, to notice the immense variety of material existences, to glance at the animated forms of living beauty, to scrutinize the chemical properties of created substances, and to pour, if possible, the light of truth on rolling worlds. Let us even venture to step back beyond the threshold of creation—venture to lift the dark curtains of primeval night, and muse upon that original, eternal material, that slumbered in the deep bosom of chaos, and out of which all the tangible substances we see and admire were made. That eternal substance is *electricity*, and contains all the original properties of all things in being. Hence all worlds and their splendid appendages were made out of electricity, and by that powerful, all-pervading agent, under Deity, they are kept in motion from age to age. Electricity actuates the whole frame of nature, and produces all the phenomena that transpire throughout the realms of unbounded space. It is the most powerful and subtile agent employed by the Creator in the government of the universe, and in carrying on the multifarious operations of nature. Making a slight variation in the language of the poet, I may with propriety say—

> ' It warms in the sun, refreshes in the breeze,
> Glows in the stars, and blossoms in the trees;
> Lives through all life, extends through all extent
> Spreads undivided, operates unspent;
> Breathes in our souls, informs our mortal part
> As full, as perfect, in a hair as heart;
> As full, as perfect, in vile man that mourns,
> As the rapt seraph, that adores and burns;

It claims all high and low, all great and small;
It fills, it bounds, connects, and equals all."

It is immaterial to what department of this globe and its surrounding elements we turn our attention, electricity is there. Wherever we witness convulsions in nature, the workings of this mighty, unseen power are there. It writes its path in lightning on the sullen brow of the dark cloud, and breathes out rolling thunder. Though cold and invisible in its equalized and slumbering state, yet it is the cause of light and heat, which it creates by the inconceivable rapidity of its motion and friction on other particles of matter. It is the cause of evaporation from basined oceans and silvery lakes—from majestic rivers and rolling streams, and from the common humidity of the earth. It forms aerial conductors in the heavens, through which this moisture in vapory oceans is borne to the highest portions of our globe, and stored up in magazines of rain, and snow, and hail! It is electricity that, by its coldness, condenses the storm, and opens these various magazines in mild beauty or awful terror on the world. It is electricity that, by the production of heat, rarefies the air, gives wings to the wind, and directs their course. It is this unseen agent, that causes the gentle zephyrs of heaven to fan the human brow with a touch of delight—that moves the stirring gale—that arms the sweeping hurricane with power—that gives to the roaring tornado all its dreadful eloquence of vengeance and terror, and clothes the mid day sun in light. It gives us the soft, pleasing touches of the evening twilight, and the crimson blushes of the rising morn. It is *electricity* that, by its effects of *light* and *heat*, produces the blossoms of spring, the fruits of summer, the laden bounties of autumn, and moves on the vast mass of vegetation in all the varieties and blended beauties of creation. It bids winter close the varied scene. It is electricity that, by its most awful impressions, causes the earthquake to awake from its Tartarean den, to speak its rumbling thunder, convulse the globe, and mark out its path of ruin.

If we turn to man, and investigate the secret stirrings of his nature, we shall find, that he is but an epitome of the universe. The chemical properties of all the various substances in existence, and in the most exact proportions, are congregated and concentrated in him, and form and constitute the very elements of his being. In the composition of his body are involved all the mineral and vegetable substances of the globe, even from the grossest matter, step by step, up to the most rarefied and fine. And, *lastly*, to finish this masterpiece of creation, the brain is invested with a living spirit. This incomprehensible spirit, like an enthroned deity, presides over, and governs through electricity, as its agent, all the voluntary motions of this organized, corporeal universe; while its living presence, and its involuntary, self-moving powers cause all the involuntary functions of life to proceed in their destined course. Hence human beings and all animated existences are subject to the same grand electrical law that pervades the universe, and moves all worlds under the superintendence of the involuntary powers of the infinite Spirit.

On this principle, it will be plainly perceived, that as man is subjected to the same common law that pervades the universe, so *electricity* is the connecting *link* between MIND and MATTER. As it is co-eternal with spirit or mind, so it is the only substance in being that mind can directly touch, or through which it can manifest its powers. It is the servant of the mind to obey its will and execute its commands. It is through electricity, that the mind conveys its various impressions and emotions to others, and through this same medium receives all its impressions from the external world. It is by electricity that the mind contracts the muscles, raises the arm, and performs all the voluntary motions of this organized body. This I will now proceed to prove.

It will be readily perceived by every one acquainted with electrical science, that if I can find an individual standing in a *negative* relationship to myself, or by any process render him so, then I, being the *positive* power, can, by producing electrical impressions from my own mind upon his, control his muscles with the most perfect ease. This is evident, because the *posi-*

tive and *negative* forces electrically and magnetically blend, are equal in power, and paralyze each other; or, on the contrary, produce motion. This great and interesting truth I will prove to a demonstration, by experiments upon ladies and gentlemen in this audience, while they are entirely awake, and in perfect possession of all their reasoning faculties. Before I proceed to produce these astonishing and even startling results, I will, in the first place, prove that ELECTRICITY is the CONNECTING LINK between MIND and inert MATTER, and is the AGENT that the mind employs to contract and relax the muscles, and to produce all the *voluntary* and *involuntary* motions of the body.

To bring this before you in the most plain and intelligible manner, I would first remark that the brain is the fountain of the nervous system, from whence it sends out its millions of branches to every part of the body. Indeed, the brain is but a congeries of nerves, and is the immediate residence of the living spirit. This spirit or mind is the cause of all motion, whether that motion be voluntary or involuntary. It wills the arm to rise, and immediately the arm obeys the mandate; while the *very presence* of this mind in the brain, even though wrapped in the insensibility of sleep, produces all the involuntary motions of the vitals, and executes the functions of life.

To establish the fact that *electricity* is, indeed, the *connecting link* between the MIND and the BODY, I would in the first place distinctly remark, that mind cannot come in direct contact with gross matter. My mind can no more directly touch my hand, than it can the mountain rock. My mind cannot touch the bones of my arm, nor the sinews, the muscles, the blood-vessels, nor the blood that rolls in them. In proof of this position, let one hemisphere of the brain receive what is called a stroke of the palsy. Let the paralysis be complete, and one half of the system will be rendered motionless. In this case, the mind may will with all its energies—may exert all its mental powers—yet the arm will not rise, nor the foot stir. Yet the bones, sinews, muscles, and blood-vessels are all there, and the blood as usual continues to flow. Here then we have proof the most irresistible, that mind can touch none of these; for what the mind can touch it can move, as easily as what the hand can physically touch it can move. Our proof is so far philosophically conclusive.

I would now remark, that it is equally certain my mind can touch some matter in my body, otherwise I could never raise my arm at all. The question, then, arises, What is that mysterious substance which the mind can touch, as its prime agent, by which it produces muscular motion? In the light our subject now stands, the answer is most simple. It is that *very substance* which was disturbed in this paralysis, and that is the nervous fluid, which is animal electricity, and forms the connecting link between mind and matter. Mind is the only substance in the universe that possesses inherent *motion* and living *power* as its two PRIMEVAL EFFICIENTS. These two seem to be inseparable, because there can be no manifestation of power except through motion. Hence MIND is the first grand moving cause. It is the *first link* in the magnificent chain of existing substances. This mind wills. This mental energy, as the creative force, is the *second link*, and stirs the nervous force, which is electricity. This is the *third link*. This electricity causes the nerve to vibrate. This is the *fourth link*. The vibration of the nerve contracts the fibre of the muscle. This is the *fifth link*. The contraction of the muscle raises the bone or the arm. This is the *sixth link*. And the arm raises dead matter. This is the *seventh link*. So it is through a chain of seven links that mind comes in contact with dead matter; that is, if we allow the creative force—the *will*—to be one link. This *will*, however, is not a *substance*, but a mere energy, or *result* of mind. To be plain, it is mind that touches electricity—electricity touches nerve—nerve touches muscle—muscle touches bone—and bone raises dead matter. It is, therefore, through this concatenation or chain, link by link, that the mind gives motion to and controls living or dead matter, and not by direct contact with all substances. Hence the proof is clear and positive, that the mind can come in contact with, and by its volition control, the electricity of the body, and collect this subtile agent with fearful power upon any part of the system.

It is evident that the mind holds its residence in the brain, and that it is not diffused over the whole system. Were it so, then our hands and feet would think, and in case they were amputated, we should lose part of our minds. If, then, the MIND, invested with ROYALTY, is enthroned in the brain—and if the mind command the foot to move, or the hand to rise, then it must send forth from its presence an agent, as its PRIME MINISTER, to execute this command. This prime minister is ELECTRICITY, which passes from the brain through the nerves, as so many telegraphic wires, to give motion to the extremities. On this principle, how easy it is to understand the philosophy of a paralysis. The nerve, as the grand conductor of the motive power, is obstructed by some spasmodic collapse, and the prime minister cannot pass the barrier that obstructs its path. In this case, the mind, as the enthroned monarch, may WILL the arm to rise, but the arm remains motionless. But remove that barrier, the agent passes, and the arm must rise. Hence it is easily seen, that all motion and power originate in mind.

I have now brought before you the connecting link between mind and matter, and through this have shown you the philosophy of the contraction of the human muscles through mental energy. This has ever been, and still is, considered an inscrutable mystery in Physiology. Whether it is now revealed or not, is submitted to your decision. To my mind, the argument in its defence is irresistible.

Having clearly and philosophically established the truth, that electricity, in the form of nervous fluid, is indeed the connecting link between mind and *inert* matter, the question now presents itself—If the mind continually throws off electricity from the brain by its mental operations, and by muscular motion, then how is the supply kept up in the brain—through what source is it introduced into the system, and how conveyed to the brain? I answer, through the respiratory organs electricity is taken into the blood at the lungs, and from the blood it is thrown to nerves and conducted to the brain, and is there secreted and prepared for the use of the mind. It will be impossible for me to argue this point fully unless I explain at the same instant the philosophy of the circulation of the blood. As I differ also with physiologists on this point, and as I do not believe that the heart circulates the blood at all, either on the hydraulic, or any other principle, so I will turn your attention to this subject.

The philosophy of the circulation of the blood is one of the grandest themes that can be presented for human contemplation. While discussing this matter, it will be clearly made to appear how electricity is gathered from the surrounding elements, carried into the system and stored up in the brain to feed the mind with impressions. I desire it to be distinctly understood, that when I speak of the *electricity, galvanism,* and *magnetism* of the human system, or of the *nervous fluid,* I mean one and the same thing. But before I proceed to notice the philosophy of the circulation of the blood, and the secretion of the nervous fluid, I will first make a few observations in relation to the *nerves* and *blood-vessels,* so that I may be distinctly understood.

I have already stated, that the brain is the fountain of the nervous system, and that both its hemispheres are made up of a congeries of nerves. They both pass to the cerebellum; and the spinal marrow, continued to the bottom of the trunk, is but the brain continued. In the spinal marrow, which is the grand conductor from the brain, is lodged the whole strength of the system. From this spinal marrow, branch out thirty-two pairs of nerves, embracing the nerves of motion and those of sensation. From these branch out others, and others again from these; and so on till they are spread out over the human system in network so infinitely fine that we cannot put down the point of a needle without feeling it—and we cannot feel, unless we touch a nerve. We see, therefore, how inconceivably fine the nervous system is. In all these millions of nerves there is no blood. They contain the electric fluid only, while the blood is confined to the veins and arteries. I am well aware that the blood-vessels pass round among the convolutions of the brain, and through them the blood freely flows to give that mighty organ action; but in the nerves themselves there is no blood. They are the residence of the living mind, and its prime agent, the electric fluid.

Though I have frequently, in my public lectures, touched upon the philosophy of the circulation of the blood, and hence those remarks were reported and published in my "Lectures on the Philosophy of Animal Magnetism, in 1843," in connection with my views of the connecting link between mind and matter, yet I have never taken up the subject in an exact, full, and connected detail of argument. This I will now proceed to do in connection with the secretion of the nervous fluid.

I would, then, in the first instance remark, that the air we breathe, as to its component parts, is computed to consist of twenty-one parts OXYGEN, and seventy-nine parts NITROGEN. Electricity, as a universal agent, pervades the entire atmosphere. We cannot turn the electric machine in any dry spot on earth without collecting it. Oxygen is that element which sustains flame and animal life. Neither can exist a moment without it, while nitrogen, on the contrary, just as suddenly extinguishes both. The atmosphere, in this compound state, is taken into the lungs. The oxygen and electricity, having a strong affinity for moisture, instantly rush to the blood, while the nitrogen is disengaged and expired. The blood, being oxygenized and electrified, instantly assumes a bright cherry-red appearance, and by this energizing process has become purified and prepared for circulation. The lungs, and the blood they contain, are both rendered electrically *positive;* and we know that in electrical science two positives resist each other and fly apart. Hence the lungs resist the blood and force it into the left ventricle of the heart. The valve closes and the blood passes into the arteries. Hence arterial blood is of a bright cherry-red hue. It is by the *positive* force of electric action, propelled through every possible ramification of the arterial system till all its thousands of minute capillary vessels are charged. Along these arteries and all their thousands of capillary branches are laid nerves of involuntary motion, but no nerves whatever attend the veins. Why is this so? Why is it, that nerves, like so many telegraphic wires, are laid along the whole arterial system in all its minute ramifications, but that none are laid along the venous system? I press this question—Why do nerves attend the arteries, while none attend the veins? I answer, that nerves are laid along the arteries to receive the electric charge from the *positive* blood that rolls in them, which charge the blood received from the air inspired by the lungs. But as the venous blood is *nega-*

tive, it has no electricity to throw off, and hence needs no attendant nerves to receive a charge—because that very electric charge, which the blood receives from each inspiration at the lungs, is thrown off into the nerves by friction, as it rolls through its destined channels in crimson streams. At the extremities of the arterial system—at the very terminus of its thousands of capillaries, the last item of the electric charge takes its departure from the positive blood, escapes into the attendant nerves, through them is instantly conducted to the brain, and is there basined up for the use of the mind.

The arterial blood, having thrown off its electricity as above described, assumes a dark—a purplish hue. It enters the capillaries of the veins, which are as numerous as those of the arteries. The blood is now *negative,* and as the lungs, by new inspirations, are kept in a *positive state,* so the venous blood returns through the right ventricle of the heart to the lungs, on the same principle that the *negative* and *positive* forces rush together. There it is again electrified and oxygenized, changed to a bright cherry-red color, is again rendered *positive,* and is thus purified and prepared once more for arterial circulation. We now clearly perceive that it is electrically the blood circulates, and electrically it recedes from, and returns to, the lungs through the two ventricles of the heart. The heart does not circulate the blood at all, as physiologists contend. The heart is the SUPREME REGULATOR of this sublime and constantly ebbing and flowing OCEAN of crimson life, with all its majestic rivers and frolicking streams, and determines **with exactness how rapidly the whole shall flow.**

LECTURE IV.

Ladies and Gentlemen:

I have in my last Lecture touched upon the philosophy of the circulation of the blood, the nervous system, and the secretion of electricity upon the brain, which I call the nervous fluid. As this part of my subject must, on account of its importance, possess peculiar interest to us all, I desire to dwell upon it a few moments longer.

From the arguments already offered, it will be clearly perceived by every philosophic mind, that the circulating system is in reality *two* distinct systems. The *first* is the ARTERIAL SYSTEM, that carries the *positive blood*, which is, as before stated, of a bright cherry-red color, and is ever flowing from the heart to the extremities. The *second* is the VENOUS SYSTEM, that carries the NEGATIVE BLOOD, which is of a purple color, and is ever flowing from the extremities to the heart. To these two circulating systems, the heart, with its two auricles, two ventricles, and valves, is exactly adapted, so as to keep the *positive* and *negative* blood apart, and to regulate the motion of both

And it will be perceived that the nervous system most perfectly corresponds with what I have said of the circulating system. I mean that nerves of involuntary motion are laid along the arteries to receive the charge of electricity from the *positive* blood that flows in them. These views of the circulation of the blood are strengthened by the fact, that the blood contains a certain portion of iron; and we well know that iron becomes a magnet only by induction, and loses its magnetic power the moment the electric current passes from it. Hence the blood, through the agency of the iron it contains, can easily assume a *positive state* at the instant it receives the electric charge from the air at the lungs. It can then pass into the arteries, and by friction throw off its electricity into the nerves, and again assume a *negative state* as it enters the veins.

I now consider the ELECTRIC or MAGNETIC CIRCULATION of the blood philosophically and irresistibly proved. Hence the position which many assume, that the heart circulates the blood on the hydraulic or vacuum principle, is utterly unfounded in truth. And that the heart, in accomplishing this, exerts a force, as they contend, of more than one hundred thousand pounds, is too preposterous to be believed. I grant that the heart is the strongest muscle in the human system; but who can for one moment believe that its motive power is equal to fifty tons? The heart, as I have already observed, does not circulate the blood at all; nor on the contrary does the blood cause the heart to throb. The heart and lungs both receive their motions from the cerebellum, which is the fountain and origin of organic life and involuntary motion. Hence the involuntary nerves from the cerebellum throb the heart and heave the lungs, and the electricity contained in the air they inspire, circulates the blood and supplies the brain with nervous fluid, as I have already explained.

Perhaps, however, the inquiry may here arise, What proof is there that the involuntary nerves from the cerebellum throb the heart and heave the lungs, and that the blood is not made to circulate from the same cause?

This double interrogatory is easily answered. Insert, for instance, a surgical knife between the joints of the vertebræ, and cut off the spinal marrow below the lungs and heart—all the parts below this incision will be so completely paralyzed, and voluntary motion and sensation so entirely destroyed, that we have no power to move the limbs by any volition we may exert; nor have we any power to feel, even though the paralyzed limbs should be broken to pieces by a hammer, or burned with fire. Yet in these immovable and unfeeling parts the blood continues to circulate as usual through the veins and arteries. This is proof positive that the blood is not made to flow by any power whatever invested in the cerebellum, but, as before proved, by the *positive* and *negative* forces of that electricity contained in the air inspired by the lungs. But let the spinal marrow be severed above the lungs and heart, and both will be instantly paralyzed and cease their motions ; yet the last inspiration taken in by the lungs will cause the blood to circulate till it floods the right ventricle of the heart with venous blood, and empties the left ventricle of its arterial blood. This is proof the most irresistible, that the HEART AND LUNGS ARE MOVED BY AN INVOLUNTARY NERVOUS FORCE ORIGINATING IN THE CEREBELLUM, while the blood is circulated by the *positive* and *negative* forces of that electricity which is taken in with the air at the lungs. The lungs merely act as a double force-pump to bring in the surrounding atmosphere, extract from it a proper supply of the vital principle to feed the bright and burning flame of life, and to reject and expire the dregs unfit for that end. This is perhaps as much as it is necessary to say in relation to the circulation of the blood, and the constant secretion of the nervous fluid from the arterial blood to the brain. I now turn to the philosophy of disease, and will be brief as possible.

It is generally supposed by medical men, that there are innumerable causes for the various diseases in existence, and that even one disease may have many causes in nature to produce it. But I contend, that there is but one grand CAUSE for all diseases, and this is the disturbing of the vital force of the body. There is in every human being a certain amount of electricity. This is, as I have said, the most subtile and fine material in the body; is the power, as has been shown, that moves the blood; and is the agent by which the mind, through the nerves, contracts the muscles and produces motion. And as all the convulsions and operations in nature and in man invariably begin in the invisible and finest substances in being, and end in the most gross, so electricity, in the human system, is the cause of all the effects there produced, whether salutary or otherwise. When this electricity is equalized throughout the nervous system, the blood will also be equalized in its circulation, and the natural result is health. But when it is thrown out of balance, the blood will, in like manner, be also disturbed, and the natural result is disease; and the disease will be severe or mild in the same ratio as the vital force is more or less disturbed.

I am well aware that medical men are much inclined to examine the patient's pulse, and watch the movements of the blood. They seem to think that nearly all diseases originate in the blood, and hence, under this impression, hundreds of specifics, or nostrums, have arisen to purify the blood, as though it contained some foreign properties that rendered it impure, and that these, by some medical treatment, must be extracted or removed from the system. But all this is fallacious, as the blood contains no foreign properties to render it impure. The blood becomes impure only through a disturbed circulation. It can be purified by no other substances in being, except what are contained in the air at the lungs. These are oxygen and electricity. The whole blood in the body must, every few moments, be passed through the lungs to be purified and preserved from putrefaction. If the circulation, in any part of the body, be obstructed, or thrown out of balance, so that the blood cannot pay its timely visit to the lungs, it must become extravasated and impure. If, in any part of the body, there is a complete obstruction, so that the blood is entirely retained, then inflammation, ulceration, and corruption must ensue.

I now turn directly to the subject, and call your undivided attention to the philosophy of disease. The operations of the mind, and the nervous system of man, have been too much overlooked by medical men, who have paid great attention to the blood, and to the more gross and solid parts of the body. But it is evident that disease begins in the electricity of the nerves, and not in the blood. Electricity is the starting point. From thence it is communicated to the blood, from the blood to the flesh, and from the flesh to the bones, which are the last effected. It begins in the finest, and ends in the grossest particles of the system. The unseen are the starting powers.

I have already remarked that the brain is the fountain of the nervous system, and sends forth its millions of branches to every possible part and extremity of the body. This nervous system is filled with electricity, which is the agent or servant of the royal mind, who, as monarch, holds his throne in the brain. From thence the mind, by its volitions, controls one half of the electricity of the system. It controls all that is contained in the voluntary nerves, but has no such control over the other half, which is confined to the involuntary nerves.

Though there is but one grand cause of disease, *which is the electricity of the system thrown out of balance*, yet there are, nevertheless, *two modes* by which this may be done. It may be done by mental impressions. And so it may be done by physical impressions from external nature. I will first notice how diseases are produced by *mental impressions*.

Millions of our race have been swept from the light of life to the darkness of death by various diseases caused by mental impressions. Misfortune and distress have fallen upon many a father, a mother, and many a child. They have shut up in their bosoms all these mental woes, and brooded over their misfortunes in secret, concealed grief. Melancholy took possession of the heart, the vital force was disturbed, the system was thrown out of balance, disease was engendered, and they went to their graves.

I am now addressing this audience. The action of

my mind has called the electricity of the system from the extremities to the brain. The blood has followed it. My feet being robbed of their due proportion of the vital force, are, in the same ratio, cold, and hence, this is, so far, disease. And unless I ceased speaking, and suffered a reaction to take place, it would bring me to my grave.

A man accumulates a fortune of two hundred thousand dollars. He loses one half of it, and is hurled in distress. He broods over his misfortune. The mind is in trouble; it shrinks back on itself. The electricity of the system, this servant of the mind, leaves the extremities and approaches the brain, the throne of the master. The blood follows on; the excitement becomes great, and he believes he shall die in an almshouse. He is a monomaniac. Suppose he now loses the other half of his fortune, and his mind will become involved in still greater distress. This mental action calls an increased quantity of electricity, that is, of nervous fluid, to the brain, and an equal amount of blood follows on. He is now entirely deranged, and his feet are incessantly cold, because the brain has robbed them of their due proportion of the vital force. Now do you not perceive, that if these forces are dispersed from the brain, and the circulation equalized, that his reason will be restored? There is not too much of blood and electricity in the system, but there may be too much in any one department of the system. I will now suppose him once more in possession of his reason. Now bring him intelligence that his darling child is crushed to atoms. The mind suddenly shrinks back on itself; the electric, or nervous fluid, instantly darts to the brain, like a faithful servant to see what distresses the master. The blood as suddenly follows the servant. The storm rages, and a fit ensues. Let the news be still more startling, and the congregated forces will, in the same ratio, be increased upon the brain, and he drops a corpse! So we perceive that, in all these instances, there is but one cause of disease. The only difference we have witnessed in the effects produced, was a gradually increased action, occasioned by an increased power of the same cause, even from the slightest excitement, gradually up to that fearful point where it produced instant death. An instance analagous to this, transpired here among you, in the case of the distinguished statesman, John Quincy Adams. Perhaps too much anxiety and thought for the welfare of his country, at his advanced age, called the forces to the brain, and the brilliant lamp of reason and life was extinguished! He has entered on other scenes!

I have thus far confined my remarks to effects produced upon the brain by the electro-nervous fluid and blood, which were called there by the various emotions, passions, and sensations of the mind. But that these forces should invade the territory of the brain, and produce such results, depends, however, upon the condition of the brain as to its comparative physical strength with the other parts of the system. In this view of the subject, had the same misfortunes as to loss of property above stated been visited upon this same individual when his brain was firm, a different disease would have been the result. Suppose that his brain, as to its physical structure, had been strong and firm, but that his lungs had been weak. Now let the same misfortunes befall him. His mind again shrinks back on itself; the electro-nervous force, as before, starts for the brain, but is not allowed to enter this palace of the distressed monarch, and it stops at the lungs, the weakest and nearest post. The blood next follows on in pursuit of the servant, and takes up its abode with him. Inflammation sets in, and, if the trouble of the monarch continues, tubercles form, ulceration takes place, and death ensues. It was consumption.

But suppose the lungs had been strong, and that the stomach had been, by some trivial circumstance, rendered the weakest part. The electro-nervous fluid and blood would, in this case, have gone there, and taken possession of that post. Inflammation, canker, with morbid secretions would have ensued, and even ulcers might have been formed. The digestive organs would have been weakened, and dyspepsia, with all its horror of horrors, would have been the result. If the liver had been the weaker spot, the same forces, under the same mental impressions, would have congregated there, and produced the liver complaint. If the stomach and liver had both been strong, and the spine weak, it would have been a spinal complaint. If all these had been physically firm, and the kidneys weak, the same forces would have produced a disease of the kidneys. And if all in the regions of the brain and trunk had been firm, and a mere blow had been inflicted upon the hip, knee, or any part of the lower limbs, the electro-nervous force and the attendant blood would have gone there, and produced the white swelling, or any other species of inflammation and distress. So we perceive, that the same CAUSE, under MENTAL IMPRESSIONS, may produce any of these diseases. As to the character of the disease, it merely takes its name from the organ or place in the body where it may locate itself. Hence diseases differ one from another only as the various diseased organs, their motions, secretions, and functions may differ—or as the various located parts of the body invaded by disease may differ from each other. But the producing CAUSE of all these diseases is one and the same. It is the ELECTRO-NERVOUS FLUID of the body.

Having said all that I at present deem necessary in relation to the disturbing of the nervous force by MENTAL IMPRESSIONS, I will now turn your attention to the disturbing of the nervous force by PHYSICAL IMPRESSIONS

As the mind in distress—in secret melancholy and grief—has disturbed the nervous force, which has engendered disease by calling the blood and other fluids of the body to its presence, and thus sent millions to their graves—as it has produced all the diseases we have mentioned and even hundreds more—so the same diseases and hundreds more are also produced by the nervous force when it is disturbed by *physical impressions* from external nature.

I am well aware that *mental* and *physical* impressions may be termed *causes* of disease; but it will be remembered, that medical men contend that there are *remote* and *proximate* causes of disease. I am on the latter, and contend that there are not thousands of *proximate* causes, but only *one* grand PROXIMATE CAUSE of disease, and this is the disturbing of the nervous fluid, or throwing the electricity of the system out of balance; and that diseases begin in the electric force of the nerves, and not in the blood. They begin in the invisible and finest substance of the body, and end in the gross. Hence the same cause that produces monomania, produces entire derangement, fits, headache, and even the common excitement of the brain in a public speaker. The same cause produces consumption, dyspepsia, liver complaint, spinal affections, pleurisy, cholera, dysentery, inflammations, fevers, etc. This subtile, *disease-causing* principle, is the ELECTRO-NERVOUS FLUID. When equalized throughout the system, it is the cause of health, for it controls the blood and other fluids, and when thrown out of balance, it is the cause of disease. Hence the minister of health and sickness—of life and death—is within us, and is one and the same principle. As electricity is the efficient cause of all convulsions, calms, and storms in nature, and of all the pleasing or awful phenomena that transpire in earth, air, or ocean, or in the vegetable or mineral kingdom, so, as man is but an epitome of the universe, it is electricity in the form of nervous fluid that produces all the convulsions, calms, and storms in his own system.

We have seen the various secret stirrings of electricity in the human nerves under *mental impressions*, in producing insanity, fits, consumptions, etc. We witness the same mournful results when that subtile power is moved by *physical impressions*. A wet foot, for instance, may throw the electro-nervous fluid out of balance, and this subtile force may suddenly check the lacteal or other secretions, and also produce insanity, or fits, or by locating itself upon the lungs, it may produce consumption. The fact is, that the electro-nervous fluid, when disturbed at the extremities, or on the surface of the body, always retires inward, and locates itself upon the weakest organ, or upon some weak portion of the vitals—the blood follows, and disease is the result. As I have fully explained this when noticing mental impressions, so there is no occasion of my par ticularizing. I will merely say, that a sudden exposure to a damp air, sitting upon a cold rock, lying upon the ground and suddenly falling asleep, or sitting with the back to a current of air while in a perspiration—all, or any of these, may at times disturb the electro-nervous force, and arouse this *disease-causing power* from its slumberings. This may throw the blood out of balance, and by locating themselves upon the weakest organ or weakest part of the system, engender disease. Or the nervous force may be disturbed by eating or drinking too much or too little of wholesome substances, or by eating and drinking unwholesome or poisonous substances, and all these correspondent diseases produced.

It is now clearly seen how *mental* and *physical* impressions disturb the electricity of the system, which locates itself upon the weakest organ, calls the blood to its aid, and brings disease, pain, and death. So we perceive, that the same nervous fluid which, when equalized, produces health, is, when thrown out of balance, the cause of disease. The whole electricity of the nerves is, of course, one hundred per cent. Fifty per cent. is under the voluntary control of the mind, and belongs to the voluntary nerves, and the other fifty per cent. is under the control of the involuntary powers of the mind, and belongs to the involuntary nerves. Now if the whole fifty per cent. of either of these forces, which when equalized is health, should be suddenly collected upon any one organ, it would be the destruction of that organ. If the mind, on hearing bad news, or by some sudden distress, should call the whole fifty per cent. of electricity under its control to the brain, apoplexy and death must ensue. This would be done by a *mental impression* on the voluntary nervous force, causing the mind to shrink back on itself and become passive. But the same melancholy result could be produced by eating, drinking, or some other *physical impression* on the involuntary force over which the mind has no such control. Hence it will be understood, that all diseases, originating under mental impressions, are produced by the fifty per cent. of voluntary nervous force. But those diseases, originating under physical impressions, are produced by the fifty per cent. of involuntary nervous force, and over which the mind has no control.

If either of these electro-nervous forces, to a certain amount, should be called to a muscle, it would be pain. If called to a still greater extent, it would be inflammation; and if the whole fifty per cent. were called there, it would be mortification, and the ultimate and absolute destruction of the muscle. The same result would follow in case either of these forces were called to any organ in the system. It would be the destruction of that organ.

There are three kinds of pain: *First*, a pain produced by negative electricity, which attracts the blood to the spot, and is ever attended with inflammation,

Second, a pain produced by positive electricity, which repels the blood, and, though equally severe, is never attended with inflammation. *Third*, a pain produced by the confused mixture of the two forces, and consists in a burning, itching, or prickly sensation, and is often very distressing.

I have now given you a few hints on the philosophy of disease, which are of course novel to you all; but they are, nevertheless, as interesting and important to the welfare of our race, as they are novel and strange. Medical men have ever noticed the great effect that the mind has upon the body, both as it regards a disastrous or salutary result. Hence they keep up the brightest hopes of their patients as to recovery, and carefully guard every one against uttering to them a word of discouragement. These effects they have seen, but not understanding the connecting link between mind and matter, the true philosophy of disease has been by them entirely overlooked, and in relation to this science they may after all cry "*humbug.*" But this will avail them nothing, for truth, after all, will stand unshaken, and be appreciated by after generations, when opposition shall have been interred, with no hope of its resurrection. In view of our subject, so far as it regards mental impressions, we see the supreme importance of maintaining a reconciled state of mind. Equanimity of mind is the parent of health, peace, and happiness and the noblest test of the true Christian. When we see thousands always restless, complaining of cold and heat, and wet and dry—complaining of their own condition, and finding fault with others, and dissatisfied with the events of Providence—we need not marvel that so many complain of indisposition and disease. **This state of mind produces them. So beware.**

LECTURE V.

LADIES AND GENTLEMEN:

When we reflect how extensive a field the philosophy of disease naturally occupies, and how vast a range we must take in order to inspect minutely its several parts, it will then be seen that my remarks, in my last Lecture, have been brief in comparison with the vastness of the subject. I flatter myself, however, that my views are understood, and that the importance of the doctrine of mental and physical impressions, in relation to disease, is clearly seen, and fully appreciated by you all. I believe it to be founded in immutable truth, and that it will survive the crush of empires and the revolution of ages.

Having brought forward the PHILOSOPHY OF DISEASE in my last Lecture, I now turn to the RATIONALE OF ITS CURE in this.

In discussing the doctrine of mental impressions, I have clearly and irresistibly proved that the mind by shrinking back on itself in fear, melancholy, and grief, in the day of adversity, misfortune, and distress, can disturb the electro-nervous fluid, and allow it to concentrate itself upon any organ of the body and engender disease. If, then, the mind can disturb the equilibrium of the nervo-electric force and call it to some organ so as to produce disease, then the mind can also disperse it, equalize the circulation, and restore health. This it can do by a mental impression, admitting the impression to be sufficiently great. For example: A man in possession of five thousand dollars is riding homeward on horseback in the evening. He is within a mile of his house. He is weary and his head aches so severely that he is obliged to walk his horse. He is so indisposed and faint that he can but just keep his saddle. From a lonely dismal spot at the road side, a robber springs and seizes his horse's bridle—presents a pistol, and exclaims, "Your money, or your life!" The rider, with a loaded whip, and at the impulse of the moment, suddenly strikes the robber's arm. This causes the pistol to discharge, and adds to the confusion of the moment. The rider, scarcely knowing what he is about, puts spurs to his horse. He darts off at the top of his speed. Before he is aware, he is at his own door. He dismounts and finds himself safe. The vital force is driven to the extremities, and his hands and feet are warm. Where is his headache now? It is gone. The supreme impression of his mind drove the electro-nervous fluid from his brain—the blood followed it—a reaction took place, and he was well. Is there any thing strange in this?

No. Then there is nothing strange in this science, for it is the curing of diseases by the doctrine of impressions.

I desire it to be distinctly understood how this power operates. Remember mind touches the electro-nervous fluid, moves it—and this fluid moves the blood. Electrical Psychology is the doctrine of impressions, and the same disease that mind, or even physical impressions can cause, the mind can remove, if the patient be in the psychological state. Because mental impressions to any extent we please can be produced upon him. It is therefore immaterial from what source a disease may arise, or what kind of a disease it may be, the mind can, by its impressions, cause the nervous fluid to cure it, or at least to produce upon it a salutary influence. If exposure to heat or cold, dampness or dryness, or to any of the changing elements, should call the nervous fluid to the lungs, and disturb the circulation of the blood, so as to produce inflammation, the mind could disperse and equalize it, and thus effect a cure as readily as though this inflammation of the lungs had been brought on by melancholy and grief, or by any other mental distress. Or if these exposures had caused any other disease or pain in the system, the mind could have had the same power to remove it, as though it had been caused by mental distress. Or if by eating, drinking, or by sedentary habits, dyspepsia had been produced, the mind could have had the same power to produce a salutary result, or even to cure it as though it had been caused by mental distress. I do not mean that a cure can be effected by the electro-nervous force, *through mental impressions*, if there be any organic destruction of the parts diseased. The consumption, for instance, could not be cured if the lungs were ulcerated; sight could not be restored if the optic nerve were destroyed; nor could deafness be removed if the auditory nerve were destroyed. In these cases, even, medical remedies, it must be granted, would be of no avail, because there is no foundation on which to build. In all I have said, or may say in regard to cures, I have reference only to curable cases. I mean, that the fifty per cent. of electro-nervous force, under the control of the mind, could effect a cure where there is no organic destruction, and where there is, at the same time, a sufficiency of vital force left to build upon, so as to be able to produce a sanative result. Nor do I mean to be understood that this science alone can at all times cure. It may require medicines to co-operate with it. As diseases are produced through mental and physical impressions, so through mental and physical impressions they must be cured.

Medicine produces a physical impression on the system, but never heals a disease. If a disease were ever healed through medicines, it was healed by the same sanative power as though it had been done by a mental impression in accordance with the teachings of Electrical Psychology. This is evident; because the sanative power is in the individual, and not in the medicine. Medicines and mental impressions only call that sanative principle to the right spot in the system so as to enable it to do its work. The following example will explain my meaning on this particular point:

You enter a garden and see a peach-tree with its fruit not fully grown, but so heavily laden, that one of its limbs is partially split from the trunk. The gardener is aware that if it be neglected till the fruit grows to maturity, the limb will be entirely parted from the tree and die. He carefully raises the limb till the split closes, and puts under it a prop to keep it to its place. He winds canvas around the wounded part, and over this he puts tar. Now there is certainly no healing principle in the prop—there is none in the canvas—nor is there any in the tar. The prop merely sustains the weight of the limb, and keeps the split together; the canvas is wound around it to prevent the tar from entering the split; and the tar was applied to protect the whole from the air, rains, and external elements; while the tree is left to the *inherent operations of its own sanative principles*. The sanative principle being in the tree, it must heal itself. So the healing principle is in man, as much so as it is in the tree. The healing principle in the tree is the *invisible electro-vegetative fluid.* This moves and equalizes the sap, and the sap affects the wood. It is the electricity of the tree that does the work ; and this electricity is under the control of its vegetable life. So the healing principle in man is the *invisible electro-nervous* fluid. This moves and equalizes the blood, and the blood affects the flesh. It is the electricity of the system, under the control of the mind.

The position is incontrovertible, that the healing principle is in man. Admitting it to be electricity, or what I call the electro-nervous fluid of the system, it is then easily seen that there is no healing principle in medicine, and it is also understood what effect medicine must have upon the system in order to produce a salutary influence. It must equalize the electricity, as before remarked, and call it to the proper spot, so as to enable it to do its healing work. Hence, if the mind can so operate upon the fifty per cent. of the electro-nervous force under its control, as to equalize it, then it follows, as a matter of course, that the same healing result will be obtained as is effected by medicine. In either case there is no difference in the healing power. In both instances it is the same. The only difference is, that in the one case the healing power was made to act by the mind, which produced its *mental* impression, and in the other case by the medicine, which produced its *physical* impression.

It may now be asked, If medicine has no healing

property in it, then how can an emetic remove impurities from the stomach by vomiting the patient? In reply I would state, that it has never done so. In this I desire to be distinctly understood. I mean that an emetic is not the vomiting principle. The vomiting principle is in the man. It is the electricity of the system. The electro-nervous fluid of the brain is the vomiting principle. Let us understand the philosophy of this. Emetics, whether *mineral* or *vegetable*, possess those peculiar chemical properties that cause immense secretions. This effect is the whole secret of their power. An emetic, taken into the stomach, produces secretions most freely from the glands of the stomach, from the mucous membrane of the lungs, from the glands of the trachæ, and from the glands of the mouth and tongue. It robs them of their moisture which is continually accumulating upon the stomach. The parts being robbed of their moisture by this artificial action, the electricity from the nerves follows it, because electricity has a strong affinity for moisture. When a sufficiency of the electric force is drawn from the brain, and the blood having in the same ratio followed it, the countenance becomes pale—an expansion and collapse of the stomach takes place, and vomiting is the result. This is its philosophy. In proof of the fact, electricity cannot be gathered in damp weather. The moisture, for which **it has a strong affinity, holds it.**

LECTURE V.

After all I have said of medicine and its operations, it may yet be supposed that it possesses some healing principle, and that the emetic does vomit the patient. Why then will it not vomit a dead man? The answer is, because the vital force is gone, and the emetic is powerless. But why will it not vomit the man when he is worn out with disease and near his end? I answer, because the vital force in the man, on which vomiting depends, is wasted; and as it does not exist in the medicine, so the emetic, in its chemical action having no material to work upon, or to call to its aid, is powerless.

If this is not satisfactory to your minds in the settlement of the question whether the vomiting principle is in the medicine or in the patient, I will pursue the subject still farther. Suppose while eating strawberries and cream, you tell a sensitive lady that she has taken into the stomach a worm, or even a fly—she stops eating, and in a minute she vomits freely. How is this, when she has swallowed, in fact, neither worm nor fly? I answer, that the vomiting principle is in the brain. She believed that she had taken into the stomach what was stated; she kept her attention steadily and most intently upon it—and the mind threw the electro-nervous force from the brain to the stomach, until there was a sufficient quantity to produce an expansion and collapse of the stomach, and cause vomiting. Now the vomiting in this case and in the case of the emetic was occasioned by one and the same thing, and that is the electro-nervous fluid. The only difference in the two cases is, that the emetic called it from the brain by a *physical* impression, and the mind forced it from the brain by a *mental* impression.

If the vomiting principle is not in us, why then does it turn the stomach to see an animal eating any thing very filthy, like the dog returning to his vomit? If this principle is not in us, how can it produce nausea? How can the motion of a vessel, and sometimes even the motion of a carriage, produce vomiting, unless it exists in the nervous force of the brain? Why will a fall, or blow upon the head, produce it.

The same is true in relation to cathartics, which excite the secretions of the glands, but of other glands than those affected by an emetic. A cathartic excites the secretions of the mucous glands of the alimentary canal. This draws the electric action from the brain, but mostly from the nerves on the surface of the body there, and produces its results. I have been thus particular upon the action and operation of emetics, as this one hint is sufficient to lead any reflecting mind to a correct impression of the relation in which medicines stand to the human system. They are the mere props and supports of some weak part, to aid nature in restoring herself to health and vigor. A cathartic, taken into the stomach of a very sensitive individual, will produce the result of an emetic; and an emetic, too long in effecting its end in the first stomach, will, after passing the duodenum, produce the result of a cathartic in the second stomach.

I have now said all that is necessary in relation to the curing of diseases by the ELECTRO-NERVOUS FORCE, and have clearly shown how this force can be made to act by mind, or by medicine. I will now give advice in relation to avoiding disease and preserving health, which it will be well for every one to observe who is desirous of securing this inestimable blessing. As life is dear to all, I shall be pardoned when I say that medical gentlemen are mad who administer medicine in silence to the patient without candidly informing him what the medicine is, and what effect or effects he intends it to produce. If the patient were thus instructed by a physician in whom he had full confidence, then he would be in constant expectation of the anticipated effect; and the mind, by its mental impressions, acting in concert with the physical impressions of the medicine, would produce a salutary and happy result. I grant that this information cannot be given to infants, nor to deranged persons; but it should be done in all possible cases.

In order to preserve health, *the body should be kept clean, and the mind pure and calm.* There are extremes in every thing, and these should be carefully avoided. The body should be carefully washed all over, or bathed, except the head, in water moderately cool. No soap should be used in either case, and the process should not occupy more than *three* or *four* minutes. It should be briskly rubbed with a coarse towel, and mostly downward, so as not to disturb the minute scales that cover the pores. In cold weather, colder water should be used than in moderate weather. Indeed, the water should be about the temperature of the elements. But in freezing weather the body should be merely immersed, and almost immediately extricated, and the washing process should not occupy more than a moment of time. In cold weather, twice per week is sufficient; and in warm weather, every alternate day is abundant, in ordinary cases. Too frequent washings and bathings, and of too long continuance, to persons in ordinary health, is deleterious, as it destroys too much of the natural oil of the skin, which the Creator has supplied to give it a soft and silky texture. The system of hydropathy has great force, if rightly managed. In cases of heat, or inflammation, warm water should be applied, and the reaction would be coolness; and in cases of cold feet, they should be washed on going to bed each night in cold water, till they remain continually warm. The coldest water will extract the frost from a frozen hand, whereas if it were immersed in the warmest water that could be borne, it would perhaps destroy it, so as to render even amputation necessary. But if the hand be burned or scalded, immersing it in the warmest water that can be borne, or holding it to the fire, will produce a salutary result, even though the remedy be a harsh one. On this principle, you see the inconsistency of cold water applications, and even of ice to the head in brain fevers, or where there is a severe inflammation of the brain, occasioned by a fall, a blow, or any concussion.

I now turn the attention of ladies and gentlemen to eating, drinking, and wearing apparel, and will endeavor, in few words as possible, to show the bearing of these upon the human constitution.

Our bodies are made up of the elements, and, as I have already observed, are an epitome of the universe. In order to insure perfect health, we should subsist entirely upon the provisions, whether vegetable or animal, that are produced in that part of the earth where we were born and reared, or in that part of the earth where we intend to spend our days. And, moreover, our wearing apparel should also be the product of the same section where we live. Cotton should never be worn where the snow covers the earth, or in that part of the earth's latitude where it cannot be raised. Hemp, flax, cotton, wool, and silk may be worn with perfect safety in those latitudes of the earth's surface where they can be cultivated. The Creator's works are perfect. He has established complete harmony between the vegetables, and the soil where they grow, and the climate that fostered their existence and warmed them into life. He, therefore, who eats the food belonging to his own latitude, who drinks the water that gushes from his own springs, and wears the clothing produced in his own climate, establishes a perfect harmony and aptitude between his own body and the surrounding elements. I mean that he does this in case he uses these blessings temperately, as not abusing them.

The truth of this will appear perfectly clear, if we have a correct understanding of inuring ourselves to another climate, entirely different from the one to which we have been accustomed. I will therefore call your attention to the PHILOSOPHY OF BECOMING ACCLIMATED.

The mineral kingdom lays a foundation for the vegetable, and the vegetable for the animal kingdom. It is therefore perfectly clear that no animals could have had an existence till there were vegetables, because an *animal* is but a *vegetable* of the *second* growth. Each latitude of the globe has vegetables peculiar to itself, and these make up all the varieties that exist on earth. But the same species of vegetables differ from each other in different latitudes, as far as the climates and elements or soils may differ from each other. An apple, pear, or peach, grown in forty degrees north latitude, differs considerably from the same fruit raised in thirty degrees north latitude. This is certain, because it is the result of surrounding elements that gave it being. The same may be said of corn, wheat, and rye in different latitudes. And as animals are but vegetables of the second growth, hence the same animals vary in accordance with their latitudes. The beef, mutton, and pork, raised in thirty and forty degrees north latitude, are therefore unlike, each being adapted to its own climate and the vegetables that sustained them.

I have already stated, that our bodies are made of the water, the vegetables, and animals upon which we subsist, and are adapted to the climate and surrounding elements where we were born and reared. Our bodies are continually wasting away, and by food and drink are continually repaired. We lose the fleshy particles of our bodies about once a year, and the bones in about seven years. Hence in seven years we have possessed seven bodies of flesh and blood, and one frame of bones. We have not now, in all probability, a particle of flesh and bones we had seven years ago. The water we have drank, and the flesh and vegetables we have eaten, having made up the component parts of our bodies, cause us to hanker and long for the same substances of which our bodies are composed. Like substance in us calls for like substance without, to supply the waste of the system. This is habitude.

Now suppose we suddenly change our climate from forty to thirty degrees north latitude. The air, water, fruits, vegetables, and flesh all differ. The old particles composing our bodies, and brought from forty degrees north latitude, fly off as usual. This produces hunger and thirst, and we supply our wants by the water and food of thirty degrees north latitude, and continue for weeks to do so. This creates a conflict between the old substances of our bodies and the new flesh and blood continually forming, throws the electro-nervous force out of balance, and engenders disease. If we live and struggle on, for about seven years, we become ACCLIMATED, because our old flesh and bones, formed by the substances of one latitude, have disappeared, and our entire systems are made up of the substances of another latitude. Hence we see the danger of changing our positions on the globe to any great extent, which may, however, in some instances, prove beneficial to the constitution. Such is the PHILOSOPHY of being ACCLIMATED.

In view of what I have now brought forward, it will be clearly perceived, by ladies and gentlemen, that we should confine ourselves to the water, fruits, grains, and animal food, and even to the medicines produced in that climate where we live, and reject those of distant latitudes and foreign climates. To drink tea and coffee, and eat oranges, lemons, citrons, pineapples, and the productions of all parts of the globe, is like changing, in some measure, our climate for another, or for several others, and thus keeping up a continual conflict between the elementary particles that are constantly entering the composition of our bodies. There is an incessant war waged between the climate where we live, and the productions of another region, and those of our own. To all this, add the clothing of other distant climes to be worn by us, and who can marvel that almost every man, woman, and child is complaining of some indisposition, or else groaning under disease and pain? Abandon luxuries of foreign growth; avoid dissipation; keep your bodies clean; your minds calm and contented; eat the productions of your own climate; drink the clear crystal water of your own spring; wear the flax, hemp, cotton, or wool that is raised in your own latitude; take all the rest of sleep that your nature and temperament require; have your hours of study, labor, exercise, and serious contemplation all regulated; and be temperate in all things. Follow these directions, and no doctor will enter your house. If you must have tea, use sage, pennyroyal, and hemlock. These are wholesome, and habit will transform them into luxuries far transcending the nerve-destroying plant of China.

It is impossible that the Creator could have erred in adapting all the fruits, grains, and other vegetable substances to each latitude of the earth, so that man and other creatures can subsist there in health, peace, and happiness. And man no more requires the products of other climes to increase these blessings, than the animals around him, who find not only their food and drink, but even their medicines produced by the soil on which they tread, without resorting to foreign importations. At the novelty of these ideas you may smile, but they are based upon immutable truth, and established, constituted, and sustained by HIM who founded the pillars of strength and beauty that support the fabric of nature, and must stand till they shall fall.

LECTURE VI.

Ladies and Gentlemen:

The nature and importance of Electrical Psychology I have clearly and philosophically argued, in a free, unchained, and fearless expression of my thoughts. For this, even if I have erred, I am entitled to your approbation, rather than your condemnation. For what is man, when he makes himself a cowering, cringing slave to the opinions of others, and tamely bows to win the momentary smiles of popular applause from the passing crowd? What I have said in relation to this science, has been the sincere breathings of my own convictions. I have, therefore, reasoned fearless of consequences; and if I have in so doing met your approbation, I rejoice at it; if I have met your disapprobation, I regret it—yet you will pardon me when I say that I cannot alter my course and accommodate myself to the opinions of others, however elevated may be their stations. Fully sensible of the duty I owe to my fellow-men, and to the Supreme Ruler of the universe, and when I discharge this to the best of my ability, I little care what men may think or even say of me.

If, however, what I have argued of the human system—the electro-nervous force—the connecting link between mind and matter—the circulation of the blood—the philosophy of disease—the rationale of its cure—the laws of health, and the philosophy of being acclimated—if these excite your surprise, ladies and gentlemen may then prepare themselves for still greater surprise in the arguments now to be offered on spirit, and the creation and government of the universe. Being myself perfectly unshackled and free, I shall exert myself in that freedom while pursuing this department of my subject.

In my introductory remarks in my THIRD Lecture, 1 took a general survey of the powers and operations of electricity throughout the empire of nature. We saw its secret workings, and its alternately sublime or awful manifestations. But all these operations and convulsions, however magnificently grand, will appear but as the drop of the bucket to the fountain, when compared with the UNSEEN POWER that stirs the universe. Electricity, so swift in its movement as to rival the lightning glance of thought, and so inconceivably awful in its rending force as to convulse the globe to its centre, is yet as nothing, and less than nothing, compared with that Eternal One who arms it with power—who gives it all its expansive force, and who makes it the messenger of his attributes to both nature and man. With his finger he has written the truth of this science on every object throughout the realms of nature. It is written in the beams of the mid-day sun—in the descending rains and gentle dews. It is written in the flowery field and shady grove. It is written in stars on the scroll of night. It is written in lightning on the bosom of the dark cloud. It is written deep in sympathy on the soul, and controls the most powerful affections and stormy passions of the human heart.

In this Lecture I will turn your attention to SPIRIT, or MIND—by which I mean one and the same thing—and will endeavor to prove the existence of an Infinite Spirit.

Though the powers of mind and its complicated operations can be seen, felt, and in a good degree comprehended, yet, after all, we know but little of mind as it regards its *properties*, or *substance*. Some suppose it to be absolutely and positively *immaterial*, because it is purely spirit. Others believe *mind* to be the result of organism, and contend that it cannot exist without a brain, which is the grand organ that secretes thought, even as the liver secretes its bile, or the stomach its gastric juice! The former of these suppositions is the one generally adopted by the Christian community who believe spirit to be an *immateriality*. The latter supposition is embraced by those Christians who wholly rely upon the resurrection of the body for the future existence of the spirit. They are called Materialists, because they make out the spirit to be no substance at all, but merely the result of organized matter. Of this faith was the celebrated Dr. Priestly. This latter position is also adopted by the Atheists, who contend that spirit cannot exist independent of an organized brain ; and as they reject the Christian hope of the resurrection, so they contend that mind is extinguished in the night of the grave, and sleeps in nonentity, to wake no more. Hence the idea of a God, as an intelligent Spirit, they regard as a freak of fancy—a mere chimera of the human brain. Both of these positions as it regards spirit I reject, and will give my reasons for doing so.

I reject the *immateriality* of the spirit, because that which is positively and absolutely *immaterial* cannot of course possess either length, breadth, thickness, nor occupy any space. Indeed, it cannot, in this case, possess any form ; and that which possesses no form, cannot, in the nature of things, occupy any space. And to talk of a thing having an existence, which, at the same time, has no form, nor occupies space, is the most consummate nonsense. Hence an *immateriality* is a nonentity—a blank nothing. On the other hand, if *mind* is merely the result of organism, and if it cannot exist independent of an organized brain, then who made the first brain ? Did it not require an intelligent spirit to organize its several parts, and adapt the eye to light, the ear to sound, and make these organs the inlets of sensation to the inhabitant in that brain ?

Surely the brain did not make itself, for this would only be saying, that the brain acted before it existed!

Having given my reasons for rejecting both these ideas of *mind*, I am now ready to introduce the question, What is MIND? I answer, it is a substance—an element—as really so as air or water, but differs materially from all inert substances in being. I regard *mind* as living and embodied form—as that incomprehensible element whose *nature* it is to possess *life* and *motion*, as much so as it is the nature of other substances to possess inertia. Hence, mind is, in these two respects—namely, *life* and *motion*—directly the opposite of dead matter.

In the first place I will start with the assertion that there must be in the universe an Infinite Mind. It is impossible, in the very nature and constitution of things, that an absolute perfection of substances can be philosophically maintained without this admission. For the truth of this position I rely upon motion. By MOTION, then, I am to prove the existence of an Eternal Mind.

In the first place permit me to remark, that inherent motion is not an attribute common to all substances in nature. This globe, as a body, is moved by the *positive* and *negative* forces of electrical action. And all the operations of nature in the earth and elements are carried on by the same power. Whether it be crystalizations, or petrifactions, the growth of vegetation, or its decomposition—motions and changes in air and water—or the crumbling particles of the mountain rock—all the motions, visible and invisible, that transpire in the mineral and vegetable kingdoms, and in all their multifarious operations, are produced by electricity, which is the universal agent appointed to keep up the order and harmony of the universe. And yet it is certain that electricity does not possess inherent motion as its attribute. Motion belongs to one substance only, and that is mind.

There is certainly as much order in the universe as there is in the human body. Let us, then, look truth calmly in the face. Each organ of the body performs but one function. The eye sees—the ear hears—the olfactories smell—the glands taste—the heart throbs to regulate the blood—the hands handle—the feet walk, and the liver secretes its bile. The eye never hears, and the ear never sees. So there is but ONE SUBSTANCE in nature whose attribute is inherent motion, and that is MIND. Not one single part of the human body possesses independent motion. Electricity is there also the grand agent to move the limbs and vitals, and the living mind is the only moving power.

The point upon which I am now entering is one of most deep and thrilling interest. It is no less than to prove the existence of an Eternal Mind from *motion and the absolute perfection of the chain of elementary substances.* But while accomplishing this, I must call to my aid the relative subtilties of different portions of matter with which we are surrounded. Let us, for a moment, turn our attention to a few of the most obvious substances in nature, and then glance at her absolute perfection as a whole. Let us carefully notice the gradation these substances occupy toward each other in their relation to motion, and then the intrinsic beauty of the subject will appear. I will begin at the heaviest matter that may first suggest itself to my mind, and leisurely pass on, rising higher and still higher, through its various grades, up to that which is more and more rarefied, subtile, and light, till we arrive at that which must necessarily possess inherent motion, and therefore living power.

The heaviest of gross substances in existence is the most difficult to move, and hence must be at the greatest possible distance from motion. Though there are several solid substances heavier than lead, yet I choose to begin at this, as the idea I wish to convey is all that is worthy of your consideration in the present argument. Lead, then, on account of the density of its particles, is difficult to move. Were it the heaviest substance in nature, it would take its position farther distant from motion than any other substance. Rock being more easily moved than lead, takes its relative position nearer to motion. In like manner earth is more easily moved than rock. Water is more easily moved than earth. Air is more easily moved than water. The gaseous fluids are more easily moved than air, and electricity is more easily moved than the gaseous fluids.

It will now be perceived, by ladies and gentlemen, that as we mount the rounds of the ladder in the magnificent scale of material substances, there is a gradual approximation toward motion. Each substance as we rise, being more rarefied and light than the one below it, is of course nearer to motion than its grosser neighbor. And it will be perceived by every philosophic mind, that we cannot continually approximate motion without at last reaching motion, or that substance to which motion belongs.

We have now mounted from lead up to electricity; and though as we rose we found each successive substance more easily moved than the one below it, still we have not as yet found a single material that possesses inherent motion as its attribute. Lead, rock, earth, and water are moved by impulse. Air is moved by rarefication, and electricity is moved by the positive and negative forces. True we have mounted up, as before remarked, to electricity, but even this cannot move, unless it is thrown out of balance in relation to quantity as to its *positive* and *negative* forces. In such cases it flies, equalizes itself, and again sinks to rest. I am fully sensible that electricity is a fluid most inconceivably subtile, rarefied, and fine. It is computed to take four million particles of our air to make a speck as large as the smallest visible grain of sand, and yet electricity is more than seven hundred thousand times finer than air! It is almost unparticled matter, and is not only invisible, but, so far as we can judge, it is imponderable. It cannot be seen—it cannot be weighed! A thousand empty Leyden jars, capable of containing a gallon each, may be placed upon the nicest scale, and most accurately weighed. Then let these be filled with electricity, and, so far as human sagacity can determine, they will weigh no more. Hence to our perception, a thousand gallons weigh nothing.

As electricity, in regard to motion, stands upon the poise, being completely balanced by the positive and negative forces, that equalize each other, so it is easily perceived, that if we mount one step higher, we must come to that substance whose nature it is to move, and the result of that motion is thought and power. It is MIND. Hence it will be distinctly perceived, in view of the argument now offered, that we cannot, as philosophers, stop short of *motion* in the highest and most sublime substance in being. This conclusion, as the result of the argument, is absolutely and positively irresistible, and challenges refutation.

When we mount up in our contemplations through the various grades of matter, and see it continually brightening as we progress onward in our delightful career of rapture, till we arrive at that sublimated substance which can neither be seen nor weighed—which moves with a velocity of twelve million miles per minute, and can travel around this globe in the eighth part of a second, we are struck with astonishment and awe! But as this is not the last link in the immeasurable chain, we are forced to proceed onward till we arrive at the finest, most sublime, and brilliant substance in being—a substance that possesses the attributes of inherent or self-motion and living power, and from which all other motion and power throughout the immeasurable universe are derived. This is the INFINITE MIND, and possesses embodied form. He is a living being. This Infinite Mind comes in contact with electricity, gives to it motion, arms it with power, and, through this mighty unseen agent, moves the universe, and carries on all the multifarious operations of nature, whether minute or grand. Hence there is not a motion that transpires amidst the immensity of his works, from rolling globes down to the falling leaf, but what originates in the ETERNAL MIND, and by Him is performed, through electricity as his agent. Mind is, therefore, the absolute perfection of all substances in being; and as it possesses self-motion as its grand attribute, so it is, in this respect, exactly the reverse of all other substances, which are, of themselves, motionless. MIND, or SPIRIT, is above all, and absolutely disposes of and controls all. Hence mind and its agent,

LECTURE VI.

electricity, are both imponderable—are both invisible, and coeternal.

As the Eternal One wraps clouds and darkness round about him, and holds back the face of his throne, so many do not believe in his existence, because he is unseen, while all the visible objects of creation are to them so many realities. But the very position here assumed is an erroneous one. The very reverse of this is true. What is seen is not the reality, but is only the manifestation of the *unseen*, which is the reality. Let us carefully look at this point. There is an apple-tree; it is plainly seen; but is that tree the reality? No; but it is the result of an *invisible* cause, and that *unseen* cause is the reality. But what was it? I reply, that it was not even the seed, but the *life* of that seed was the reality; and that *unseen life* possessed the embodied form of that tree. All its shapes and colors were there. By coming in contact with the soil and moisture, in a proper temperature of climate, it was enabled to throw out its own invisible and living form. First, then, the life; next the seed in which it dwells; next the trunk of the tree appears. Then its limbs and branches—its buds, leaves, blossoms, and fruit again end in living beauty. It began in life, and in seed or life it ended. It performed an electric circle. The tree, then, is nothing more than a visible outshoot—an ultimate of an invisible substance, which is **the reality**.

All the powers and operations of nature are lodged in the unseen and finest portions of matter—they pass on through every grade, and end in the gross and heaviest parts. The unseen power that stirs the earthquake and convulses the globe is the *reality*. It passes through every grade of matter, and ends in rending the solid rocks and hurling cities in the vortex of ruin. The power that moves this globe in its orbit at the rate of sixty-eight thousand miles per hour, is an invisible agent, moved by omnipotent Power—for all operations and effects begin in the finest substance in being, which is the unseen cause, and therefore the reality. Hence it is the same in nature as in the human system, as I have already shown in my arguments on the philosophy of disease. The disease begins in the finest substance of the body—in the electricity of the nerves—passes on to the blood and flesh, and ends in the bones. There is, indeed, but one common mode of operation in nature and in man.

Ladies and Gentlemen—I desire now to turn your attention to one important point in relation to mind, which has been entirely overlooked by philosophers. I mean its *involuntary* powers. To speak of the *involuntary* powers of mind will certainly produce a singular impression on your hearts; and the strangeness of the idea may, perhaps, fill you with surprise. But strange as it may appear, it is nevertheless true that mind possesses the two grand attributes of *voluntary* and *involuntary* power. These two constitute the mind as a living being of embodied form. If mind make use of electricity as its agent, then it must possess the voluntary and involuntary powers to meet the positive and negative forces in electricity. If this be not so, then the Infinite Mind cannot be the Creator and Governor of the universe; because it is by his *voluntary* power that he creates a universe, but it is by his *involuntary* power that he sustains and governs it. Each of these powers, from a philosophical necessity, and from the very nature of his being, perform their own peculiar functions, and in perfect harmony preside over their own respective departments. It is the peculiar province of the voluntary power of the Infinite Mind to plan, arrange, dispose, and create worlds and their inhabitants, and it is the peculiar province of his involuntary power to govern and control these worlds and their inhabitants through the fixed laws of nature. Let us reason this point, and its consistency will appear.

In the first place—if the voluntary power of the Creator governed the universe, then no possible contingencies could happen—and nothing once commenced could ever perish prematurely. For instance: if God determined to create a human pair, and by his voluntary power commenced the work, they could not perish when his work was but partially accomplished. They are destined to come to maturity, invested with the true lineaments of form—and destined to gaze upon each other as perfect specimens of living beauty. If not, then God in his voluntary and absolute determinations can be thwarted and disappointed.

The first male and female, at least, of each species, were produced, and the whole living chain of animated existence was placed upon this globe by the voluntary powers of God, without any previous parents from whom they received their being. They were not born, but created, for there is philosophically and strictly a very wide difference between being *created* and *born*. The *former* we call miracle, the *latter*, an order of nature. To produce a human pair without a previous father and mother, is not in the order or power of nature, for she never changes her mode of operation in the production of her animated existences.

The same is true in relation to the vegetable kingdom. The whole species of vegetable life was produced by the voluntary powers of God. In the order of nature there never was an acorn but what grew on an oak; and there never was an oak but what came from an acorn. Geology proves that there has been a period when there were no vegetables or animals on this globe. Which then was first—the acorn or the oak? If you reply that the acorn was first, then there was an acorn that did not grow on an oak. If you say that the oak was first, then there was an oak that did not come from an acorn. Whence then is the starting point of creation, if there is no God? for nature cannot start herself, as this would only be saying that she acted before she existed. Whether the Creator, in the first place, produced by his voluntary powers the seeds or the plants, is of no consequence to my present purpose. It is enough to say, that they were brought into existence without any parent stock, and in performing this work there could be no uncertainty, nor could any thing perish prematurely, because it was under the voluntary powers of the Infinite Mind.

But after this globe was created, and the first link of every species of vegetable and animal life was moved into existence by the voluntary powers of the Creator, it then naturally and of philosophical necessity passed from the control of the *voluntary* powers to the control of the *involuntary* powers of the Infinite Mind, and by them to be governed through the established laws of nature. Here then casualties may naturally arise, but no where else under the government of the Supreme.

This view of mind removes the many difficulties and perplexities we encounter, when we contemplate the unchangeable character of the Creator in the government of the world. Millions of our race are continually perishing by premature birth! The eye was most skillfully organized and adapted to see light, but saw it not. The ear was formed—all its vocal chambers were arranged, and the whole adapted to the reverberations of sound, but it never heard. It had hands, but they never handled—feet, but they never walked—lungs, but they never breathed—and a mouth, but it never spoke, nor tasted food.

Again—how many millions of our race die under ten years of age! And though they were constituted, and ripening for the enjoyment of the social and domestic affections, and the multiplication of their race, yet they were prematurely cut off, and left no progeny on earth. Now if these events are under the government of the voluntary powers of the Creator, would he not, I ask, be arrested in the execution of his voluntary will, and would not his designs fail of being accomplished? The conclusion is absolutely irresistible, for how can we judge of *designs* only as we see the adaptation of means to ends? If an eye and ear are formed, and adapted to light and sound, does not this prove the will and design of God, that the one shall see, and the other shall hear? It does. If then the infant prematurely dies and never sees an object, nor hears a sound, are not those two organs formed in vain, and are not the design and will of the Creator both frustrated? If the girl that died at ten years of age, and never bore nor nursed children—if it is admitted that she did not answer the full measure and end of her existence, in common with her sex, is not then the will of God rendered abortive, and do not his designs in this case fail? It must be so, if the government of the world is under the voluntary powers of the Infinite Mind.

That this part of my subject may be understood, and its consistency clearly seen, I will endeavor to present it before you in a very plain and simple form. I will take for illustration the human mind in connection with this body. We have two distinct brains—the cerebrum, with its two hemispheres and six lobes, commencing at the frontal part of the skull, and occupying the greater portion of the cavity; and the cerebellum, which occupies the back portion of the skull. The spinal marrow, extending through the vertebræ to the bottom of the trunk, is but the continuation of these two brains. From the spinal marrow branch out, as I have before stated, thirty-two pairs of nerves, embracing both the nerves of motion and those of sensation. From these again branch out others, and in thousands of ramifications carry out the full power of both brains into every part of the system.

The cerebrum is the great fountain of the voluntary nerves, through which the voluntary powers of the mind ever act. The cerebellum is the fountain of the involuntary nerves, through which the involuntary powers of the mind ever act. Though the voluntary and involuntary nerves from these two brains seem to blend in the spinal marrow, yet they preserve their distinct character, even to their final termination in the system, and execute the functions appertaining to their own office in producing voluntary and involuntary motion. Such is the residence of the living mind, which seems to hold its throne in the medulla oblongata, at the fountain-head of the voluntary and involuntary nerves. From thence my mind, by its volitions, controls all the voluntary motions of my body, through the cerebrum. At will I move my hands in any possible direction I please to handle substances, and at will I move my feet to walk.

But over the throbbings of my heart, the ultimate heaving of my lungs, the circulation of my blood, and the digestion of food by the stomach, I have no voluntary control. Awake, asleep, at home, abroad, the heart continues its motions, and the functions of life are executed, whether I will it or not. These then receive their motions from the involuntary powers of my mind, acting through the cerebellum. That these are all moved by mind is certain—because, take the mind or spirit from the body, and all motions, whether voluntary or involuntary, instantly cease.

I will now make an application of this to the Infinite Mind, in creating and governing the universe. If, for instance, you make machinery of various kinds, these are your own creations, for they are made by the voluntary powers of your mind. If you cultivate the earth, and raise grain and the various vegetables, to sustain your existence, these again are your own creations, for they are produced by your voluntary powers. You prepare them, by various processes, for your use—you cook and place them on the table. You eat them, and thus far they are under your voluntary action. But the moment they are eaten, your creations are finished, and the whole, naturally and of philosophical necessity, passes beyond your direct volition, and is subjected to the involuntary powers of your mind. These now take charge of this new creation, and govern it in all its involuntary motions and revolutions, according to the fixed laws of the organized system.

In like manner the voluntary powers of Deity are unchangeably employed in planning, arranging, and creating new worlds, and systems of worlds, and peopling them with inhabitants. When the whole of any such system is finished, and all its laws established for the rolling of worlds, and for the operations of the mineral, vegetable, and animal kingdoms, the whole naturally passes, according to the principles of philosophical necessity, from the action and control of his voluntary, miraculous power, and submits itself to be governed through the fixed laws of the universe, by the involuntary powers of the same Infinite Mind. As the bare presence of the human mind in the brain causes the heart to throb and the functions of life to proceed, even when that mind is wrapped in sleep so profound, that not a thought is stirring in its voluntary department, so the bare presence and majesty of the

Infinite Mind, even if he should not exercise a thought, would cause all worlds to roll through immensity, and cause all the operations of nature in the mineral, vegetable, and animal kingdoms to proceed on in their ceaseless changes; for these are under the control of the involuntary powers of the Deity, acting through the laws of the universe.

LECTURE VII.

LADIES AND GENTLEMEN:

IN my last Lecture the momentous question was presented for our consideration—Where is the starting point of all motion and power, whether voluntary or involuntary, in both nature and man? The transcendent importance of this question clothes it with the eloquence of its own splendor. I have humbly endeavored to answer it by showing that all motion and power originate in mind. And surely the idea that mind possesses the attribute of innate motion and living power, is both majestic and sublime. I have shown that mind has two grand forces. I mean its voluntary and involuntary powers, by which the world was created and is governed. I have proved the existence of the Infinite Mind from *motion and the absolute perfection of material existences.* I have shown that mind must be some substance, and not the result of organism, nor an absolute *immateriality*, which is but a *nonentity.*

I am well aware that thought, reason, and understanding are considered to be mind, and that these are *immaterial*. But they are not mind, as I have clearly proved in my Lectures on the Philosophy of Mesmerism. Thought and reason are but the results of mind. What is it that thinks and reasons? It is the mind. Then mind is something distinct from these mental operations, which are only its effects. When the voluntary powers of the mind are stilled in sleep, reason and thought are gone. Hence if these are mind, then the mind is annihilated in sleep. But if we admit mind to be a substance, a living and spiritually organized being, then all is plain. Sleep stops its motion, and thought is gone. Remove that pressure, and release the mind, and instantly it resumes its inherent motion, and the result of that motion is thought and power. On this point I add no more, but refer you to my Lectures on Mesmerism to learn my views more fully.

I now turn your attention to the subject of creation. Entering upon this, I feel the incompetency of my feeble powers to do it justice. Like a drop to an ocean, or an atom to a universe, any possible representation of the intrinsic grandeur of this subject must fall so far short of its reality, as to render any attempt at an adequate description the unpardonable presumption of impotent folly. Yet, as we are endowed with reason, and as the inspiration of the Almighty hath given us understanding, so we are bound, by the very laws of our being, to extend our researches to the utmost verge of our mental capacity. He who would curb the human intellect and say *this* or *that* is a subject with which we have no right to meddle, and into which we have no right to inquire, is not only recreant to duty as an intellectual and moral being, but betrays his own ignorance, and proves himself a scientific bigot. Give the mind full scope and sea-room—let it feel the deep stirrings of its own powers, and soar, if it can, into the light of eternity, and survey the very throne of God, and him who sitteth thereon; and, if possible, let it scan the secret energies of his creating fiat, and even examine the raw material out of which worlds were manufactured.

It is the most commonly received opinion in the Christian world, that God made all things out of nothing. It is true the inspired book does not say, or even hint this. It simply says—" In the beginning God created the heavens and the earth;" but it does not add the words—*out of nothing*. It is absolutely and philosophically impossible, in the very nature and constitution of things, that something can be made out of nothing. It implies, at the same time, a contradiction in terms. We cannot form even a notion in our imaginations how much of nothing it would take to make the least imaginable something. I am speaking of *nothing* in the strictest sense of the word. But using the word *nothing* in its common acceptation, we can easily perceive how all things could have been made out of nothing. When all visible objects are removed from a room, we say *there is nothing in it—it is empty.* Yet we know that it is filled with air, because we continue to breathe. But if the air, by a force-pump, were removed from an air-tight room, we might, with much more propriety, say *there is nothing in it ;* yet electricity would be there. If solid substances were therefore made out of air, in an empty room, we could say that they were made out of nothing, for the room, according to the usual mode of expression, had nothing in it. But admitting the air to have been extracted from the room, and nothing but electricity left, and if solid substances were produced from this ethereal and invisible fluid, we could with much more apparent consistency say, that they were made out of nothing. In this sense, I grant that all things were made out of nothing. Paul says—" The things that are seen were not made of things that do appear." Here he plainly states, that the substances *seen* were made of *invisible* substances, or such as did *not appear*—for by *things* he only means *substances.*

If, however, it be said, to *create* must mean to bring into existence something from nothing, I have only to say, that this is not so; for it says, " God created man out of the *dust* of the earth." Here he created him out of something—it was out of dust, and yet it was creation. The Hebrew word rendered *create,* more strictly means to gather together by concretion, or to form by consolidation—but never can it mean to bring *something* into existence from absolutely and positively *nothing*. I therefore contend that all things were made out of electricity, which is not only an invisible and imponderable substance, but is primeval and eternal matter. It contains the invisible and imponderable properties of all things in being. That this is electricity is certain, because there is no other substance with which the Infinite Mind could have come in direct contact, so as to have produced by his creating power the solid and visible substances that compose the globe. It is, as I have already proved, in my third and fourth Lectures, philosophically impossible for mind to come in direct contact with any substance in nature except electricity. Hence electricity contains the elementary principles of all things in being, and contains them in their original, invisible, and imponderable state.

There must be something eternal. God, duration, and space exist of philosophical necessity, and that space was eternally filled with primeval matter. When I say that they exist of necessity, I mean that the contrary of space and duration cannot possibly be conceived. If infinite space were filled with an infinite globe, it would be space filled. If that globe were struck out of existence, it would be space empty. Filled or empty, it would still be *space*. As space exists of necessity, it is absolutely and positively eternal, and hence could never have been created nor changed. The same is true in relation to duration. Duration must have rolled on, even if there had been no revolutions of suns and worlds to mark its periods. The contrary cannot possibly be conceived. Hence duration and space both exist of philosophical necessity, and are absolutely eternal. Endless duration is the age of Jehovah, and space is the empire in which he dwells and reigns. This space was eternally filled with mind and invisible matter in its original state. They both exist of philosophical necessity.

Hence matter is eternal, because if there ever had been a period when there was nothing in existence as it regards matter, then nothing would now have been, for nothing cannot create itself into something. The same is true in relation to mind. If there ever had been a period when there was no mind in existence, then no mind could now have been, for mind could not have created itself, as this would be admitting mind to have acted before it existed. Hence mind and primeval matter are both coexistent and coeternal. Indeed, the one could not exist without the other, because that electricity, which is original and eternal matter, is the body of God. All other bodies are therefore emanations from his body, and all other spirits are emanations from his spirit. Hence all things are of God. He has poured himself throughout all his works. He has poured spirit from spirit's awful fountain, and kinlled into existence a world of rationals. On this principle it will be seen, that the Eternal Mind is not absolutely omnipresent, while his electrical body is, because it pervades immensity of space. Mind must be enthroned, and not diffused over the whole body. And as the mind of Jehovah actuates his body, so he produces impressions throughout the boundlessness of space, and makes himself instantly felt throughout the immensity of his works, even as the human mind, which is located in the brain, still makes its presence felt throughout the body, even to every possible extremity, and produces the impressions of its existence on others.

Mind or spirit is of itself embodied and living form. It is spiritual organism in absolute perfection, and from mind itself all form and beauty emanate. The body of man is but an outshoot or manifestation of his mind. If I may be indulged the expression, it is the ultimate of his mind. Hence every creature in existence has a body which is the shape of its mind, admitting that the physical laws of the system were not interrupted in producing the natural form of the body from mind. The serpent is all length—is all concentration, and no wonder that he can charm the bird and other creatures around him. What a singular mind the lobster must have, for he has a singular body!

We touch the finger to any substance, and in the finger we appear to feel it. But this is not so, because all feeling is in the mind. If we amputate the arm or leg, yet the fingers and toes as usual can be felt. For instance, we move a finger or wield the arm. How is this done? I answer this question by saying, that the mind has its spiritual fingers, arms, limbs, and all its lineaments of form corresponding to those of the body. The mind holds its throne in the brain, and possessing in itself the power of feeling and motion, it merely stirs its spiritual fingers, or wields its spiritual arm, and through the electric action of the nerves, which are laid, like so many telegraphic wires, between the two, the natural finger and the natural arm are compelled to make an exactly correspondent motion. This solves the mystery why the man who has his arm amputated, even up to the shoulder, yet feels his arm and his fingers as long as he lives, and often feels in them an itching sensation, or even pain, and that, too, at the same distance from his body which the fingers and arm occupied before amputation took place. All operations, convulsions, and motions begin in the unseen substance of the body, and end in its gross and solid parts. These are last moved, and last affected. This is not only so in muscular motion, but throughout nature.

Having the great principles of mind and matter before us, I will now proceed to notice the creation of worlds. I have already remarked, that all the chemical properties of all substances in existence, belonging to our globe and its surrounding elements, were made out of electricity. Hence electricity contains all the elementary principles of all things in being. The ancients supposed there to be but four elements—namely, *earth*, *air*, *fire*, and *water*. It so happens, however, that *heat* is no element at all, any more than *cold*. It is merely an effect of substances in motion, produced by their friction. Though the ancients supposed there to be but four elements, yet as the science of chemistry advances onward toward perfection, more elements are detected. I believe that about forty have been already discovered, yet we have no reason to believe that even these are all. I will suppose, however, that there are one hundred elements belonging to this globe. Then there are one hundred elements in electricity, out of which this globe was created. We will step back in our imaginations to that period when this globe, as such, had no existence. For the sake of perspicuity, we will suppose one hundred cords to be fastened on those one hundred elements in electricity. Please to bear this fact in mind.

Now, as the Eternal Mind can come in direct contact with electricity only, so he exerted his voluntary powers that constitute his creative energy, and condensed those one hundred elements that constitute electricity, down to a more gross and dense state, each element sliding down its own cord in its progress toward creation. Though mind can directly touch nothing but electricity, yet electricity, as the universal agent under Deity, can touch all substances in being. The Creator again acts, through another volume of electricity upon those one hundred partially condensed elements, and moves them down a grade farther onward toward their ultimate, or created state. And thus the work progresses; wave successively following wave down its own cord, till they all become air. Hence air contains the one hundred elements; and all the chemical properties of all things in being are involved in it. And so the work of creation progresses, under the never ceasing action of the Infinite Mind, from whom all motion and power emanate, till those one hundred elements are made into water. Hence water contains all the chemical properties of all things in being. Matter, from its invisible electric state, has now become visible in the crystal, volatile, and colorless state called water. The whole one hundred elements are here in solution; and from water, which is the universal solvent of nature, earth, and all mineral and crystalized substances were made. Boyle has proved, that by transmutation, as he terms it, nature turns water into earth; and Bishop Watson, in his "Chemical Essays," admits the same, and says, "it has never been disproved by any writer." Boyle should not have said that *nature*, by transmutation, does this; but that the CREATOR, by his own power of inherent motion, turns water into earth. I resume this interesting subject.

The one hundred elements, having reached the lower extremity of the one hundred cords, have now attained their ultimate created condition and form, and the finished globe, in all its youth, beauty, and variety, appears. At the top of those cords are the one hundred elements in their original electrical state, resting in their own invisibility; and as we descend we see the continual change each successive wave passed through, as the whole one hundred substances were, under the action of the Creator, gradually approaching their created state, till at length they emerged from invisibility and chaotic night into the light of day, and rendered the variegated beauties of their created forms visible to the eye of the beholder.

The globe being finished, it required electricity, the original substance out of which it was made, to be brought upon it by the Creator, so that his infinite mind, through this agent, might come in contact with it, in order to move and govern it, not only in its revolutions by the attractive and repulsive forces, but in producing all the changes and operations in its mineral, vegetable, and animal kingdoms. As this great work is submitted to the involuntary powers of the Infinite Mind, and as mind cannot come in direct contact with gross matter, so the beauty and simplicity of the subject appear in the grandeur of the idea, that electricity, being uncreated and eternal matter, is the only substance that mind can touch, and hence is the great physical agent the Creator employs in the government of all worlds. The unchanging laws of the universe are but the unchanging thoughts of God. Ladies and gentlemen, I desire you to bear in mind that it requires electricity, the very substance out of which the globe was made, to govern it by its positive and negative forces under the energy of Infinite Power.

As this subject is somewhat intricate, permit me to be very explicit in making myself understood. When I say that it requires electricity to govern the globe, I mean as follows: Electricity, being the uncreated substance, is the *positive* force, and the globe, being the created substance, is the *negative* force. In the next place it will be clearly perceived, that all the substances existing in the globe as so many ULTIMATES, exist in electricity as so many PRIMATES. For instance: If there is gold in the globe, then there is gold in electricity, out of which it was made. If there is phosphate of lime in the globe, out of which the shells of the ocean and bones are formed, then there is phosphate of lime in electricity, out of which it was made. The gold in electricity is in a gaseous and invisible state, and is the *positive* force, and the gold in the globe is in a solid and visible state, and is the *negative* force. As the positive and negative forces always come together, so the gold in electricity entirely controls and mineralizes the gold in the globe, but lets its ninety-nine kindred elements alone. Each one keeps its own cord of communication from top to bottom—from *primate* to *ultimate*—from *positive* to *negative*.

LECTURE VII. 131

The same is true, not only of the gold, and of the phosphate of lime, but also of the ninety-eight remaining elements. The whole one hundred elements in electricity, as the *positive* forces, are brought to act upon the one hundred corresponding elements of the globe, as the *negative* forces, and thus not only move it on its axis, and in its revolutions around the sun, but produce all the changes and operations in these elementary substances of which the globe is composed.

These ideas of the creation and government of the world are in reality sublime. And when we reflect that the Infinite Mind comes in contact with electricity, and, through that eternal, invisible agent, governs all worlds by his involuntary powers, sublimity rises into infinite magnificence, and overwhelms the soul with awe!

The sun being pure electricity is, of course, a cold, invisible body. He is placed, as is supposed, in the centre of a retinue of worlds composing our planetary system, and that to these worlds he gives light, heat, and vegetation. But to my mind it is evident that there can be no light above our atmosphere which surrounds the globe to the height of about fifty miles. As electricity travels from the sun to the globe in never-ceasing streams, so when it strikes the top of our atmosphere it becomes faintly visible, and not before. This is proved by the morning and evening twilight, when the sun is so far below the eastern hills as to strike the very top of our atmosphere, apparently on a level with our fields, and affords a feeble light on account of the thinness of our air at that height. But as it rises higher, its rays shoot deeper, and the air growing denser as they approach the earth where we stand, till they touch it, the friction on the particles of air is of course greater, and the light and heat are rendered more intense by this density of atmosphere, and by their final reflection and reaction from the globe. Hence could we rise to the top of our atmosphere, the sun would disappear, and we should there be shrouded in total darkness. Electricity is cold and invisible, and as it travels from the sun to the globe at the rate of twelve million miles per minute, so it sets the particles of the air on fire by the rapidity of its motion and friction. Such is the philosophy of the morning and evening twilight, which never has been, and cannot be explained on any other principle than the electrical invisibility of our sun, and the absence of all light above our atmosphere. And electricity, thrown from the sun to the globe, is the mode employed by the Creator to bring it to its full growth and perfection, as a meet habitation for man.

As electricity is, in its one hundred elements, continually pouring from the sun upon the globe, why does it not continue to increase it in bulk? I reply that it does, and hence its entire creation, as to its size, vegetables, and animals, is not yet perfected, but will be in future ages. Its distance from the sun, and its exact relation to surrounding worlds, will then forbid its increase in bulk. The human body, when completely developed by food and drink, ceases its growth, even though the same sustenance, both in quality and quantity, is continued. This I will more fully explain, and hence the cause of the variation of the compass, which in philosophy yet remains inscrutable, will be made to appear.

Comets are declared by Newton and others to be melted globes, and he computed the heat of one to be several thousand times hotter than that of red-hot iron, and that it would take a comet the size of this globe, fifty thousand years to cool to its centre. Comets move in very elliptical orbits, and are deemed, on this account, to be very eccentric bodies. The cause of this is, that while they are chained by the attractive and repulsive forces to keep a circle, yet as they are propelled in a straight line, sky-rocket-like, by their own internal gaseous flames that stream in their course, so their orbits are elliptical. As they cool, their own internal force is lessened, and their orbits become more circular, because there is less trespassing on the attractive and repulsive forces, which, if left to their own operation, independent of foreign influences, would move all worlds in perfect circles. Immensity of space is not square, for then worlds would move in a square, but it is round, if I may be indulged in the expression in regard to that boundless field, "whose centre is everywhere, and its circumference nowhere." Electricity, uninfluenced, always moves in circles.

The globe yet moves in an elliptical orbit, because its bowels are melted lava, and perhaps not more than one hundred miles in depth of its crust are as yet cooled. And the two hundred volcanoes now in existence, are so many spiracles to the subterranean furnace, and continually throw off the gaseous substances generated in its bosom, and cause it to transgress in some measure the attractive and repulsive forces that move it. As it cools, it continually approximates, in its orbit, nearer to a circle. This will cause the variation of the compass to continue, till its own internal forces cease to affect its motion, and allow the law of attraction and repulsion to move it in a perfect circle around the sun. And when it shall perform an exact circle in its annual revolution, it will be perfectly finished as to its size, and yet the quantity of electricity thrown upon it from the sun, will be the same as it now is, and ever has been. But this redundancy will be thrown off at its north and south poles, and in such increased quantities as to warm and enlighten those extremities of the globe, and bring them into the fruitfulness and bloom of the garden of Eden. Then the variation of the compass will cease, inasmuch as the cause will be removed that produces it. The cause of its variation is the elliptical orbit in which our globe moves, and its continual and

LECTURE VII.

unceasing approach to a circle. And when that circle shall be obtained, the globe will be finished, and the variation of the compass will disappear.

The globe is yet in its infancy—yes, in the embryo of its being—and it will require many thousand years to finish it. And this must be done, because under the voluntary powers of the Creator, nothing can perish prematurely. Many species of vegetables and animals now in existence, will become extinct, and disappear from the page of the naturalist, and others of a more improved and superior character will be awakened into being. They will be perfectly adapted to the future and ultimate perfection that this globe, under the energies of the Infinite Mind, is destined to attain. Its creation will then be perfected. The soil upon which we *now* stand, will *then* be some deep stratum in its crust, containing our present vegetables and animals in a state of petrifaction. These will be pronounced, by coming generations, the strange nondescript remains of past centuries, and afford to the future geologist and naturalist abundant materials for their loftiest speculations. This subject, in connection with the boundlessness of the universe, and the successive creation of worlds, I should like to pursue to a greater extent, but lest I weary your patience, I now turn your attention to the creation of the vegetable and animal species.

As globes were successively produced, so vegetables and animals were not created at once, but successively through a long series of intervening ages. Does not the Creator act through the established laws of generation in producing the human species? He does. While I freely admit that God originally produced man by what we call *miracle*, yet by miracle I only mean, that the first human beings were produced without any parent stock from whom they received their existence through ordinary generation, as we witness in the present day. And they were evidently produced full-grown, otherwise they could not have sustained their existence by procuring their own food, because the infant is helpless. But the miracle by which existence was thus conferred was not contrary to the laws of nature, but was effected by the voluntary powers of Deity exerted through the laws of nature. It was thus he established both the vegetable and animal kingdoms, not simultaneously, but successively and progressively through various ages, from the lowest vegetable life up to man, who is the glory of this lower world.

While I contend that the Creator produced the whole vegetable and animal creation at first, without any parent stock or the ordinary mode of generation, yet I would not be understood to say that there were no germs of life existing as a primordial cause adequate to the effect produced. But while I contend that there were, for instance, no acorns, nor other seeds in being, yet it is evident that the germ necessary to produce an acorn or an oak eternally existed in God. Hence the spirit of all life, whether vegetable or animal, even from the highest reasoning powers, through every link of the animal chain down to the lowest creature, and through every link of the vegetable chain, eternally existed in God, and is absolutely immortal. The whole of this immense variety combined in Deity constitutes the fullness and perfection of the ETERNAL MIND. Hence the lowest animal or vegetable life is but a part of the lowest life in God's spirit, which is the correspondent germ from whence it emanated. And the matter that forms the visible substance of all animal and vegetable bodies eternally existed in electricity, which is the original, invisible, and immortal condition of inert matter, and constitutes the body of God. Hence God and electricity are both immortal and eternal. From electricity, which is the invisible body of God, have emanated all the visible substances that constitute globes, and from the fullness of his spirit have emanated all life, form, and motion. And as all organism exists in spirit, so each animal and vegetable have developed a physical body corresponding in form to the germ of life they received from the inexhaustible fountain of the Infinite Mind.

If God does not create through the laws of nature, but by miracle, in the arbitrary sense it is generally understood by Christians, he would in this case have finished the globe before he produced the vegetable and animal kingdoms, and then moved them both into existence at the same time. But he can not, from the very nature of his perfections, suspend the production of life while forming a globe of dead matter, because he pours forth simultaneously and unchangeably all his perfections which are transmitted through correspondent laws for the production of life, so far as a globe may be finished. And as this globe was progressively forming through successive ages, and one elementary department finished before another, so the successive creation of plants and animals, as geology proves, is easily and rationally accounted for.

God could not create a fish until there was water adapted to its existence. And the moment the water was perfected, it stood in a philosophical aptitude to the marine laws of the universe, and through these emanated from the Creator that portion only of his spirit which stood in aptitude to the aqueous department, and this spirit became the living germ or life of that fish, and produced its body through the positive and negative forces of electric action. Hence the body of this fish was but the developed and visible shape of its mind. But as the water was progressively created, and for many ages covered the earth before dry land appeared, therefore, while in its turbid and unfinished state, many of the inferior species, from the lowest life up to shell-fish, and from thence up through every grade, existed before the most highly organized and perfect fish was created. And each of these grades, in like manner, through the laws of nature received their life from the infinite fountain of spirit, which became the germ of their being. The various shapes of their organic structures were but visible manifestations of the various shapes of their minds, and the most perfectly organized fish in the ocean involves in his body the organism of all below him, and his intelligence is equal in amount to the intelligence in all.

It is evident that vegetables, in some form, must have preceded animals, for an animal is but a vegetable of the second growth. May there not be a marine vegetation of as great variety and abundance in the caverned vales of the ocean as there is on earth? Of this, however, we are certain, that terrestrial plants and trees could not have been created till the dry land appeared, because the Deity does not create by any arbitrary mode of procedure, but through the immutable laws of nature. As soon as the dry land stood in a philosophical aptitude to the laws of the universe, and as the Spirit of the Creator gives out, like the sun, its unchangeable and never-ceasing emanations, so it communicated a portion of itself as the germinating principle of life, and vegetation appeared, commencing at the humblest and most imperfect formation of plants, and rising higher and still higher in the beauty of organic perfection, till the noblest fruit-trees and most powerful sons of the forest stood erect, and the finest organized plants and most beautiful flowers graced creation, and robed the new-born earth in smiles.

As each of these vegetable tribes rose in succession, one above another with increasing splendor, so each superior tribe involved in its own perfection the perfection and organism of all below it. For instance, the *first species* of plants on the yet marshy earth was ordinary; the *second*, more perfect, retained its own, and involved all contained in the *first ;* the *third*, still advancing, retained its own perfection, and involved all contained in the one below it; the *fourth* makes its appearance one grade higher, and involves all the organic perfections of the *three* below it. And should we be able, in this vast range, to find the thousandth different species, that thousandth one would retain its own, and involve all the complicated beauties of organic structure and life contained in the 999 below it; because, as the form of the earth, in its progressive creation, became more and more perfect and dense, each rising vegetable species, standing in a full and exact aptitude to all the laws of nature then in action, so far as the globe was finished, would avail itself of all the life from the Creator which thus far acted through, and filled these laws.

It was the same, as we have already noticed, with all animal life in the ocean. Each higher involved in itself the perfections of all below it. It was the same with all animated beings in earth and air. The amphibious animal is, of course, the connecting link between the aqueous and terrestrial race. From the humblest land animal up to man, the same grand law obtains. Each higher involves in its constitution the perfections of all below it, even up to man. When the earth was finished, man was produced. And all the laws of nature in relation to this globe being in action, so in man's organism was involved the organism of the whole animal and vegetable creation, and in his spirit was involved the spirit of all life and intelligence in universal nature below him. And, standing in a complete relationship to the finished globe and all its perfect laws, he, of course, drank in a portion of all the perfections contained in the Infinite Spirit, and hence he was strictly in the image of God. Man is, therefore, in every sense, a perfect and grand epitome of the universe. As he is in the image of his God, he stands at the fountain-head of creation, and drinks in all the powers of universal nature, and is sustained by being fed with a due portion of both spiritual and physical sustenance. His mind is fed and developed with impressions as his body is with food.

God is a spirit, and in his spirit are involved all life, all form, and the germinating principle of all animal and vegetable spirit. And in his body, which is electricity, are involved the invisible and ethereal substances of all inert matter, out of which all globes and the bodies of all creatures were produced. In God is, therefore, involved the invisible and primal essence of all matter and spirit existing in all globes and their inhabitants.

But, after all, what is spirit? It is that substance which possesses self-motion, intelligence, sensation, and power. Spirit is a union of two grand forces. The *first* is voluntary; the *second* is involuntary. The *first* is the grand magazine in which are stored up all the voluntary powers of Infinite Intelligence. All the schemes, plans, and arrangements that appertain to all worlds and their countless inhabitants are there. The *second* contains all the involuntary powers of the Infinite Mind by which all worlds and their inhabitants, after having been created, are controlled through the fixed laws of nature. The *first* plans, arranges, and creates through the laws of its own omniscient being, which become the laws of the universe; and the *second* controls, moves, and governs all worlds and their inhabitants through the fixed laws of nature. The *first* is the positive force; the *second* is the negative force. The *first* is male; the *second* is female. Hence of the male and female we may say, that the one begins in the *voluntary*, and the other in the *involuntary power* of the Infinite Spirit. They both run through every department of the universe, and thread universal nature.

There are likewise two electricities, called the **positive** and *negative*. The positive is *male*, the negative is *female.* The male electricity belongs to the heavens; the female electricity belongs to the earth. The male and female also extend through every possible link of the immense vegetable chain, as well as through every link of the animal chain, and retain their separate existence and equal powers in the positive and negative electricities, which are the primeval, eternal, and invisible efficients of all visible matter.

Nature, as a whole, is one entire and absolute perfection, and stands in this beautiful relationship to the Creator, from whom she emanated. All the objects of creation, upon which we gaze with so much admiration—all the diversified glories of the landscape—the mineral, vegetable, and animal kingdoms, taken in one grand whole—are an exact and visible impression of the eternal perfections of his own character and invisible being, even as the stamp impresses the wax and leaves its perfect image. Nature is the visible daguerreotype shadow of his own invisible being. She is the offspring of God. The poet breathes out,

"Man, bear thy brow aloft! view every grace
In God's great OFFSPRING, beauteous NATURE's face."

Creation is therefore no arbitrary act in God, but, like the ever-streaming rays of light from the sun, it is the natural result, the visible emanation and outshoot of his own invisible existence, and was progressively created through the laws of the universe, and as soon as that part of the globe in which life was to be produced stood in a finished relationship to those laws. Hence the laws of nature are but the result of the unchanging thoughts of God. One part of the globe was finished before another, and the creation of life, both vegetable and animal, was in like manner progressive, from the lowest grade and most imperfect organism, step by step, up to man, who is the perfection of all, and is in the image of God.

In this view of our subject it will be perceived that spirit is a substance eternal in its nature, and not the result of an organized brain, and that man has not received his existence by climbing gradually from the lowest link of the vegetable or animal chain up to his present perfection and grandeur. He was never in his creation a vegetable, or even a lower animal; was never a mushroom or a plant, a tadpole or a horse, as some writers contend. His existence was never ingermed and involved in any one or all of the six grand links of the living chain below him, which naturalists divide into the *vegetable*, the *pisces*, the *saurian*, the *aves*, the *marsupial*, and *mammalia kingdoms*, making man the seventh link. Throwing aside the useless technicalities of foreign language, these seven links of the living chain embraced in the seven grand kingdoms of nature can be expressed in plain English. Their rising order is as follows: First—The vegetable kingdom. Second—The fish kingdom. Third—The reptile kingdom, embracing lizards, turtles, crocodiles, etc. Fourth—The bird kingdom. FIFTH—The pouch kingdom, embracing all who protect their young by carrying them in pouches. SIXTH—The breast kingdom, or those that suckle their young; and SEVENTH—Man.

It will also be perceived, in view of my position, that gross, inert matter cannot be transmuted into mind—cannot possibly secrete mind—nor can it, in any sense whatever, become spirit through any refining process, as is contended for by some. In this case it must have preceded God, and hence on this principle God is not eternal. In the face of this theory, there must have been a period when there was nothing but inert matter in being, and if all motion originates in mind, how then was dead matter set in motion so as to produce spirit or mind through a successive series of elementary transmutations?

The same is in like manner equally true of each and every link of the animal chain below man. The monkey was never a bird nor a fish, and the horse was never a snake nor an oyster. The horse-kind, for instance, however much they may have been improved by amalgamation, have ever retained their circle, and have never broken from their link in the chain, and emerged into any other link above them. The same remarks are equally applicable to the vegetable chain. The rose-bush can never become an oak, nor the oak a peach-tree. The family involved in each link, however much they may be improved by amalgamation or culture, can never break their circle, nor emerge into another link above them. The individual life of every link of the whole animal and vegetable chain is an emanation from the Infinite Mind, and each acting through its correspondent law, and through that elementary department of the globe to which this law is unerringly adapted, has manifested its own invisible form in the visible body it produced. What the life of the seed is to the production and shape of the plant, the mind of each creature is to the production and shape of its body. Hence the brain does not produce mind, as the atheist contends, but mind was the original germ that produced and developed the brain. All vegetable life, as well as animal, is therefore a species of mind. They are both emanations from the Creator, are both immortal, and will retain their separate existence and identity without end.

Substances, in their infinite variety, pay a visit to time, assume visible forms, so as to manifest their intrinsic beauties for a moment to the eye of the beholder, and then step back into eternity, and reassume their native invisibility in their own immortality. As man is now constituted, were there but one object presented for his contemplation, the mind would soon become wearied and disgusted with sameness. But the infinite variety and beauty of the animal and vegetable creation here presented by the Deity, open to the mind sources of inexpressible and never-ceasing delight. It seems irrational, therefore, to conclude that the whole chain of being, which is perfect on earth, will be struck out of existence (except man, who is the highest link), and leave a cheerless blank in the realms of glory. For one, I expect to meet the whole animated chain, and to witness immortal groves, unwithering plants, and never-fading flowers in that world where death, and pain, and change shall be no more.

LECTURE VIII.

Ladies and Gentlemen:

The query may perhaps now arise in your minds, What bearing has the subject of the creation of this globe, and the original materials out of which it was made, advanced in the last Lecture, upon the science of Electrical Psychology? The answer to this query will be fully made to appear in the arguments I have to offer on the present occasion. I have already stated in my third Lecture, that man is an epitome of the universe, and that the chemical properties of all the various substances in existence are congregated in him, and form and constitute the very elements of his being. I have stated, that in the composition of this body are involved all the mineral and vegetable substances of this globe, even from the grossest and heaviest matter up to the most rarefied and light. And *lastly*, to finish this masterpiece of creation, I stated that the brain was invested with a living spirit, that, like an enthroned deity, presides over, and governs, through electricity as its agent, all the voluntary motions of this little, organized, corporeal universe; while its living presence, and involuntary self-moving powers, cause all the involuntary functions of life to proceed in their destined course. Hence human beings, and all animated existences, are subject to the same common electrical law that pervades the universe, and moves all worlds under the superintendence of the involuntary powers of the Infinite Spirit.

That all substances are incorporated in the body of man is irresistibly true, otherwise he could not inure himself to all, even to the most deadly poisons, and render them, in a good degree, harmless in his system. He may so accustom himself to the use of tobacco, rum, or even opium, that he can take into the stomach a quantity sufficient to produce the death of several individuals, while he himself will experience from it but a slight effect. He may even commence the use of arsenic in small quantities, gradually increasing the dose, till he gets incorporated into his system a sufficient quantity to kill, for instance, five men. As in this case it forms a part of his body, so it causes a longing for it in proportion to the quantity in the system. Should he now take a portion sufficient to kill five men, it would only produce a balance of power with that already in his system. It would meet the demand. This is habitude. But should he take one portion more, sufficient to kill any other man, he would die. Now it would be impossible for a man to inure himself to any such substances, unless there were some small particle in the composition of his body on which to build. Hence it is philosophically true, that man is an epitome of the universe, and that all the elements, in exact proportions, are most skillfully combined in his system, by the hand of the Creator; and these proportions should never be disturbed and thrown out of balance by dissipation.

Having these facts distinctly before us, I would now state, that if there are one hundred elements in the globe which was made out of the same number in electricity, then there are one hundred in the composition of man's body, for he is but an epitome of the universe. As his body was created out of the dust of the earth, and is but a vegetable of the second growth, so it is the same as though it had been originally made out of electricity. And as the globe, after its creation, required electricity, the original substance from whence, under Deity, it sprung, to move, control, and govern it, so, after man was organized, and his brain invested with a living spirit, it required electricity, the primeval substance out of which he was made, to be inhaled with the air into his lungs, and carried to every part of his system, and by which, under the impulse of mind, it must be moved, controlled, and governed by the positive and negative forces that move all worlds. You now perceive what connection Electrical Psychology has with the creation of our globe. It is a science that involves the electrical theory of the universe, and all the multifarious operations of nature.

We know not, as yet, how many elements there may be in existence. I desire it, however, to be distinctly borne in mind, that if there are one hundred in electricity, which is primal and eternal matter, then there are one hundred in the globe, one hundred in the vegetables that the globe produces, and one hundred in the human body, which is sustained by, and, therefore, made up of vegetables. The stomach is the great workshop of the system, to manufacture new materials to supply the demand occasioned by its constant wastes. The food and water taken into the stomach contain the one hundred elements to meet the supply of the one hundred that are contained in the composition of the body. Electricity, containing also one hundred, is inspired by the lungs, communicated to the blood, from the blood to the nerves, and conducted to the brain, and there laid up for the use of the mind, as I have explained in my THIRD LECTURE. This electricity is sent by the involuntary powers of the mind from the cerebellum through the pneumagastric and other involuntary nerves to the stomach, to produce digestion. The one hundred elements in electricity meet the one hundred corresponding elements in the food, and convert the whole mass into one homogeneous chyle. This is done by the positive and negative forces, without the least confusion or interference of one element with its kindred elements. The nutritious parts of this chyle are taken up by the absorbents, and, in the form of serum, are thrown into the circulating system, and transmuted into blood. The blood is the universal solvent of the system, containing, in solution, all the chemical properties that are to constitute the body, even from its finest particles down to the solid bones—the same as water is the universal solvent of nature, out of which all the constituent principles of this globe are formed, through electrical action.

The finest particles of the blood are taken up, and, by the positive and negative forces of electricity, are transmuted into flesh, tendons, bones, and all the substances that constitute the animal economy, and by the same forces the old particles of the body are thrown off, to mingle again with those of the globe. When I say that all this is effected by the one hundred electrical elements, each acting upon its own element in the food, without interfering with any of its ninety-nine kindred elements, I desire to be distinctly understood. In order to express clearly so intricate an idea, I will take one of these elements, and carry it through in all its principal bearings.

Phosphate of lime is the substance that forms our bones. It may not be a simple element, but in order to convey my ideas on this point, I will consider it so. As our bones are continually wasting away, so this waste must be supplied; and as they are often fractured, so they require new particles to reunite them by ossification. Hence there must be phosphate of lime in our food as well as in electricity. This is certain, because that hard, bony-like substance collected on the teeth in the act of mastication, is from the phosphate of lime in our food and water. Having these facts before us, I now turn to the point under consideration, and ask your undivided attention.

The food is taken into the stomach. The phosphate of lime in electricity being the *positive* force, moves from the brain—from the cerebellum—through the involuntary nerves to the stomach. It takes hold of the phosphate of lime in the food, which is the *negative* force, and leaves the other ninety-nine elements of the food unmolested. This is perfectly philosophical, for the *positive* and *negative* invariably rush together. It converts this phosphate of lime into chyle, and takes it up through the absorbents, and transmutes it into serum and blood. This phosphate of lime from the food now forms a constituent part of the blood. In the next place, the phosphate of lime in electricity takes hold of the phosphate of lime in the blood, and moves it on through all its destined avenues till it reaches the liver, which, while it secretes the bile, seems to act as the bolter of the system, to separate these one hundred elements to be distributed to their destined, correspondent parts of the body. The phosphate of lime in electricity extracts the like substance from the blood at the liver, conveys it to the various bones of the body, transmutes it into an osseous substance, and lays it down, particle after particle, and thus forms anew the solid framework of the system, while the dregs are passed off through the urinary secretions. But before it lays down the *new*, it removes the *old particle* by its repulsive force, and compels it to fly off by insensible perspiration. Fully sensible that I am now understood in reference to the operation of this one element, I am satisfied that you understand me also in relation to the operations of the other ninety-and-nine, in carrying on the work of digestion to keep up the repairs of the body.

These ideas, though somewhat intricate, are nevertheless interesting and sublime, as they unfold the relation in which man stands to the globe, to surrounding worlds and his Creator, as an epitome of the universe. If their novelty produce surprise in any breast, yet this is no reason that they should awaken resentment, or kindle indignation against the speaker. We are finite beings, can know but little, and we should ever be ready and willing to freely express our thoughts reciprocally to each other, independent of the opposition of men. By this mutual interchange of sentiment and feeling we should increase in knowledge, and grow wiser and better. Indeed, we need not go, in our contemplations, out of ourselves to learn the great principles and operations of both mind and matter, of God and his works. As it regards human research, the words of the poet are unchangeably true, and must stand unshaken when thrones and kingdoms fall. He immortalized his verse when he breathed out,

"The proper study of mankind is MAN."

I now turn to another department of my subject, equally interesting. I mean the DOCTRINE OF IMPRESSIONS, by which both nature and man are thrown out of balance, made sick and cured. In this also we shall see the relation between man and nature.

The philosophy of disease I have briefly, but faithfully argued in my FOURTH LECTURE, and shown how it may be produced by both mental and physical impressions. Hence there is no occasion that I should weary your attention by ranging that field of pestilence and death. I shall confine my observations principally to nature, and even in these I shall be brief. The law of EQUILIBRIUM is the grand central LAW of the universe. It holds over nature the reins of government, and allows her, in her operations and changes, to stray, but not too far, from the central track. She may rise above, or fall below this law, but to its mandate she must ever bow, and at stated periods resume her medium course.

Electricity, being a universal agent, produces all the phenomena and changes that transpire in our globe and its surrounding elements. By heat, which is an electrical effect, the air is rarefied and water is evaporated. When the rarefication of the air is carried to an extreme, then that portion of the earth and its inhabitants suffer. Nature is diseased, and the denser portion of the atmosphere is, at length, aroused from its slumberings and armed with force. The sweeping hurricane rushes, or the dreadful tornado roars in its awful movement to fill up, and rescue that rarefied and diseased portion of the air, and continues its force till an equilibrium is attained in her aerial realms. At this point all action ceases, and nature is well. She was cured by her own impressions.

In like manner evaporation may continue till the air is filled, in its upper regions, with vapors. As electricity has a strong affinity for moisture, it leaves the drier portions of the atmosphere near the earth, and ascends to the moist and vapory regions above. By this process electricity is thrown out of balance. The man who has had a broken bone, even years ago, or who is subject to rheumatism, will feel an inconvenience in that spot, or in his system, as harbingers of the approaching storm. The cause of this is, that he does not inspire as much electricity as usual with the air into the lungs, and feels the inconvenience. And the storm will surely burst, if there are no upper currents of air to disperse the vapor. The electricity being thrown out of balance condenses the vapors into thick clouds by its coldness, and thus darkens the heavens. The lightnings flash, the thunders roll, the rains descend, and the war of elements will continue till that subtile fluid is equally dispersed throughout the atmosphere. Nature having gained her equilibrium, in her electrical realms, is at rest. By these awful impressions of her voice she is cured. Here it is distinctly perceived that electricity is a cold body, because it condenses the storm, and when its quantity is sufficiently great it produces hail, even in the warmest weather in our southern climates. In these few ideas we see also the philosophy of storms.

Even the globe may be sick. She may have a bowel complaint. By the confined air and continually generating gases in the lava contained in her bowels she is thrown out of balance. The earthquake awakes from slumber, and springs from its dreadful couch. It starts to discharge its force at the nearest volcano. In its fearful march it sounds its rumbling thunders and convulses the globe. Flames start up through fissures of the opening earth, and from the bottom of the ocean burning islands arise! Volcanoes bellow and disembogue. Their lava overwhelms devoted cities, and their shock hurls others in crumbling ruins! A reaction takes place, an equilibrium is produced in her subterranean realms, and she is well. By these awful impressions of her own power she is cured.

I might extend my observations to every visible department of nature, and notice her more minute operations, but these few remarks, in reference to her **most stupendous** and obvious convulsions, are sufficient to give you my ideas how she becomes diseased by being thrown out of her equilibrium, and how she is cured by the inherent force of her own impressions. As man, then, is an epitome of the universe, the full force of my arguments on the philosophy of disease and the rationale of its cure, advanced in my FOURTH and FIFTH LECTURES, will be clearly seen, and the relation in which man stands to the universe will be more distinctly understood.

As I am now on the doctrine of impressions, I take the liberty to say, that we should endeavor, at all times, to keep ourselves *positive* to the surrounding impressions of nature. We take disease much more easily to fall asleep in an unhealthy spot than to keep awake. While traveling in stages through some low, damp, and unhealthy places in the southern states, and where the mail stage runs both night and day, the traveler unused to that climate should be careful to take short naps during the day, so as not to fall asleep in the night stage. It renders him *passive* and *negative* to the surrounding IMPRESSIONS of nature, when she receives no salutary influence from the beams of the sun. These impressions become the *positive* force, and the electricity of the air inspired by the lungs enters the system, disturbs the nervous force and the circulation, throws the whole out of balance, and disease ensues.

LECTURE VIII.

A citizen of Charleston, South Carolina, may ride out, in warm weather, three or four miles into the country, and, returning the same day, will experience no inconvenience from the change. But should he remain over night and sleep there, he would, in all probability, have an attack of what is there called "*the country fever*," and in a few hours he might be a corpse, as it is considered to be even more fatal than the yellow fever. On the contrary, a person from the country visiting Charleston and returning the same day, receives no harm. But should he remain over night, and sleep there, the same mournful results might ensue. My views on the *philosophy of becoming acclimated*, in my SIXTH LECTURE, will throw some light on this point. And when we reflect that a person, while awake, is *active* and *positive* to surrounding impressions, we can easily perceive that he resists them, and consequently avoids disease.

In view of the above, it will be readily perceived why one person, even in the wakeful state, will take disease much more easily than another. Those who are firm in mind as a rock, are immovably calm, and have no fear of disease, even when some startling malady visits their neighborhood. These will not take it, even if they visit the bedside of the sick. This determined action of their minds throws a constant and powerful current of the electro-nervous force from their brains and systems, keeps them positive to surrounding impressions, and enables them to resist their force. But those who are in constant fear of some disease, who are always complaining of their feelings, pains, and aches, keep themselves constantly unwell by thus concentrating their thoughts upon their own systems, and watching each movement. When fever or cholera visits their neighborhood, these are the very persons who are in danger of an attack. Even fleeing to another section will not save them, unless this circumstance should be the means of changing their thoughts and removing their fears. The difficulty is, that fear, as Dr. Mason Good remarks, depresses the vital energy of the muscles, and slackens the motions of life. It causes the mind to shrink back on itself, and to render the system negative to the surrounding impressions of the elements, and thus engenders disease. More than one half the cases of cholera that have occurred during the past year, owe their existence to the fears and excitements of such persons, who, if they had not heard that it was in their midst, would not have been afflicted with it

The cholera is a sudden collapse of the whole cuticle, occasioned by the electricity of the nerves at the surface suddenly retiring to the stomach and bowels. The pores of the skin being closed, the blood and other fluids follow the electricity, and retire internally. The venous circulation is obstructed and weakened, and the fluids seem to rush to the stomach and bowels, and immense secretions ensue. Intense fever and inflammation in the entire alimentary canal aggravate the other difficulties, and the storm bursts in fearful terror. The external and internal parts of the system being thrown out of balance in their electrical action, and the arterial and venous circulation having lost their equilibrium, the most dreadful cramps and convulsions ensue. All that is necessary to effect a cure is, to procure a reaction from the centre to the surface, and thus restore the usual equilibrium between the arterial and venous circulation, by equalizing the electricity of the system.

What I have now argued in relation to keeping the mind positive to surrounding impressions, will account for the well-known fact, that an individual sitting with his back to a current of air, while in a state of perspiration, will take cold much sooner than if he faced it. The cause is obvious. The front part of the brain contains the positive electro-nervous forces, under the control of the voluntary powers of the mind, and the back part contains the negative electro-nervous forces, under the control of the involuntary powers of the mind. As the positive forces, under an absolute volition of mind, resist all external impression, so the fact is readily seen why they have more power than the negative forces to resist disease, or any encroachments that may be made upon the system.

I would now remark, that the science of Electrical Psychology, being the doctrine of impressions, throws an immense flood of light on the human mind, and its susceptibility to the most strange and unreasonable impressions in the power of man to conceive. There are some minds so constituted, that it is absolutely impossible for them to resist the impressions that others may make upon them. This science unfolds what was considered an inscrutable mystery in relation to the conduct of several individuals who perished in the excitement of the Salem witchcraft. Persons of well-known character—yes, of a *stainless* moral reputation—were executed on their own confession! They were charged with being bewitched, and with having bewitched others. They plead guilty to the charge, firmly believed it to be true, and, on their own confession, were sentenced to die, and were cut off from the land of the living. They were in the psychological state. In my public experiments, I have taken persons who are naturally in the *psychological state*, and have produced such impressions upon them. I have made them confess that they were bewitched, and that they had rode on broomsticks through the air to bewitch others, and deserved to die.

Hundreds of instances have occurred in our world, where persons have been charged with murder, have confessed themselves guilty of the deed, and, on that confession, have been solemnly sentenced to die. And yet, before the day of execution arrived, the supposed murdered man was found alive in some distant section, and hurried home just in time to save an innocent fellow-creature from an ignominious death. Turn to the criminal calendar, and you will find some most striking instances of this character, and that, too, in our own country, and even in New England, the boasted land of light and morals. All such persons were naturally in the *psychological state*, and really believed what they confessed. How many may have, through such means, innocently lost their lives, the opening scenes of eternity alone can disclose. Judges and jurors have yet to learn that no man should be hung on his own confession. If he must die, let it be in the face of the most indubitable evidence, and, even then, let him be recommended to mercy, for often murder, as well as suicide, is committed under some strange hallucination of mind.

LECTURE IX.

Ladies and Gentlemen:

Much has been advanced in relation to mind and matter, their various operations, powers, and manifestations, and the countless mental and physical impressions of which they are susceptible. I have also said not a little of the electro-nervous force, as the agent of the mind, and how the functions of every part of the system are executed under its energy. I have proved it to be the connecting link between mind and inert matter, and the agent by which the Creator moves all worlds through the boundless fields of space. I have shown the connection existing between man and nature, and the relationship he sustains to her as an epitome of the universe. As I have made electricity the grand agent that, under mind, moves on all the multifarious operations appertaining to the human system, it may be asked, what proof is there to establish this truth, independent of what has already been offered? If the arguments already advanced to prove that mind touches and moves electricity as its prime agent, are not sufficient and entirely satisfactory, I will then refer you to a visible and tangible experiment, the result of which you can witness, and thus test the truth of my position.

Let any gentleman of eloquence, feeling, and pathos strip up his sleeve, and lay his bare arm on a table where it shall be perfectly at rest; let him then repeat some impressive poetry, or any prose sentences of stirring eloquence, paying no attention to his arm till his feelings are moved, and at that instant he will see his arm covered with what are called goose-pimples. If he cease speaking, they will gradually disappear, as his mind sinks into calmness. Indeed, he can see them rise and fall with his feelings and emotions. These are occasioned by the redundant electricity which is thrown to the surface by the strong emotions and positive impulses of the excited mind. These pimples rise up at the root of each hair, and as hair is a non-conductor, and resists electricity, so the internal pressure of the electro-nervous force, propelled to the surface by the mind, causes these minute eminences to arise. Electricity is, in its nature, a cold substance. Hence, when the weather is cold, the air, being dense, contains an excess of electricity and oxygen. These, being inspired by the lungs in greater quantities than usual, brace the system, and render these pimples in the same ratio more prominent and visible than in warm weather. This circumstance confirms the proof that it is electricity moved by mind, that causes these to rise when the feelings are excited by an eloquence that causes even cold chills to pass over the body.

The proof now produced I consider to be absolutely and positively irresistible, and abundant to satisfy any philosophic mind, that electricity is the connecting link between mind and inert matter, and is, therefore, the agent through which the mind manifests its motions and powers. But should this not be sufficient to send a bold and firm conviction to the mind of the greatest skeptic, then I will endeavor to carry the proof still farther, and firmly nail the matter beyond his power to remove it. I will show him how abundant the proof is by which this position is sustained. Let the skeptic place himself on an insulated stool, with his arm entirely bare, and charge his body from a powerful electric machine. The hairs and pimples will rise up even as they do under an intense action of the mind. When the body is electrically charged on an insulated stool, even the hairs of the head rise up erect, and the same result follows when the mind is greatly excited by fear or moved by strong and stormy emotions.

If these evidences are not sufficient to strike the skeptic speechless in his opposition, then let him take a needle, and, after satisfying himself that it has no magnetic power to attract the smallest atom, let him insert it in the nerve of an animal, and it will become sufficiently magnetic to take up fine iron filings. Indeed, ladies and gentlemen, I have no doubt that the naked arm, under sufficiently strong and stirring emotions of mind to raise those pimples, would, while in that condition, produce an effect upon the electrometer.

We now perceive why the mind, when involved in trouble and distress, has so powerfully affected the body, not only in bringing upon it various diseases, but often sudden, or even instant death. And we moreover see why the mind, when calm, serene, and happy, when buoyant with hope, and animated with confidence, faith, and joy, has produced such powerful and salutary results in removing pains and diseases. We see why, under the energy of such a favorable state of mind, warts, and even king's-evil, cancers, and various tumors have been made to disappear.

Dr. John C. Warren, of Boston, Massachusetts, states, in his work on tumors, that a lady called upon him to ask his advice in relation to an experiment she thought of trying on a tumor with which she was afflicted. It was to rub it with the hand of a dead person; and, as she had a good opportunity, she asked Dr. Warren whether she had not better improve it. He states, that he at first thought of dissuading her from it, but sensible of the power of the imagination, he advised her to try the experiment. She did so, and in a few weeks the tumor disappeared!

Dr. Warren calls it the imagination; but it is the effect of a mental impression, as I have just stated, producing the result by the action of electricity through the voluntary nerves. The philosophy of this is simple, and in a few words I will notice it.

The old particles of our flesh are thrown off through the electro-nervous force of the involuntary nerves, and by the same force the new particles from the blood are laid down in their stead. Hence the wastes and repairs of the system are about balanced. We change, as I have stated, the fleshy particles of our bodies about once per year, and the bones in seven years. While, therefore, the involuntary nerves are keeping up this balance of power between the wastes and repairs of the flesh, so the same tumor that is thrown off once per year with the other particles of the body, is gradually replaced each year by the same involuntary electro-nervous force from the new particles of the blood. Over this the mind has no direct control, because it acts through the voluntary nerves. Hence when the mind is under the influence of confidence, faith, hope, and joy, organic activity is heightened, and by keeping the mind upon the tumor while in this happy state, and believing it will disappear, creates a surplus of action at that spot through the voluntary nerves, and this surplus action throws off this surplus protuberance to return no more. Such is the philosophy of what is called imagination.

The point being understood how the electro-nervous fluid removes a tumor, the query may now arise in your minds, Why does it heal a wound or cure a dis-

LECTURE IX.

ease? In answer to this question I would first remark, that I am well aware that the healing properties are in the individual, or in the electricity of the system, and not in the medicine. And the question, *Why does the electro-nervous fluid heal*, has been indirectly considered in my last Lecture, when explaining the process of digestion. Because if all things were made out of electricity, then it is certain that electricity contains all the elementary principles, and therefore all the healing properties of all things in being. All the balms, oils, and minerals in existence are contained in electricity, and in their most skillfully combined proportions. This electricity is inspired with the air into the lungs, and passed through the blood into the nerves of the brain, and becomes the electro-nervous fluid. It is the positive, moving power, in all its one hundred elements, and meets the same one hundred kindred elements that compose the body, and are the negative power. And the positive and negative forces coming together, and the one hundred elements in electricity meeting the one hundred of the same kind in the body, each tending to its own, produce the healing result, on the same principle that they produce digestion, repair the system, and equalize circulation. For a full explanation of this point you will please call to mind my remarks on the digestive process in my last Lecture, and the whole will be easily comprehended.

I now leave this point and call your attention to the brain, which is the palace and throne of the mind, where it dwells and reigns. I shall briefly notice its operations in its earthly house, point out the connection between the voluntary and involuntary nerves through which the mind acts, and conclude by noticing the philosophy of sleep.

I have stated in a former Lecture, that each individual has two distinct brains—namely, the cerebrum, which occupies the frontal part of the cranium, filling the principal part of its cavity, and the cerebellum, which occupies the back portion of the cranium. The voluntary nerves belong to the cerebrum, through which the voluntary powers of the mind act, and the involuntary nerves belong to the cerebellum, through which the involuntary powers of the mind act. And though in their intricate convolutions through every part of the cranium, they seem to interweave and blend in ten thousand ways, and both dive into the spine, and there combine to form the spinal marrow, yet by some secret charm they preserve their entirely distinct character as to their voluntary and involuntary powers, and thus carry out the separate forces of both brains into every part of the entire system.

Our voluntary powers by which we reason, and by which we move our limbs and bodies, being the positive force during our wakeful moments, soon tire, and require the refreshment of sleep to restore them. But our involuntary powers, by which the heart and lungs are moved, and the functions of life performed, commence their career of action at birth, and often continue it, without any apparent weariness, for seventy, eighty, or even a hundred years. They, however, tire at last, and also require sleep. But when they sleep, it is death. Natural sleep, which involves the sleep of the voluntary powers only in a state of entire insensibility, is so far on the road to death. It is the half-way house to the land of silence. By natural sleep our exhausted voluntary powers are restored, we wake up refreshed, our weariness has disappeared, and we are prepared for renewed action. There is at the same time another important end gained by our insensibility in sleep. The involuntary powers, being left free from the exciting action of the voluntary powers, were allowed to gradually slacken their movements, and regain their true and healthful equilibrium.

In order that this part of my subject may be distinctly understood, I must point out the connection between the voluntary and involuntary powers, and the manner in which they may reciprocally affect each other. Our pulsations are more frequent in the evening than in the morning. This is owing to the mental and physical action of our voluntary powers during our wakeful moments. They, being the positive force, trespass upon the involuntary powers, which are the negative force, and hence one grand object of sleep is to allow the heart to come down to its due natural slowness of pulsation. The voluntary powers, being the positive force, can of course trespass upon the involuntary, till they become tired out and sink to rest in the sleep of death. This I will endeavor to make plain by the following circumstances.

In the barbarous ages of the world, criminals have been, in some instances, doomed to die through deprivation of sleep. Guards, who took charge of them by turns, both night and day, were ordered to keep them incessantly awake. This they did do by touching them with some instrument of torture, and sometimes with fire, whenever exhausted nature would yield to repose. In such instances the pulsations of the heart are gradually increased above their usual throb, becoming more and more frequent, till between the third and fourth day, when they rise to about one hundred and twenty per minute, which is a fever heat. And so on, gradually increasing, till the seventh or eighth day, when the pulse is only perceived by a tremulous motion, inconsistent with the continuance of life, and the sufferer expires. You now perceive that the voluntary powers, by being kept awake, trespass upon the involuntary powers till they too are tired, and fall asleep; but that sleep is death.

I have already remarked, that when our voluntary powers are exhausted they fall asleep at night, and in the morning we wake up restored. This brought us half way on our journey to the door of death, and well may sleep, in all ages, have been considered its emblem. But when the involuntary powers are entirely exhausted by pain, by fevers, or by sickness in general, they also require rest, and therefore fall asleep. This is death. Now, if there were no positive organic destruction, and could the laws of chemistry that decompose our bodies be suspended, and could the entire system, blood and all, be kept precisely in the same condition as it was when we expired, we should wake up after a few days in perfect health. This is no revery of fancy, no chimera of the speaker's brain, but absolutely and positively true, and in perfect accordance with the principles of philosophy. As this subject is new, I will take it into consideration, as it must be not only interesting, but vastly important to us all.

In the first place, we know that the serpent and toad species, the alligator tribe, and nearly all insects, fall into torpidity in winter, and in the spring they are aroused from this state in perfect health, and with regenerated vigor. Not only their voluntary, but also their involuntary powers were asleep. The breathing lungs and throbbing heart were motionless, and the circulating blood was stilled. The raccoon and several other species of animals burrow, and fall into a torpid state as winter approaches, and remain till spring without any sustenance whatever, and then make their appearance without any loss of flesh. To all these creatures the *foramen ovale*, an opening between the auricles of the heart, never closes, and hence they can live without breathing.

It may, however, be said, that this is by no means applicable to human beings, for they cannot live without breathing. How then do we live without breathing, or even without the throbbing of the heart, or the circulation of the blood, till we were born into existance? I answer by saying, that the foramen ovale was not closed, but generally closes soon after our birth takes place. We know that the new-born infant requires but little air, and can live where we should be smothered and perish. Again, there is occasionally an individual in whom this never closes. It is true, that these instances are exceedingly rare, and such persons are liable, when disease or pain exhausts the involuntary powers, to sink into a torpid state, which has been mistaken for death. The lungs and heart suspended their motions, the blood ceased to circulate, and the limbs grew stiff and cold. Thousands in this condition have been prematurely buried, came to life, struggled, turned over in their coffins, and perished. On being disinterred they have been found with the face downward. Some, placed in tombs, have revived, been accidentally heard, and fortunately rescued. And though they expired with a distressing disease, yet they awoke to life in health.

An instance of this kind occurred in New Jersey,

where an individual was apparently in a state of death. He was cold and motionless. The lungs heaved not; the heart in its pulsations was stilled; the blood was stagnated in its channels, and had ceased to flow. His funeral was two or three times appointed, the friends and neighbors assembled, and through the entreaties of the physician it was postponed to another time. He at length awoke from this state to life, and awoke in health. Some call this singular condition, where circulation is suspended, a trance; but it is the sleep of the involuntary powers in those individuals only where the foramen ovale is not closed. In all other persons it would be death.

In view of these facts we should be warned not to inter our friends too soon after we suppose they are dead. And as death is only the sleep of the involuntary powers, so dying cannot be a painful process, but one that must afford the greatest pleasure and delight of which we can conceive. It must certainly afford as much real enjoyment to die as to lie down upon our beds and sink into natural sleep. All sufferings arise from the nature of the disease that tires out the involuntary powers, and not from the gasping struggles of the dying. The fatigues, toils, and sufferings of the day, that prepare our voluntary powers for a night's repose, are not to be taxed upon the process of our dropping into natural sleep. This is of itself pleasurable, and so is also the process of dropping into the sleep of death. In this respect it is not "the king of terrors," but the welcome angel of soothing smiles and crowning joys.

You now perceive that though the voluntary and involuntary powers of the mind are entirely distinct, and seem to act independently of each other through two distinct sets of nerves, yet there must be some secret link between the two that unites them in one bond of everlasting and indissoluble union. That this point may be settled as accurately as possible, I must call your attention to the voluntary and involuntary nerves, to determine the connection between them, and also to ascertain the throne of the mind, or in what particular part of the brain it may be located.

Though I have faithfully explained the philosophy of the circulation of the blood in my third Lecture, yet I am compelled to glance at the position in which the arterial and venous circulation stand in relation to each other, and notice the connection between them, and then see if this will not throw some light on the voluntary and involuntary nervous forces of the brain.

The circulating system is in reality two distinct systems. The *arterial* carries the cherry-red blood, which is *positive*, and ever flows from the lungs and heart to the extremities, and the *venous* carries the dark blood, which is *negative*, and ever flows from the extremities to the heart and lungs. The arterial system, commencing at the lungs and heart, divides into various branches, and these again into others, and so on, till they spread out in thousands of small blood-vessels called capillaries, too minute for the dissecting knife to trace, or the naked eye to see. Indeed, they run out and seem to end, if I may so speak, in millions of nothings. At their terminations, and in just as many millions of nothings, the venous system begins. Though there is no visible connection, that the dissector can trace between the two, yet we know that such a connection must exist, otherwise the blood could never pass from the capillaries of the arteries into those of the veins.

As the nervous system must correspond with the circulating system, so these remarks will prepare your minds for a correct understanding of my views in relation to the *voluntary* and *involuntary nerves* and the throne of the mind. The involuntary nerves have their origin in the cerebellum, which is the organ of involuntary motion, wind round in intricate mazes, and form its convolutions. They pass into the spine, and form the spinal marrow, a part of which is but the cerebellum continued, and from thence they branch out to the heart, lungs, and to all the involuntary parts of the system, so that motion may be communicated to them by the involuntary powers of the mind. They return through another department of the spinal marrow to the brain, and terminate in the medulla oblongata in thousands of nothings, by which I only mean invisible fibres. In just as many thousands of nothings, the voluntary nerves begin—wind round in like intricate mazes, and form the convolutions of the cerebrum, which is the great organ of voluntary motion. They pass into the spine and form the spinal marrow, which is but the continuation of the two brains, and from thence they branch out to all the voluntary parts of the system, so that motion may be communicated to them at pleasure by the voluntary powers of the mind.

It is evident that the same secret and invisible connection exists between the voluntary and involuntary nerves of the two brains that exists between the arteries and veins of the two circulating systems which carry the positive and negative blood. If this connection between the voluntary and involuntary nerves of the two brains does not exist, then the *voluntary powers* could not, by their wakefulness, produce the least possible effect upon the involuntary powers, so as to tire them out and produce death, nor could they even cause the least disease. And on the other hand, the *involuntary* could not produce the least possible effect upon the *voluntary* powers.

The mind is certainly not diffused throughout both brains, because a part of the brain may be destroyed, and the mind still retain all its powers and faculties. If it were thus diffused, being an active principle, it would keep every organ of the brain uniformly excited.

LECTURE IX. 179

Hence it appears most reasonable, that the mind holds its throne between the TERMINATION of the involuntary nerves of the cerebellum and the COMMENCEMENT of the voluntary nerves of the cerebrum. This will appear rational, if we reflect that any sudden, irregular motion of the heart for instance, or of any other involuntary organ, will instantly convey the warning to the mind, and bid it beware. But this sensation could not be communicated to the mind unless it held its throne between the voluntary and involuntary nerves. This, though difficult to determine, seems to be in the MEDULLA OBLONGATA. There the royal monarch sits enthroned. From the external world, through one common nerve, he receives all his impressions, and from thence he transmits them by electric telegraph to the various departments of his palace—or, to speak more phrenologically, to the different organs of the brain, and thus manifests the true impression of his character to the world.

In the light our subject now stands, the philosophy of natural sleep can be stated in very few words. Heat expands, and cold shrinks the nerves of the brain. As the *mind* is that sublimated substance we call *spirit*, and is a living being of embodied form, and being the reverse of dead matter, it is its nature to move, and the result of that motion is thought and power. By the shrinking of the nerves of the cerebrum its motions are stilled, and thought is gone. This is sleep.

I am done, and though errors may be detected, I care not. I have spoken freely, and meant to do so. And though skeptics may sneer, yet I see and feel the full weight, importance, and majesty of my subject. I have every thing to hope for in its favor, as a powerful agent to remove disease, and pain, and to succor the distressed.

LECTURE X.

Ladies and Gentlemen:

The science of Electrical Psychology is yet in the infancy of its existence, and as so many astonishing cures have been already effected under its energy while yet in the very dawn of its being, so we can at present form but a faint conception of that supreme empire over disease which it is ultimately destined in some future age to attain, or of that magnificence and power with which coming generations will see it invested. The time will come when it shall stand forth in the full vigor and beauty of its manhood, clothed in its meridian splendor, and shedding the pure light and heat of its own healing power over the millions of our race. In the great field of sciences already known to the philosopher, that of Electrical Psychology stands pre-eminent. In making this declaration I do not detract one iota from their value or greatness, but on the contrary yield to them all their grandeur. They are worthy of the Creator who established them when he founded the empire of nature, and worthy of the master spirits who revealed them to the world. They are great, and the various ranks of greatness they occupy in the scale of sciences were assigned them by that unerring Being who arranged the order and harmony of the universe, and not by erring man. Then censure me not for the declaration I make as it regards their relative importance.

I am not insensible of the fact that astronomy is a science of that peculiar and lofty character that knocks at the door of the heart, calls aloud for the most bold and daring thought, and bids it soar into the regions of unbounded space to survey, measure, weigh, and balance suns and worlds. The bare sublimity of the conception that man, who is but " an atom of an atom-world," can enter those vast dominions of the Creator and take cognizance of the grandeur of their expansiveness, the wisdom of their arrangements, the beauty of their variety, and the order and harmony of their motions, bespeaks the high origin of his nature and destiny as an intellectual and moral being. But astronomy, however vast may be its fields of brilliant suns and blooming worlds, and however strong may be its claims upon the human intellect for the exercise of its highest powers and most deep-stirring energies is, after all, but a physical science, and therefore inferior to the science of mind.

If, from this lofty and daring flight among countless suns and worlds, we descend and dive into the depths of the globe on which we tread, and should we be able to explore its dark subterranean dens and deepest caverns, even down to its centre—or should we only range its known geological departments and survey the various strata of its crust, and scrutinize the marine, vegetable, and animal remains they contain as so many deposits and mementoes marking the footsteps of nature in former ages, we shall also find a call for the deepest thought to scan the mysteries of geological science, and to search out and explain the operations and convulsions of nature in these subterranean regions. These contemplations on the heavens above, or on the structure of the earth beneath, are certainly sublime, and challenge the noblest powers of the human soul. But high as the science of astronomy may call the mind to soar, or deep as the science of geology may urge it to descend, yet these, after all, are only physical in their character, end, and aim.

But, on the other hand, the science of Electrical Psychology being the science of the living mind, its silent energetic workings and mysterious powers are as far above these and all others of a like character as mind is supreme over senseless matter. And as the object of this science is to produce such mental and moral impressions upon the sick and afflicted as shall restore them to health and happiness, and as this can positively be accomplished upon all who are in the electro-psychological state, so the vast importance and utility of this science are but faintly realized by the public at large—are but dimly seen. Even when these mental impressions can not be made upon an individual so as even to paralyze a muscle, still I can, in the great majority of cases, either cure or greatly benefit the sufferer by physical impressions upon his body, provided that he will faithfully follow my directions.

The remedies this science prescribes are always safe because its pharmacy is of God, and rests on the bosom of nature. Even in those cases where they can do no good they will do no harm. It discards those powerful, poisonous, and dangerous medicines of the old-school practice which, in their experiments, have proved so fatal to the lives of millions of our race. It selects those only from the fields of nature which grow in that part of the earth's latitude where we live, and such must be adapted to our constitution and condition by the wisdom of the Creator, who has provided both food and medicine to all animals and creatures in that part of the globe where he awakened them into existence. If we watch the actions of the animal creation we shall learn that there is, and indeed must be, as much simplicity in our medicine as there is in our food. Allopathy, Thompsonianism, Homeopathy, Hydropathy, Electropathy, and I will add, Aeripathy and Terrapathy, should never be made to exist as so many separate medical schools, but the excellences of them all, so far as they are applicable to the relief of human sufferings in any corresponding latitude on earth, should be combined into one grand system TO CURE, and call it CURAPATHY.

Water is nature's universal solvent, and when properly applied, in its various degrees of heat and cold, to the different parts of the system, either externally or internally as the case may require, it is a most powerful agent to restore the equilibrium of the circulating forces and remove disease. But water alone is not sufficient in every case. The air in its application and various temperatures should not be overlooked, nor the quality and temperature of that which is inhaled into the lungs. We can live longer without food or water than we can without air. In very warm weather, when the air is greatly rarefied by heat, let the invalid, and even the well person, descend into a dry cellar, entirely under ground, undress, and there not only breathe the pure, cool, and earth-impregnated air for half an hour or more each day, but let the body at the same time be exposed to its action. This will brace the feeble system of the invalid, gradually raising it up to soundness, and impart vigor and energy to the healthy. Call this Aeripathy. But this is not sufficient to remove every case of disease. Electricity, galvanism, and magnetism, in all their forms, should not be forgotten. Electricity is the agent of mind and the invisible power of matter. These three should be passed through different parts of the human system to ease pain, and remove nervous obstructions and nervous diseases by thus equalizing the **nervous** force. This is Electropathy, and requires not only a familiar acquaintance with electrical science, but also great skill in its correct application to the diseased.

But this alone is not sufficient. We must not be unmindful of our mother earth, nor wholly forget to lean upon her bosom. Our bodies take into their composition, not only due portions of *electricity, air,* and *water,* these three grand divisions of nature, but they also claim a large portion of earth, out of which they are said to have been formed. We are, indeed, an epitome of the universe, and stand in an exact aptitude and relationship to nature. This being so, permit me to remark, that diseased persons, during the summer season or warm months, should seek some farmer's secluded plough-field or garden, expose their naked bodies, except the covered head, for several minutes to the rays of the sun. When well heated and rubbed, cover them up in the fresh earth for half an hour or more, then wash and rub briskly with a towel, dry well in the sun, and dress. At other times, and as often as convenient, let the invalid follow the ploughman, and as he turns up the fresh earth let him breathe the air while charged with the invisible life-giving substances that rise from the ground.

As the above advantages can only be enjoyed by those in the country, what shall be done for those in cities? In order to be more explicit on this interesting point, when you build you a house make provisions for a room that can admit the sun through its windows. It might be connected with your bathing establishment, and in the same room. Have at least three articles permanently constructed like the tub in which you lie down to bathe the body. Let one be filled with a pure, rich, fertile earth—another with a light, sandy soil, and a third with clay. Here let the invalid each day bury his body in one of the first two, and remain at least half an hour, after first having exposed it to the action of the sun. Then let him wash, rub well with a towel, and dry thoroughly in the sun before dressing. But in case of severe chronic diseases, apply pure water to the clay till it becomes a mortar in which the body will sink, and let the patient bathe his body in this. If the disease is attended with inflammation, let the mortar be warm as can be conveniently borne, and then wash the body in water of the same temperature. If there is no inflammation, let the water be cold as its usual summer temperature, and wash the body in water of the same, rub briskly with a towel, and always dry thoroughly in the sun, if possible, before dressing. By this mode of treatment an empire over many diseases will be obtained, when all other modes have failed. This I will name TERRAPATHY. Simple internal medicines, of an animal or vegetable nature, may at times be taken into the stomach, but nothing of a poisonous character. I therefore repeat, that Electrical Psychology is the doctrine of mental and physical impressions to cure the sick. This can often be done without any medicine at all, by simply a mental impression, which this science involves. But when I use physical impressions, I can not restrict my action to the narrow sectarian "medical schools" set up by men, but avail myself of a free and untrammeled range in the extensive fields of nature. Hence I sum up the whole matter by re-affirming, that Allopathy, Thompsonianism, Homeopathy, Hydropathy, Electropathy, to which I add Aeripathy and Terrapathy, should never be established as so many separate medical schools. In the splendid science of Electrical Psychology I embrace the excellences of them all so far as they are applicable to the relief of human sufferings, and combine them in one grand system to cure, and call it CURAPATHY.

I presume the question will arise in some minds, why should Terrapathy, or the various applications of different kinds of earth to the body, have a tendency to cure? This question is somewhat difficult of solution, but no more so than to solve why water, air, or any medicine has a tendency to produce a sanative result upon the human system. If, however, you will recall my arguments on the philosophy of digestion in my eighth lecture, and what I said on the philosophy of cure in my ninth, you will have my answer to the question, *Why should Terrapathy have a tendency to cure?* No physician pretends to explain *why* his medicines produce certain effects upon the system. He merely knows the fact, and acts accordingly. These facts, as to the medicinal virtues of certain substances, have in many cases, at least, been learned from the animal creation or been discovered by accident. When one rattlesnake bites another, the wounded one will invariably eat a certain plant and live. A negro, laboring in the Dismal Swamp, in North Carolina, observing this, ate the same on being bitten by a rattlesnake, and was cured. Others laboring there have practiced it with the same success. Indeed, nearly every useful vegetable medicine now in possession of doctors, has been discovered by some old woman in the country, or by old hunters and Indians, and, after much learned opposition and medical sneering, it has been at length received as their adopted child, and one after another has been, after passing through a like ordeal, introduced into the medical family, and claimed as their lawful paternity. Even Peruvian bark was discovered by the Jesuits to be an excellent specific for ague and fever. For this they were persecuted by the medical profession, who sneered at the remedy, laughed its discoverers to scorn, and moved the clergy to fulminate their thunders against them and their medicine. But they have long ago adopted this persecuted child into the medical family and school. Now, they can not treat an intermittent fever without this darling. You know that quinine, which is manufactured from Peruvian bark, is in our day "all the rage" in treating ague and fever. But setting aside the manner in which the medical properties of substances were first discovered, let us come directly to the subject under consideration.

What evidence, we may now ask, is there that Terrapathy possesses any power to cure? It will be remembered that I have contended throughout these Lectures that electricity is the power that controls matter, even from the smallest particle up to the most ponderous globes, and that mind is a self-moving substance that controls electricity, and that hence all power and motion consubstantially dwell in, and emanate from mind. I have contended that the sanative principle is in the man, and is involved in the electro-nervous fluid, which is the positive force breathed in from the atmosphere, and the food taken into the stomach is the negative force abstracted from the earth, and answering to it. These two forces in man, being the *positive* and *negative*, meet together and embrace each other. All the elements of the positive electro-nervous force of the brain blend with all the corresponding elements of the negative electro-vegetative force of the food in the stomach, and digestion, which is but the transmutation of food into the elements of the system, proceeds. The body, being the medium between these two forces, is gradually and incessantly changing, by the old particles being dismissed from its service and new ones enlisted to supply the waste of this unceasing war. But the electricity inspired with the air into the lungs, in being secreted by the brain, undergoes a change from what it was in the atmosphere equal in degree and corresponding to that of earth transmuted into vegetables. This is evidently so, because in order to enable it to act upon the negative electric *force* of the food in the stomach, it must stand in the same positive relationship to *this* that the positive electricity of the atmosphere does to the negative electricity of the globe in order to transmute its earthy particles into vegetable substances. Should the electricity of the atmosphere, when taken into the lungs, remain in its unchanged state, it could never carry on a perfect digestion, so as to transmute food into flesh and bones, because a perfect aptitude between this electricity, the food, and the living body does not exist. This can only be done by electricity, after having been secreted and changed by the brain into an electro-nervous fluid. But, on the other hand, this electro-nervous fluid can not possibly transmute earthy particles into vegetables, because a perfect aptitude between these three changing properties does not exist. This can only be done by the electricities of the atmosphere and globe acting in conjunction.

Having these general facts distinctly before us, we shall now be able to discover and appreciate the fact, that TERRAPATHY possesses also, and that too in an eminent degree, its distinct powers to cure. To a candid consideration of this point I now invite your particular attention.

In my Fourth Lecture I have argued the philosophy of health and disease, and trust that the ideas there advanced are retained by you all. When the mind is serene, and its mental and moral attributes are so balanced as to act in perfect unison; when all the internal circulating forces of the body are equalized so as to move on in one harmonious and beautiful round in their destined channels; and when the body externally stands in the same well-balanced and beautiful relation to the air, water, vegetables, and earth, then health must be the natural result of this state of things, on the principle of the common law of equilibrium, in which all other laws are involved. But when any or all of these are thrown out of balance, disease ensues. How, then, are these difficulties to be overcome, the circulating forces equalized, the mind restored to its wonted serenity, and health and happiness regained? In reply to these important and interesting queries, I would in the first place observe, that it is admitted by all who are acquainted with the principles of electrical science, that the atmosphere is charged with *positive* electricity, and the earth with *negative* electricity. Each of these electricities possess, of course, the attractive and repulsive forces

Now, as all diseases are either of a positive or negative character, so they must be cured by the positive or negative electricities, or by the application of substances that contain them. We should first attempt a cure by the science of Electrical Psychology alone. Whether this, of itself, would prove successful or not, could be tested in a few moments, by an immediate trial of mental impressions upon the patient. If these were successful, the mind would resume the balance of its powers. Its peace and contentment would be restored, and by its mental energies the nervous, and other circulating forces of the body would be equalized, and health and happiness ensue. But if the disease can not be psychologically cured by direct mental impressions, then we are compelled to resort to physical remedies, and make what I call physical impressions upon the body, and through these to reach the mind, because the mind and body intermutually and reciprocally affect each other.

Suppose, then, the disease to be a *positive one*, occasioned by the positive electricity of the system being thrown out of balance. In all diseases of this character, even though they may be attended with severe pain, yet there is never any inflammation. To these make cold applications, or the positive electric forces. Opposites should seldom be used, for they can not act as permanent alteratives. Or suppose the disease to be a *negative one*, occasioned by the negative electricity of the system being thrown out of balance. All diseases of this character will be attended, not only with pain, but inflammation. To these we should apply the negative forces, which belong in a peculiar sense to the earth.

Here permit me to exhibit this interesting subject in a more definite and orderly arrangement, so as to be readily understood. Now, do you not perceive that, according to the peculiar nature of the disease, we should apply electricity, galvanism, or magnetism, or else air in its various temperatures, from the coldest to the warmest that can be borne? Do you not perceive that when the disease requires it, that water, in its various temperatures, should be applied, either externally or internally? And do you not perceive that herbs, in their various decocted combinations, or otherwise, should also, when the disease requires it, be taken internally or applied externally, and of such temperatures as to produce a salutary result? We have now descended from electricity, the finest known inert substance in being, through all the grand elementary departments of nature, down to the vegetable kingdom. Now, shall we stop here, or proceed down to EARTH, the MOTHER of us all, and draw relief from her generous bosom? Shall we stop at herbs, earth's eldest-born children, who forever hang upon her breast, or shall we approach the maternal germinating and generating power and source from whence they draw their vital being? As the earth is electrically *negative*, and peculiarly so, how supreme must her powers be over all diseases attended with inflammation! Earthy substances, in various clayey or other combinations, and in the form of poultices, either cold or warm, as the case may require, can be applied to the diseased part, and with the same convenience that we do any other substance. Or, when necessary, let the whole body be buried in soils of various kinds, in their natural vegetating temperature. Or should the disease require it, let the body be immersed in various mortars made of one or several kinds of clay, or other earthy compounds. The only thing requisite is a good knowledge of their chemical properties, and good judgment and skill *how*, and *when*, and in what manner to apply them to any given disease.

Consistent and even irresistible as all this may appear, yet the question comes up—Can any facts be produced as evidence of the sanative results of Terrapathy? Certainly; there are thousands of instances of its power. But as it has never occurred to any mind to bring it into practice as a system, so the instances of its power are merely incidental. I have made it my study occasionally for five years, and yet I am now only ready to introduce it into the service of my grand system of Electro-Psychological Curapathy, and commence its practice. But to the point.

I might refer, with more force than many are aware,

to the spittle and clay prepared by the Master, and put on the eyes of a blind man, whom he then ordered to go and wash in the Pool of Siloam, and on doing of which he received his sight. Most of Christians suppose that all this was useless, and that he employed some other agent to restore his sight besides the means he manifestly employed. But it is in vain for any one to contend that Christ practiced a fraud, by putting clay upon his eyes to produce no possible effect, and then secretly and deceptively restored his sight by some other power. It was done by the very means that he thus openly employed, and by which he pretended it was done, and without a shade of deception through fear of men. It was accomplished by the combined forces of Terrapathy, Hydropathy, and the faith and confidence inspired in the blind man's mind by a strong psychological impression.

But without any reference whatever to the Master, I will, in as few words as possible, show that the various earths possess a most powerful electro-absorbent force to draw out inflammation from the human system, and with which no other known substances in existence can compare. The smallest effect we witness on earth is often pregnant with the greatest power, and portends the most salutary or awful results. A straw shows the direction of the current, however deep its waters, or secret its irresistible movement.

Take then, for example, the sting of the bee, or the

bite of any poisonous insect, where the pain, swelling, and inflammation would be great. The moment the circumstance occurs take almost any kind of earth at hand capable of producing vegetation, moisten it with spittle or blood-warm water, apply it to the wound, and in a few moments the poison will be extracted, and every painful result arrested. But a blue or white clay soil, moistened with warm water or spittle, is preferable, if it can be obtained without delay.

As to the drawing and absorbent powers of clay and other earths, I might bring a few simple facts. For instance, let oil or grease be spilled upon the floor, and remain till the board be saturated. No soap and water can remove it—no washings can make it disappear; yet clay, rightly prepared, will extract it. Or suppose there are oil or grease spots upon a silk dress. Rub pulverized magnesia on the opposite or wrong side of the dress, then press a hot iron to the grease spot on the right side, and the whole will instantly disappear, and leave the silk as bright and fair as ever. The same result may be obtained by using pulverized French chalk on any beautiful woolen dresses or shawls. Now it is utterly impossible that these effects could be produced unless these substances possessed a supreme electro-absorbent power. Or let clothing be saturated with any substance producing the strongest possible and the most pungent and enduring scent, even that of the skunk, and when no washing, no airing can remove it, let it be buried in any soil capable of producing a free vegetation, and in three or four days the whole will entirely disappear.

The question arises—What is the cause of this? I answer by saying, that the human stomach can not, neither can that of any other animal, digest any creature swallowed alive, so long as it possesses animal life. It must die before the stomach can digest and appropriate it to the elements that compose the body, and until then the creature must sustain its existence by drawing its sustenance from the vital force of the body. So the earth can not digest, that is, decompose, any substance while that substance has either animal or vegetable life. These both draw strength and substance from her. But the moment they are dead she can digest and appropriate them to her own use, and thus invigorate and fructify herself. Hence it is seen why Terrapathy can cure. It is because all substances in the human system that are adverse to animal life and health, the earth can appropriate to herself, and so she can all essences of the most pungent smell. She digests the whole, and manufactures and re-absorbs them again into the elements that compose her maternal body. She removes every substance from the human system adverse to the laws of animal life, and leaves perfect health. Hence the supremacy of Electro-Psychological Curapathy over all medical systems in being is clearly manifest, and I add no more.

LECTURE XI.

PRIVATE INSTRUCTIONS TO THE CLASS.

THE SECRET REVEALED.

GENTLEMEN:

IN my last Lecture I have argued the supremacy of Curapathy over all medical systems in existence, for in it are combined the excellences of them all; and, in addition to these, it contains modes of treatment that no medical science as yet involves. In this peculiar position of my subject it will be perceived by all those who have paid any attention to the science of Electrical Psychology, that it is of most paramount importance to the human race, as a curative agent, and should, therefore, be understood by all, so far, at least, as to apply it successfully to the removal of disease and pain. It should be practically understood by all medical men. This will cost them only the trifling sum of ten dollars, and in the course of their practice it would be worth thousands to them, and at the same time afford them the supreme pleasure of having saved many a life, where medicine must have failed. To obtain a good knowledge of this science will require about FIVE

LESSONS OF TWO HOURS EACH; and as I am now permanently settled in New York city, I am ready to impart these instructions to all persons of *good moral character* who may call. If persons at a distance will form a class sufficiently large to warrant the expense, and address me a letter at New York, I will visit them one week, and not only give private instructions to the class, but will deliver, in the mean time, five public evening lectures besides, and perform most interesting experiments, of which the class may have the profit of the admission fee. This would generally pay their tuition, and in many instances exceed it.

I make this proposal, because hundreds of ignorant individuals have undertaken to lecture upon, and even to teach this science, who have never received any instruction from me, either verbal or written. These persons pretend to teach it, and that, too, for any price they can obtain, from five dollars down to twenty-five cents! They had better receive "*a penny for their thoughts,*" so as to adapt the price of tuition to the amount of information they impart. All the regular students to whom I have taught the science of Electrical Psychology have been laid under written obligations, and have seriously pledged their sacred honor never to teach it under ten dollars. Those, therefore, who are qualified teachers and honorable men do still continue to adhere to the obligations they signed, and charge the original fee. Those who vary from it have either forfeited their obligations, or else never learned the science as they ought; and hence the public will know who and what they are.

It is due to myself to state, that some have changed the name of this science to that of "ELECTRO BIOLOGY," and have claimed authorship as to its discovery, and have even stated that Electro Biology has no connection whatever with Electrical Psychology, but is an entirely distinct science. This I am compelled to give a most decided and unqualified denial. I have visited some of the principal places where the Biologists have lectured, and have gathered all the facts in relation to their proceedings and the character of their experiments. I am acquainted with its whole history, and the circumstances under which it received its name, and why Electrical Psychology was first called "*Electro Biology.*" Should I, in a future day, be compelled in self-defense to take this subject in hand, I shall make all the necessary disclosures, which the interest and advancement of this science may require, or justice and duty demand. For the present they must rest in my bosom till circumstances shall call them forth. I would now only say, that the science of *Electrical Psychology is identical with that of Electro Biology, and that the latter has no existence only what it draws from the former, unless it be the mere half of its name.*

I have already stated, that there are certain individuals who have gone through the country lecturing, and pretending to teach this science for one or two dollars, and even for twenty-five cents, when they could get no more, who are utterly ignorant of the human system—ignorant of those diseases that assail it, and ignorant of the common principles involved in any of the sciences. Such may be able to inform you how to close a man's eyes—how to paralyze or move his limbs, and how to make a psychological impression on his mind. But how can they teach any one its philoscphical application to disease, or to any useful medical purpose? Every man of common sense must perceive that this is impossible without the knowledge of science in general. Such incompetent individuals have done Electrical Psychology a serious injury, and in several places have brought it into disrepute.

Under all these circumstances, I feel it my duty to put an end to the worse than useless labors of such individuals, by fully explaining the secret mode of operation—how an individual may be controlled by mental and physical impressions. I would not be understood that this can be wholly done by language. It requires a visible and personal application of what the theory involves—a practical illustration as to performing experiments, and how to apply it successfully to disease. I will, however, do it faithfully, so far as language can accomplish it, and far beyond what any lecturer now in the field attempts to explain to his class of pupils. The most have failed to give satisfaction to those whom they have undertaken to instruct, and in many cases serious difficulties have occurred in relation to the sum paid for instruction. I have therefore come to the conclusion not to suffer odium in future to be brought upon this science, if in my power to prevent it. I proceed, therefore, to give the instructions to all, so that they may know how to experiment upon their fellow-men, as well as those generally who go about as lecturers and teachers of this science. In the accomplishment of this I shall be brief as possible. What requires ten hours of instruction can not, by any means, be communicated fully in two lectures of half an hour each. Yet I will embody all, and even more than is generally given to any class of pupils by those claiming to be teachers.

I would, in the first place, remark, that the Creator has stamped simplicity, as far as possible, upon each separate part of the human system. As I remarked in my sixth Lecture, each organ of the body performs but one function. The eye sees, the ear hears, the olfactories smell, the glands taste, the heart throbs to regulate the blood, the hands handle, the feet walk, the liver secretes its bile, and the stomach digests its food. The eye never hears, and the ear never sees. So there evidently is but one nerve or set of nerves through which impressions from the external world are communicated to the mind. This is certain, because the mind can receive but one idea at a time. It is immaterial how rapidly soever ideas may be transmitted to the mind, they are nevertheless successive, and two ideas can not possibly be conceived, at the same instant, by the mind. One must succeed the other. But as there are millions of nerves in the human brain, and if it were alike the office of each to communicate ideas to the mind, then as many millions of ideas as there are nerves might be transmitted to the mind at the same instant. But we are conscious that they are successively and not simultaneously conceived. We can not attend to two public speakers at once, so as to understand their ideas, if both were before us, and each addressing us upon a different subject. With the same earnestness that we give heed to the one, we must neglect the other. Indeed, there can be no doubt in relation to the fact of ideas being successively communicated to the mind, if we reflect that even one public speaker by too rapid a delivery often confuses the hearer.

The mind, as a living being of embodied form, has its spiritual brain and spiritual organs answering to the correspondent phrenological organs of the physical brain through which it manifests itself. The latter are, indeed, a production from the former, as much so as the plant and its form are a production from the life of the seed. The nerve, or family of nerves, through which impressions are communicated to the mind, and by the mind to the body, to move its various parts, is located in the organ of Individuality. All the organs of the brain, and, indeed, of the whole system, are double, and so are the senses likewise. The brain has its two hemispheres, its two eyes, two ears, two glands of taste, and two olfactories of smell. We have two hands, two feet, and the heart has its two auricles and two ventricles. The organ of Individuality is also double. It is located in the centre of the lower part of the forehead, sends off branches to the optic, auditory, and olfactory nerves—extends through both hemispheres of the brain, passes down the spinal marrow, and in its course sends off branches to the arms and lower limbs, and, indeed, to all the voluntary parts of the body. Hence all voluntary motion originating in mind is communicated to the organ of Individuality, and from thence is transmitted through correspondent nerves to that part of the body where the mind directs motion to be made. Hence the organ of Individuality is the one that constitutes our individualism, or personal identity, and by which we identify all individual objects in the external world. And though this organ, like all the other phrenological organs of the brain, is made up of a congeries of nerves, yet I am satisfied that it has but one single identical nerve that is moved by a mental impression, and that one moves by sympathy the whole family of nerves dwelling in that organ; and thus motion is communicated to every voluntary department of the body where the mind, as the motive power, directs.

For illustration of the above, suppose a pebble were thrown into the centre of Lake Superior. It would displace its waters, and produce a circle. That circle would produce a *second*, and that *second* would produce a *third circle*, and so on, each continuing to lessen in its action until it apparently died away. But though imperceptible to the naked eye, yet the successive action would be continued even to the distant shores, and move every drop of water from the centre to the circumference. And not only so, but that pebble would displace, by sympathy, every particle of water in the basined lake, even to its greatest depth. This is evident, because if a rock, half the size of that mighty lake, were thrown into its centre, the universal disturbance of every particle of water would be evident and perceptible. On the same principle, a pebble—yes, a single grain of sand—would produce the same result, only on a smaller scale. So the centre nerve (if I may so speak) of the organ of Individuality is moved by a mental impression, and this movement communicates motion by sympathetic impulse to each and every voluntary part of the body where the mind directs. Is not this the true philosophy of what we call *sympathy* existing between the different parts of the human body and the various attributes of the soul, and between one individual and another? And is not this the true philosophy of *personal identity*, on the mystery of which so much has been written? Did not the mind of man possess a *spiritual* organ of Individuality corresponding to the *physical* one of the brain, how then could either personal identity or sympathy be recognized, or even exist? This one spiritual organ constitutes the unity of all the attributes of the mind, spirit, soul, or whatever you please to call that part of man which is to exist immortal in a future world. The phrenological organs of the human brain are but a daguerreotype manifestation—a result of the correspondent spiritual organs of the living mind. They constitute the physical apartments of the earthly house which is fitted up as a temporary residence for the in visible inhabitant within, during its continuance here.

Having clearly placed before you those interesting points that involve the ever sweet and pleasing doctrine of sympathy, I will now proceed to instruct you how an individual can be *electrically* and *psychologically* controlled. This is a subject involving vast utility as a curative power to the sick and distressed, and is therefore full of deep and stirring interest to every feeling heart. To control is to cure. In order to affect an individual, and to successfully control his mind and muscles, it is, in the first place, necessary that he should stand in a negative relation to the operator as to the doctrine of impressions. Some persons are naturally in this condition, were born in it, live in it.

and will die in it. Others are not in this state, and hence means must be used to bring them there before they can be controlled. In order to determine whether an individual stands in this negative relation to yourself, as the operator, you must first proceed to take the communication, as we term it. This is invariably and philosophically done through the medium of two points. I care not whether it be effected by visible contact or otherwise, it is still done through the medium of two points, or the negative and positive electric forces, and through the same nerve, or family of nerves, that constitutes, phrenologically, our individualism or personal identity.

Before I proceed to notice the most easy, sure, and direct mode by which an electro-psychological communication may be established, I will, in the first place, speak of the philosophy of communication in general. It is evident that the *positive* and *negative* forces of the two electricities pervade all nature. These I call in my seventh Lecture the *male* and *female* electricities. These two forces not only permeate, more or less, all substances in nature, but they also unceasingly emanate from them in electric circles. Hence, as man is a part of the universe, he constantly takes into his system large portions of electricity with the air he inspires, with the water he drinks, and with the food he eats. And by mental and muscular action, and the common operations of animal life, he unceasingly throws it off through the nervous force. On passing from his system into the surrounding elements, it forms around him his electric or magnetic circle. How large this circle may be is as yet to us unknown. Hence, when two individuals come within a certain distance of each other, their circles meet, and touch each other at two points. And if one of these individuals is in the electro-psychological state, the communication will be taken through the positive and negative forces. And though this communication was taken without personal contact, yet it was done through the nerve that constitutes our individualism or personal identity. A communication in this manner can be established with those persons only who are very sensitive. As only about one in twenty-five is naturally in this state, so I can step before an audience of a thousand persons, state to them what I intend to do, so that all shall understand me; then request them all to close their eyes firmly, and say, *You can not open your eyes!* and forty out of the thousand will be unable to do so. All this can be performed in five minutes after entering the hall.

It is, however, certain, that no effect can be produced till you establish a thorough communication between yourself and the subject through the nervous force of the organ of Individuality that constitutes his personal identity. And as the centre or moving nerve of this organ has sympathy with all the voluntary nerves of the system, and as they reciprocally affect each other so you can establish a psychological communication by touching any part of the system where voluntary nerves are located, and particularly of those individuals who are very sensitive and impressible. But the most natural mode to get a good communication, and the one least liable to be detected by the audience, is to take the individual by the hand, and in the same manner as though you were going to shake hands. Press your thumb with moderate force upon the ULNAR NERVE, which spreads its branches to the ring and little finger of the hand. The pressure should be nearly an inch above the knuckle, and in range of the ring finger. Lay the ball of the thumb flat and partially crosswise, so as to cover the minute branches of this nerve of motion and sensation. The pressure, though firm, should not be so great as to produce pain or the least uneasiness to the subject. When you first take him by the hand, request him to place his eyes upon yours, and to keep them fixed, so that he may see every emotion of your mind expressed in the countenance. Continue this position and also the pressure upon this *cubital nerve* for half a minute or more. Then request him to close his eyes, and with your fingers gently brush downward several times over the eyelids, as though fastening them firmly together. Throughout the whole process feel within yourself a fixed determination to close them, so as to express that determination fully in your countenance and manner. Having done this, place your hand on the top of his head and press your thumb firmly on the organ of Individuality, bearing partially downward, and with the other thumb still pressing the ULNAR NERVE, tell him—*you can not open your eyes!* Remember, that your manner, your expression of countenance, your motions, and your language must all be of the most positive character. If he succeed in opening his eyes, try it once or twice more, because impressions, whether physical or mental, continue to deepen by repetition. In case, however, that you can not close his eyes, nor see any effect produced upon them, you should cease making any further efforts, because you have now fairly tested that his mind and body both stand in a positive relation to yours as it regards the doctrine of impressions.

There is yet another mode of communication that I have discovered, which is far preferable to the one just noticed, is supreme over all others, and will remain so till Omnipotence shall see fit to change the nervous system of man. This is the MEDIAN NERVE, which is the second of the brachial plexus. It is a compound nerve having the power of both motion and sensation. It is located in the centre of the upper part of the palm of the hand near where it joins the wrist. In order to take the communication through this medium, you must take the subject by the hand with the palm upward, and place the ball of your thumb in the centre of his hand near the root of his thumb, and give a moderate but firm pressure. The astonishing nature of the impression can only be equaled by the result produced. It is a nerve of voluntary motion as well as sensation, and therefore belongs to, and has its origin in, the cerebrum. True, like the other nerves, it can be traced directly no farther than the spinal cord, yet there is no difficulty in determining its origin to be in the cerebrum, because that is the organ of all voluntary motion, even as the cerebellum is the organ of all involuntary motion. This mode of communication transcends all others, and will answer in all possible cases, even upon persons the most difficult to control, as well as upon those who are the most sensitive and impressible. I care not how you obtain the communication with an individual—whether it be without contact, or by touching any part of the body, yet the communication must ultimately be established through the MEDIAN NERVE as the centre telegraphic force from the organ of Individuality, through which organ all ideas and all impressions are transmitted from the external world to the mind, and through that same organ are transmitted by the volitions of the mind to the different parts of the body. Even if the communication is taken by pressure on the *ulnar nerve*, yet it is nevertheless communicated by sympathy to the MEDIAN NERVE, and through which alone the communication becomes perfect. There is no question, in my mind, that the *optic*, the *auditory*, and the *olfactory* nerves, as well as those of taste, are but branches of the same common nerve by which impressions or ideas are transmitted to the mind through the organ of Individuality. Those whom I have instructed, will please to remember this. I desire you, and all, in order to experiment with power, to keep up a perfect uniformity in taking the communication through the MEDIAN NERVE, and through this to transmit the electric current to the brain and electrify the body.

I am aware that the exact location of this nerve is somewhat difficult to find, unless you are personally instructed. If you succeed in closing the subject's eyes by the above mode, you may then request him to put his hands on his head, or in any other position you choose, and tell him, *You can not stir them!* In case you succeed, request him to be seated, and tell him, *You can not rise!* If you are successful in this, request him to put his hands in motion, and tell him, *You can not stop them!* If you succeed, request him to walk the floor, and tell him, *You can not cease walking!* And so you may continue to perform experiments involving muscular motion and paralysis of any kind that may occur to your mind, till you can completely control him, in arresting or moving all the voluntary parts of his system. When this is accomplished, we say, for the sake of convenience, *he is in the electrical state.*

You may, perhaps, not be able to affect him any further; and as you can not know how this matter stands without the trial, so you will next proceed to produce mental impressions by operating upon his mind only. If he is entirely in the state, you can make him see that a cane is a living snake or eel; that a hat is a halibut or flounder; a handkerchief is a bird, child, or rabbit; or that the moon or a star falls on a person in the audience, and sets him on fire, and you can make him hasten to extinguish it. You can make him see a river, and on it a steamboat crowded with human beings. You can make him see the boiler burst, and the boat blow up, with his father or mother, brother or sister, or wife or child on board. You can lay out the lifeless corpse before him in state, cause him to kneel at its side, and to freely shed over it the tears of affection and bereavement. You can suddenly show him a boy or girl, and he sees in them the lost father or mother standing before him, and gives the warm embrace. You can change his own personal identity, and make him believe that he is a child two or three years old, and inspire him with the artless feelings of that age; or that he is an aged man, or even a woman, or a negro, or some renowned statesman or hero. You can change the taste of water to that of vinegar, wormwood, honey, or of any liquors you please. In like manner you can operate on his hearing and smelling, as well as on his sight, feeling, and taste. When you can produce such mental hallucinations as these on all his senses, or thousands of others that may suggest themselves to your mind, we say, for the sake of convenience, that he is in the *psychological state*.

I have thus far confined my remarks to that class of individuals who are *naturally* in the electro-psychological state, and shown you clearly how a communication in its various modes may be taken, so as to successfully control them both physically and mentally. The average number of persons in the United States who are naturally in the psychological state is about one in twenty-five. These can be cured of any functional diseases with which they may be assailed, by simply performing upon them the experiments I have just named, or any others of a like character. And not only so, but upon such any surgical operation may be performed without the slightest degree of pain, and that, too, while they are wide awake, and in perfect possession of all their reasoning faculties. But while only one in twenty-five is entirely in this state, and naturally so, yet there is, perhaps, one in twelve who is partially in the state, and on whom experiments can be performed to a greater or less extent. All these, in connection with those on whom you can produce no effect whatever, are to be subjected to a process to bring them into the electro-psychological state, and we see, too, how vastly important it is that this, if possible, should be done. This, indeed, would be the noblest triumph ever achieved by man. It would be a triumph over disease and pain, and prepare the human race to wear out with age.

In order to bring about this result, I know, at present, of no better process than the following: Take pure zinc and silver, with a copper wire, as a conductor, passed through the zinc, so as to come in contact with the silver. For convenience, take a piece of zinc the size of a cent, but somewhat thicker, and imbed a five-cent piece in its centre, and pass a small copper wire, as a rivet, through both. Place this coin in the palm of the hand, with the silver side up, and request him to bring it within about a foot of his eyes. Let him take a position, either sitting or standing, which he can retain twenty minutes or more, without any motion of his feet, hands, lips, head, or any part of his body. He must remain motionless as a statue, except the natural winking of the eye. His mind should be perfectly resigned and kept entirely passive to surrounding impressions. The eyes should be placed upon the coin as though they were riveted there, and during the whole twenty or twenty-five minutes they should, on no consideration, be raised to look at any person or object whatever, and the spectators should be still as the grave. If the eyes have a tendency to close, he should not strive to keep them open, but let them close. Follow nature. In a public audience, when lecturing, you should seat, if possible, a class of thirty persons. When the time has expired, collect your coin so as relieve the class from their wearisome position, and then try each individual, always taking the communication in the manner I have described, and proceed to experiment upon them the same as you do upon those who are naturally in the state. If one sitting do not bring them entirely into the psychological state, then let it be repeated on the next evening, and so continue on till the work is consummated. All, with few exceptions, can be, by perseverance, brought into this state. Some are naturally in it—some are brought into it by *one sitting*—some by *two*—some by *three*— and some may require a *hundred sittings* of half an hour each before they can be brought to the participation of this inestimable blessing. No two individuals are alike impressible in any thing whatever, whether it be mental effort, moral power and moral suasion, or physical endurance. Hence we should not be surprised, that they all differ from each other as to nervous impressibility in this science, and that, too, in the same ratio as they may differ in their phrenological developments and cerebral excitability. It is enough for us to know on this point that no two individuals are in any respect exactly alike.

Having described the electro-magnetic coin which I conceive to be the best, under all circumstances, to produce the result, and having directed you how to use it, I would now apprise you, that this state may be induced by other substances as agents in nature. It may be induced by fixing the eyes upon a piece of zinc alone, and observing the directions already given. It may be induced by a piece of silver, or a piece of copper, iron, lead, or any other metal. It may be induced by a piece of wood, or any other substance in nature. Or it may be done by a mere mental abstraction, with no substance, only the surrounding elements. But when no substance is used, the process to the state is slow and tedious. Then, again, there is every possible grade of power from the feeblest substance placed in the hand up to the galvanic battery, which is more powerful than the coin I have adopted as a matter of convenience and utility. The galvanic battery I should prefer, if it could be carried in the pocket, or be accessible to all. If thirty persons should join hands, and the two individuals at the extremes of the line each take a handle of a galvanic battery, and let the current be so graduated as to be but faintly felt, and a greater number would be affected than by any other agent that could be employed. In this case, as in all others, it is to be understood, that the same stillness of muscles, the same fixed position of the eye upon some object or spot, and the same passivity of mind are to be strictly observed.

The query may now arise in the minds of some of the class—Why should all substances in existence have a greater or less tendency to produce this state? I answer, that electricity is the great and universal agent ordained by the Creator to form, to transmute, or to decompose all substances that swarm in the empire of nature. Hence all substances in existence throw off a never-ceasing electro-atmospheric emanation in a greater or less degree, otherwise they could never change. And these emanations by their impressions more or less affect all human beings according to the relative position in which they may be placed to receive and feel the force of such impressions. Therefore sleep and wakefulness, health and sickness, pain and ease, and all the various sensations and changes to which the human system is subject, are experienced. Hence when we fix our attention upon one substance, and become mentally and physically passive to surrounding impressions, we render ourselves, by this volition, relatively *negative*, as far as in our power, to the *positive* force of the substance with which we are engaged, and drowsiness, or some other cerebral change or phenomenon ensues, because by passivity the electro-nervous fluid is supplied through the lungs and stomach for the brain more freely than it is thrown off. But when we resume the activity of our mental and physical energies, we, by this volition and action, become relatively *positive* to the surrounding impressions of all substances in nature, and wakefulness, with all its attendant delights, is the result, because by mental and muscular action we throw off from the brain the electro-nervous fluid more rapidly than it is supplied through the lungs and stomach.

In order, therefore, to render the subject as simple as possible, and to establish and perpetuate a uniformity of procedure in the use of a substance to be placed in the hand, I desire you to insist upon the electro-magnetic coin as being alone sufficient, under the directions given, to induce the state. And I desire you to insist that the pressure on the MEDIAN NERVE is alone sufficient to establish a communication between the operator and the subject to perform all the experiments, both electrical and psychological, that this science may involve. Indeed, all substances, so far as their electro-emanating power extends, produce the same effect in degree as the coin I recommend. Hence, strictly and philosophically speaking, the electro-magnetic coin, as the true mode of inducing the state, is all in all. And as all possible modes of obtaining communication, whether by contact or otherwise, must meet in the organ of Individuality, through which all impressions are transmitted to the mind, and from the mind, through that same organ, to all the voluntary parts of the body, so there is strictly and philosophically speaking but one mode of taking communication, and hence the MEDIAN NERVE is all in all. If, however, you could remember the exposition I have given you on this intricate and interesting subject, you would then find no difficulty in defending yourself against the assaults of skeptical men. But as it is, I must leave you with the two simple forms I recommend—the ELECTRO-MAGNETIC COIN and the MEDIAN NERVE.

As the general points of the subject are now distinctly before you, I would next state, that we divide this science, for the sake of perspicuity, into FIVE PLANS. The first *three* regard the mediums through which persons are brought into the electro-psychological state. The *first* is through Mesmerism. Hence you will call Mesmerism plan NUMBER ONE. The *second* is the pressure on the nerve by which we detect those who are naturally in the electro-psychological state. This you will call plan NUMBER TWO. The *third* is the coin by which others are to be brought into this state. The coin you will therefore call plan NUMBER THREE. The *fourth* involves all the experiments, whether *electrical* or *psychological*, as a sanative agent, by which those who are already in this state are to be relieved of pain, cured of disease, or prepared for any surgical operation without suffering. This you will call plan NUMBER FOUR. And the *fifth*, in order to cure the diseases of those who are not in the state, involves the application of physical impressions upon their bodies, and the administering of remedies, whether externally or internally applied. This you will call plan NUMBER FIVE. On each of these five plans I now proceed to impart all the necessary information; and in as clear and concise a manner as possible.

In regard to Mesmerism, which is plan NUMBER ONE, I would say, that if you desire to mesmerize a person, who has never been put into the state, nor in the least affected, I know of no better mode than to seat him in an easy posture, and request him to be calm and resigned. Take him by both hands, or else by one hand and place your other gently on his forehead. But with whatever part of his body you may choose to come in contact, be sure to always touch two points, answering to the *positive* and *negative* forces. Having taken him by both hands, fix your eyes firmly upon his, and, if possible, let him contentedly and steadily look you in the face. Remain in this position till his eyes close. Then place both your hands on his head, gently pass them to his shoulders, down the arms, and off at the ends of his fingers. Throw your hands outward as you return them to his head, and continue these passes till he can hear no voice but yours. He is then entirely in the mesmeric state.

The reason why I desire you to throw your hands outward on returning them to his head when making the passes is, to avoid waking him by passing them upward in front and near to his body. It is a well-known fact, that by the downward passes of an electro-magnet, attached to a galvanic battery, the steel magnet becomes instantly charged so as to lift a pound of iron. But by the upward passes it becomes instantly demagnetized so that it will lift nothing. By the downward passes I mean from the bow or centre of the magnet to the extremities, and by upward passes I mean the reverse, regardless of the position in which the magnet may be held. The same applies to the human being when his mind is left uninfluenced. But if you apprise the subject when in the magnetic state, that the upward passes will not awake him, then by the force of his own mind he can retain his condition, in defiance of all the passes you may make. The mind, when in the mesmeric state, has the power of appropriating electricity or magnetism to itself, or of rejecting it, at pleasure.

In case, however, that the person whom you seat to be mesmerized is not affected, and feels no inclination whatever to close his eyes after fifteen or twenty minutes' trial, you will still proceed, as directed, to make the passes, and continue them also for fifteen or twenty minutes. Then take him again by the hands, as at first, and continue this position about the same length of time, then resume the passes, as before directed, and continue these two modes of operation alternately till about an hour is consumed at a sitting. Before you leave him, reverse the passes for the space of a minute or so, as though waking him up, even though you see no visible effect produced. On the next day, give him another sitting of an hour; and so on, day after day, till you get him into the mesmeric state. Remember, that all the influence you produce upon him at one sitting, however minute or imperceptible it may be, he fully retains to all subsequent daily sittings.

When a person is in the mesmeric state, whether put there by yourself or by some other one, take the communication by NUMBER TWO and awake him by the upward passes; or else do it by an impression, as follows: Tell him, "I will count *three*, and at the same instant I say *three* I will slap my hands together, and you will be wide awake and in your perfect senses. Are you ready?" If he answer in the affirmative, you will proceed to count—" *One*, TWO, THREE!" The word *three* should be spoken suddenly, and in a very loud voice, and at the same instant the palms of the hands should be smitten together. This will instantly awake him. Those who are thus aroused from mesmeric slumber to wakefulness are, with few exceptions, in the electro-psychological state, and you can immediately proceed to experiment upon them. Here, then, is an individual who was brought into this state through NUMBER ONE, and he stands in a negative relation to you as it regards the doctrine of impressions, and his body is principally charged with *negative* electricity, which is from the earth, and which alone is susceptible of being successfully controlled.

Having given you all the necessary directions how to mesmerize, and how to bring a person into the electro-psychological state through NUMBER ONE, and shown the relation in which he stands to you as the operator,

I now proceed to instruct you in relation to NUMBER TWO. This can be done in a very few words, as it has been already pretty fully noticed. In the first place, you may go into a public audience, or among your social friends, and take one individual after another by the hand, press the MEDIAN NERVE, as I have directed, and if you succeed in controlling some one, both physically and mentally, then such individual is recognized as in the electro-psychological state through NUMBER TWO. Though this person has never been mesmerized, nor operated upon, yet he is found to be naturally in the same state, through NUMBER TWO, as is the individual who was brought into it through NUMBER ONE. Seat them side by side, and they both feel the same nervous sympathy toward each other, are both charged with the same negative electricity, and both stand in a negative relation to you as it regards the doctrine of impressions.

Take NUMBER THREE, which is the electro-magnetic coin, and place it in the hand of an individual whom you can not affect, as you did either of the persons mentioned, and subject him to the process of looking at it as I have directed. When the time of the sitting has expired, take the usual communication, NUMBER TWO, and in case you can control him, both physically and mentally, he is recognized as brought into the electro-psychological state through NUMBER THREE. Here, then, are three individuals in the same state of nervous impressibility, charged with the same negative electricity, stand in the same negative relation to you, as it regards the doctrine of impressions, and by the same impression they can all be controlled, collectively or separately. They are all in the electro-psychological state, but were brought there through *three different plans*. But by whatever means individuals may be brought into this state, yet bear in mind, that through NUMBER TWO, either with or without contact, you take the communication, which is the secret, invisible, and subtile link of controlling power, and without which no effect whatever can be produced. Every principle of philosophy is based upon *cause, medium*, and *effect* Even the Creator himself, were he completely isolated from this globe, could produce no possible effect upon it, nor upon the inhabitants of its surface, because there would be, in such case, no medium of communication by which he could come in contact with it, or in the least affect its animal and vegetable kingdoms. Touch what nerve you please, or obtain the communication with or without contact, as you may—I care not how, yet it must be transmitted to the brain through the MEDIAN NERVE to the organ of Individuality, and from thence to the mind. Even if you press the *ulnar nerve* yet it must be by sympathy communicated from this to the MEDIAN NERVE, which is much larger, runs parallel along the arm with it to the spinal cord, and from thence they both unquestionably pass to the organ of Individuality in the cerebrum. They are both compound nerves, by which we mean, that they are both susceptible of voluntary motion and sensation, being connected with the mind as its agents to transmit the *electro-nervous fluid* to and from it, and through *which* it holds a correspondence with the external world. Through *this* it receives by impressions its messages, and through this by impressions it returns its answers. To take the communication, therefore, by acting directly upon the MEDIAN NERVE is far preferable to any other mode, and particularly so upon persons who are not very sensitive or impressible. The more remote we take our communication from this nerve, the longer we must labor to get control, and perhaps often fail, and the more feeble will be our action and impression in producing any interesting, brilliant, and startling experiments. The next best mode to get a communication is, as I have uniformly taught, through the ULNAR NERVE, and is the best mode to conceal the secret from others.

I have now briefly noticed the first THREE PLANS, through which individuals may be brought into the psychological state, and the subtile medium of communication through which they may be controlled by mental impressions. In regard to plan NUMBER FOUR I would remark, that as it involves *all* the experiments, both electrical and psychological, and as I have already sufficiently noticed these in giving directions how to perform them, so this part of my subject has been anticipated, and is fully before you. Permit me, however, to remark, that it may be well for you to know *why* these experiments are conducive to health, and how it is possible to perform an operation without pain, when the patient is wide awake and in his perfect senses. These two points I will now philosophically explain.

Why the experiments, when properly conducted, are conducive to health, is because the mind, by coming in contact with the electricity of the nerves, moves it with a force equal to the impression which the operator makes on the patient, and sends it to that part of the system to which the patient's attention is directed. Under its energy the limbs are paralyzed, so that the subject, by all his exertions, is unable to walk, nor when walking is he able to stop, and when seated it is not in his power to rise. His arms, in an instant, are paralyzed, so that he can not move them, or they are set in motion, and he has no power to stop them. By a mental impression he is made to see his clothes on fire, or the house falling, and his limbs crushed to pieces. Or he is made to see a lion, a tiger, or a huge serpent close in pursuit to devour him. Or, at pleasure, he may be wrought up to the most supreme ecstasy of joy and delight, or be made to feel, in the extreme, any other emotion or passion of the soul. These various impressions throw the electricity of the nerves to every part of the system with such power as to burst through all functional obstructions, equalize the nervous force, and also the circulation of the blood, and thus remove disease and still pain. It is a well-known fact in medical jurisprudence, that such supreme and sudden excitements have often cured rheumatism, and made even the lame walk.

On plan NUMBER FIVE, which involves the cure of persons who are not in this state, I can say but little. It embraces physical action upon their bodies, according to the nature of the disease, and impressions upon their minds so far as it is possible to produce them. It involves external applications or internal remedies, as the case may require. In a word, it involves the excellences of all medical systems in being, and sums them all up in the supreme beauties of one bright and glorious system, and that system is Electro-Curapathy. I now turn to the consideration of the last point I promised to notice.

The true philosophical cause, why a tooth can be extracted, or a surgical operation performed, without pain, is, that all feeling or sensation is in the mind, which holds its residence in the brain, and which, as a living being of immortal form, has its spiritual hands, feet, and organs corresponding to those of the body. Indeed, the body, in all its complicated organism, is but a visible daguerreotype picture of the invisible spirit in the brain, and from which it has drawn all its lineaments of form. Strictly speaking, the body itself has no feeling. If you touch, for instance, the point of a needle to the forefinger, it irritates some minute branch of a nerve of sensation. This irritation disturbs the electricity of the nerve that serves as a telegraph wire along which the disturbed electricity passes, and a shock is produced upon the identical correspondent spot of the forefinger of the spirit, disturbs the harmony of its own beautiful movements in its spiritual sphere, and this impression produces pain.

If, then, the communication between the mind and the electricity of the nerve to which you touched the needle could be cut off—if the telegraph wire should be so impaired, that the electricity could not pass to the mind to shock it, then no pain could be felt. This is always the case in palsy, when the nerves of sensation are paralyzed. Amputation could then be performed without pain. Now, excitement will cause the same insensibility to suffering and pain, if the impression be sufficiently great to produce it. This is evident, because as there is, in the human system, but a certain amount of feeling, therefore in the same ratio that you excite one part to sensibility the other parts are so far robbed. The following anecdote related to me of Henry Clay will illustrate this. It is as follows:

A gentleman on the floor in Congress, in his speech, made a severe personal attack on Henry Clay. Mr. Clay was, at the time, very much indisposed, and considered unable to speak. He whispered to the gentleman who sat next to him, and said, I must answer him, but beg of you not to let me speak over half an hour. He commenced, and was soon on wing—soaring, and uniting the language of earth and heaven in his defense, till every period seemed to shake the universe. He was aroused—was excited—his brain stirred proudly. His half hour expired, and the gentleman pulled his coat, but Clay paid no attention to the signal. He kicked his limbs, but it made no impression. He run a pin several times half its length into the calf of his leg. Clay heeded it not, spoke two hours, sunk exhausted into his seat, and upbraided the sentinel for not stopping him! He had felt nothing. Excitement called the electricity of his system to his brain, and he threw it off by mental effort. In the same degree that sensation was called to his brain the limbs were robbed.

Dr. Channing, in his sermon on the burning of the steamboat Lexington, when so many lives were lost, most eloquently explains this very point. He says:

" We are created with a susceptibility of pain, and severe pain. This is a part of our nature, as truly as our susceptibility of enjoyment. God has implanted it, and has thus opened in the very centre of our being a fountain of suffering. We carry it within us, and can no more escape it than we can our power of thought. We are apt to throw our pains on outward things as their causes. It is the fire, the sea, the sword, or human enmity, which gives us pain. But there is no pain in the fire or the sword, which passes thence into our souls. The pain begins and ends in the soul itself. Outward things are only the occasions. Even the body has no pain in it, which it infuses into the mind. Of itself it is incapable of suffering. This hand may be cracked, crushed in the rack of the inquisitor, and that burnt in a slow fire; but in these cases it is not the fibres, the blood-vessels, the bones of the hand which endure pain. These are merely connected, by the will of the Creator, with the springs of pain in the soul. Here, here is the only origin and seat of suffering. If God so willed, the gashing of the flesh with a knife, the piercing of the heart with a dagger, might be the occasion of exquisite delight. We know that, in the heat of battle, a wound is not felt, and that men, dying for their faith by instruments of torture, have expired with triumph on their lips. In these cases, the spring of suffering in the mind is not touched by the lacerations of the body, in consequence of the absorbing action of other principles of the soul. All suffering is to be traced to the susceptibility, the capacity of pain, which belongs to our nature, and which the Creator has implanted ineradicably within us."

I close by remarking, that as the science of Electrical Psychology is the doctrine of supreme impressions, so you will readily perceive why a surgical operation can be performed without pain.

LECTURE XII.

[The following Lecture upon the science of GENETOLOGY, which was then called NATALOLOGY, was delivered, by request, to the Ladies of Troy, N. Y., in the Morris Place Hall, in February, 1844. And, as it belongs to the subject of Electrical Psychology and the great doctrine of impressions that this science involves, it is here inserted in its appropriate place. The Author has generally delivered it as the last lecture of the course, to his private classes, when giving them instructions in Electrical Psychology.]

LADIES:

THE purpose for which we are now assembled is to take into consideration the science of GENETOLOGY or HUMAN BEAUTY, as founded upon the *doctrine of impressions*. I contend that the human species can be gradually improved through the harmonious operation of mental impressions, exercised by the mother, and that the time will come when they will be born into existence with just such lineaments of form as we may choose. This is no idle dream—no infatuation of a disturbed brain, but sober reality. Human Beauty has been, in all ages, admired, praised, loved, and desired by the millions of our race. Its charms have been sung by the poet in thoughts that burn; have taxed the finest conceptions of the artist and the sculptor, and have been made to breathe upon the canvas, and to speak in the marble. The charms of Beauty have been dwelt upon, and painted by the eloquent orator, and have moved the hearts of all human kind. All know and feel the power of Beauty, and ardently covet the gem.

The subject now to be considered is, whether, through the power of the mental impressions of the mother, her unborn child, during the period from conception to birth, can be moulded into beauty, and born into existence with those admirable lineaments of form that so much delight the beholder. To the candid consideration of this interesting subject I now invite attention.

That the mother can greatly affect her unborn child is unquestionably true. No one will deny, that by some sudden impulse of mind—such as extreme fear or joy, she has often produced abortion, or else greatly injured her offspring. I know of one well-authenticated case, where the mother was extremely terrified at a young cub when she was about three months enciente. It was her twelfth child, and was born an idiot, while her other eleven children were intelligent and active. It was a boy. He lived to fourteen years of age, and had many actions peculiar to the bear. There are instances, too numerous to mention, where human beings have not only acted like, but even resembled, some species of the brute or bird race.

And as the uniform testimony of mothers is, that they were frightened during pregnancy by the creature to which the offspring was likened, so no other satisfactory cause ever has been assigned for the effect produced.

A wealthy lady, in Boston, was frightened by a parrot. Her daughter, now ten or twelve years of age, is a mediocre, and her voice and manner of speaking resemble those of this bird. A lady of my acquaintance, on seeing the head of her cosset lamb suddenly crushed, brought forth a son, about six months after this occurrence, whose temples were much pressed in, and the forehead protruded as did that of the injured lamb, yet his intellect was not in the least impaired. A singular circumstance occurred a few years ago in Bunkum County, N. C. A girl was there exhibited, who was born with only one leg and one arm. A lady who was about two months advanced in her time, had a strong desire to see this girl. Her curiosity being great, she examined the deformed object with long and unwearied attention. Her friends had to force her, as it were, from the exhibition. She went home, but the image of the unfortunate girl was but too deeply impressed upon her mind to be forgotten. She conversed about it by day, and it was the subject of her dreams by night. She at length got an impression that her child would be born like the object that haunted her brain. Her time of delivery came, and her fears were realized. She brought forth a daughter with only one leg and one arm!

How often it has occurred, where a lady has had a strong desire, or longing for wine, that she has communicated the color of the liquor by impression to her child. In like manner, through strong mental impressions, she has stamped upon the unborn child a strawberry, blackberry, grape, or any fruit for which she had an ardent longing, and made it perfect both as it regards its color and shape. Endless instances of this character can be produced, and also the uniform testimony of the mother that she had a longing desire for what appears upon the child. Against this, the arguments and objections of some medical writers and their adherents are of no weight, as they are evidently entirely ignorant of the electrical philosophy of this subject. The mental impression, or longing of the mother must, however, far exceed her usual impressions in order to produce this result upon her offspring.

I am not arguing any new truth, nor the discovery of any new principle of action, but what has been known from the earliest of human records. The Bible history admits the principle even in its application to the brute race. Laban deceived Jacob by giving to him Leah for a wife instead of Rachel, for whom he had served him seven years, by tending his flocks. He then proposed, that he should serve him seven years more for Rachel. To pacify Jacob, Laban offered him what he supposed to be a poor chance for wages. He told him, that all the speckled cattle should be his. But Jacob resorted to a plan by which he sufficiently punished the selfish spirit of Laban. He put speckled rods at the bottom of the watering troughs. He kept the male and female cattle apart. There is no question, that he allowed the males to have free access to water, but kept the females away till they were very thirsty, even bellowing and bleating for water. In this condition he allowed them to mingle only at the troughs. And as water is colorless, nothing but the speckled rods could be seen by the thirsty and drinking females, and under this strong impression they conceived. But this is not all. Jacob understood his subject sufficiently well to go over the same ground again the next day, and keep up the female herd till the same great thirst returned. This would bring to their minds what seemed to them a speckled fluid, and to those already conceived the impression would continue to deepen. True, Laban repeatedly changed the wages even up to ten times; but this was of no avail, because Jacob as often changed the scene of action by preparing the causes that must philosophically produce their corresponding results in the animal economy. Hence I again assert that I am not arguing any new principle of action. I claim no such discovery, but merely claim the discovery of its philosophy, and of having reduced it to a system capable of improving and ennobling our race.

Such are its facts, and I now turn to its philosophy. Gold can be dissolved in aqua regia. A five-dollar gold piece thrown into this liquid dissolves and soon disappears, only as the whole liquid assumes the color of the gold. Let this liquid be properly prepared, and dip the ends of the two wires of a galvanic battery into it. In this liquid you may then immerse any metallic article you please. Take, for instance, a silver watch-case with your own name engraved upon it, and many curiously wrought characters and devices; immerse this in the liquid, and the positive and negative forces of galvanic action passing from the battery through these two wires into the solution will seize the inconceivably fine particles of gold and lay them upon the watch-case as solid as though they had been melted there. You may continue this process until every particle of the half-eagle shall be placed upon the watch-case, and yet the perfect identity of your name, and all the marks and characters engraved upon it, will be retained. This is called galvanizing metals. A second copper bank-plate can be made from the original by galvanism, so that every letter and mark shall be exact, and the plate be a perfect fac-simile of the original. Hence we perceive that through the positive and negative forces of galvanism, which is but one form of electricity, a perfect identity is preserved.

We will now apply this great principle to the argument under consideration. The monthly evacuations of the female are a universal solvent in which are involved exact proportions of all the constituent elements of her body. This redundancy is given her by the Creator for the propagation of her race. As soon as she conceives, the womb closes up, and this same redundant compound of her being is secreted in the womb, as the fluid in which the fœtus is immersed and swims, and is the raw material out of which its body is to be manufactured. And while I am upon this point, permit me to remark, that as soon as the child is born this same redundant substance is carried through the lacteal secretions and manufactured into nourishment which the infant draws from its mother's bosom. Hence the menses are the prepared substance to produce the child's body in the womb, and to sustain it at the breast.

Through the galvanic action of the positive and negative forces of her involuntary nerves the fœtus is formed. These forces seize the elementary particles of this solution, and convey them to the conception, which is the nebulo-centre or nucleus to which they all tend, similar to the particles of gold in solution to the watch-case. Hence if a woman were to conceive while wrapped in total darkness, and never see the man by whom she conceived, nor get the most distant impression of his image, and could she, at the moment of conception, be consigned to a sleep of profound insensibility till the time of her delivery came, she would unquestionably bring forth an offspring exactly in her own image. It would be as perfect a fac-simile of her own organism, form, and features as the second bank-plate was of the first from which by galvanic action it was produced. But while the galvanic powers of her involuntary nerves, through the positive forces, are forming the new being in her own image, the voluntary nerves, through which the voluntary powers of her mind act, are also producing their effects by moulding the new being in the image of the person on whom her mind is most powerfully placed. Hence if her self-esteem is great, and she fancies herself superior to her husband, and has great self-love, and but little regard for him, she will often consult her mirror, and her child will most resemble herself notwithstanding the impression of her husband's countenance and the features of all others around her.

But if she, on the contrary, cherishes a warm and generous affection to her husband, and if he be far distant from home and exposed to dangers on land or ocean, her mind goes with him and lingers in imagination upon his image. The child is born, but it is in the likeness of its father. If her love and esteem toward herself and husband are about equally divided and balanced, the child will be a blended picture of the two. The opposite passions of hatred and dislike will produce the same result as it regards form of features and personal appearance. Or if the mother should entertain a very high regard for her minister, doctor, or any friend, and circumstances should occur to bring him frequently to her mind, her child would resemble him. Suppose her husband should be jealous of any of these, or of some boarder in the family whom she even hated, and charge her with conjugal infidelity, she would be inclined, under such circumstances, to keep her mind upon him in detestation, fear that her child might resemble him, and when born all her fears would be realized. Such circumstances have separated many a husband and wife, and broken up many a family when the wife was virtuous, and her honor unsullied and pure as the snowflake ere it falls.

In this view of the subject it will be seen that every countenance upon which the enciente mother gazes, and every object, whether animate or inanimate, presented to her view, has a tendency to produce an impression, either favorable or unfavorable, upon the fœtus. And as all form, motion, and power belong to, and exist in, mind, and can be communicated through electric action from the mother's mind to the fœtus, so when beautiful forms and pleasing sights are presented to her with sufficient power, she transmits them by a mental impression to the embryo being as a part of its future beauty. So, on the other hand, when horrid forms and fearful sights are presented to her mind with sufficient power, and as her mind now contains these deformities she transmits them also by mental impression to her child, and perchance effects its ruin.

If we contemplate all form, motion, and power as existing in mind, and if the mind has, indeed, its spiritual arms, hands, and fingers, and limbs, feet, and toes, and of which the natural ones are only correspondent manifestations, may not, then, the withdrawing of the spiritual arm from action in the mother's mind be the cause of preventing the natural one in the foetus from being developed and produced? She deeply contemplates a girl without an arm, and hence sends no motion from her spiritual arm, and therefore produces no electric action through the corresponding nerves to organize the natural arm of the foetus, and hence her child is born without an arm. The voluntary impression of her mind may be sufficiently great to overpower all involuntary action in that part. This would account for the crush of the lamb's head, before stated, and for all mishaps being transmitted by a deep impression from the mother's mind to the corresponding part of the foetus. It would account for the color of Jacob's cattle, because all colors exist only in the rays of light which are but a result of electric action. It would account philosophically for the fact how the color of wine and the colors and shapes of berries are in like manner stamped upon the unborn being. It would account for the fact how even the mother's disposition may be phrenologically and hereditarily communicated to her offspring. By exercising too much her acquisitiveness or secretiveness—or by exciting too deeply her combativeness, destructiveness, or revengeful feelings, she may communicate these hereditarily to her child, and thus sow, in the embryo, the seeds of the future robber, liar, or even murderer. The lady, while enceinte, walks upon enchanted ground. She can not stir without touching some string that may vibrate either harmony or discord in her offspring's soul long after her head shall have been laid in the dust. Phrenology must take one step farther back. She must commence her instructions at the commencement of our embryo being. She must there take her stand at the fountain-head of existence, and thunder her lessons of eloquence as she moves down the stream of human life to the silent grave, nor cease her warning voice till the finger of death shall touch her lip.

The subject, Ladies, of Human Beauty is now fairly open before us, and its vast importance seems to awaken in your minds, as we proceed, an increasing interest. I am now ready to have the grand question introduced—How are our children to be born into existence with just such lineaments of form, or Human Beauty, as we may desire?

To answer this question understandingly, I will take into consideration the general directions to be pursued, and the means to be used in order to produce the noblest specimen of Human Beauty. I desire, at the very onset, to introduce the subject to you in its highest perfection, so far as I am able. To this end I must select a lady of brilliant talents, and who is highly educated and accomplished as an ornament of her sex, but whose features and form are but of ordinary mould. I merely desire one who is capable of producing the strongest possible mental impression. Let this lady select, before she conceives, a portrait, bust, miniature, or picture of some beautiful, talented, and distinguished individual, or the living person, she would desire her child to be like both in appearance and character. Let it be a picture that she greatly admires for its fine proportions and beauty of person. Let her keep her mind upon it until she entirely familiarizes herself with its features and form. Let her now conceive with this deep impression on her mind; and after this, let her still continue to gaze upon, and daily contemplate, the admirable grace of its form, and the charming expression of its countenance. Let her place it where it can be readily seen. Let her imbibe for this image a sentimental passion, indelibly impress it upon the heart, and interweave and blend it, as it were, with her being. Let her contemplate it by day with such intense interest and devotion as to transplant, if possible, its image to her midnight dreams. And let her constantly long and desire, and ardently hope and expect, that her child shall be like this in form and soul. These are to be her constant feelings and impressions till the day of delivery.

In addition to this, let the most admirable order, arrangement, and comfort pervade her house, and particularly her own apartment. Let its furniture be beautiful. Let it be adorned with pictures of the most pleasing and delightful landscapes embracing all the beauties and varieties of nature, and such life-like scenery as shall awaken and rouse the noblest powers of her ideality, sublimity, and imagination. Let her frequently go out to gaze upon, and contemplate nature as she is, whether on the earth beneath, or in the starry fields that mantle the bosom of night. By these means she will keep her mind in balance, and bring it into harmony with all that is grand and beautiful in the works of the Creator. And not only so, but let her soul be kept serene. Let her passions not be excited. Let her anger, jealousy, and vengeance remain in slumber, and no language be used to ruffle her tranquillity. I am speaking of a highly educated, accomplished, and talented woman. And, lastly, let her food be wholesome, plain, and prepared to her wishes, and adapted to her appetite. Let these directions be faithfully observed during her entire period of gestation, and her child will be moulded in the image of the picture, or living person she contemplated, and be born into existence a noble specimen of Human Beauty; and under proper phrenological culture it can be borne on in the path of improvement, and finally elevated to the highest physical beauty, and intellectual and moral perfection of our nature.

I have now considered what I call a perfect case, the noblest specimen of man. And in order to produce this happy result, we perceive that the mother must be highly educated, enlightened, and refined. It depends more upon her than the father. If the father should possess the talents of an angel, and the mother be deficient in intellect, her offspring, particularly the sons, would never rise above mediocrity. In such case the best intellect is in favor of the daughters. But reverse it, and let the father be deficient, and the mother highly talented, and she will produce intelligent children of both sexes, but this intelligence will be far more strongly developed in the sons than in the daughters. An instance can not be found where an imbecile mother ever produced a man of sterling talents, even though the father, as such, were most eminently distinguished. All talented and great men have had great mothers who, even if they were uneducated, still possessed the elements of original greatness.

Owing, therefore, to this great diversity of intellectual, moral, and physical beauty and deformity in females, it can not be expected, that the grand period will soon arrive when all these difficulties will be surmounted, and when our race shall attain that physical, mental, and moral beauty which our subject involves, foreshadows, and insures. Comparatively but few females are as yet qualified to successfully introduce their offspring into existence in Human Beauty, yet the most deformed and ignorant female can be instructed and directed how to improve her progeny. Her children again can be still farther improved and elevated, and so on to succeeding generations till the end, we contemplate, shall be obtained, and the highest hopes, and the brightest mid-day dream of the philanthropist, as to the perfection of humanity, shall be consummated.

My argument, thus far, relates to those of the female race who are not yet in the electro-psychological state, but who are still capable of gradually perfecting their progeny in proportion to the strength and power of their impressions, and thus moving them onward to the fair fields of Human Beauty. But in all these cases it can be effected by the wife only, independent of her husband. But there are many who are naturally in the psychological state, and millions more who, by a slight exertion, can be brought into it. Upon all such a mental and moral impression can be made to any extent we choose. In all these instances it would be in the power of the husband to select the portrait or picture in the likeness and beauty of which he would desire his child to be moulded. And by producing the impression psychologically upon the mind of his companion once or twice per day, the end would be obtained, and in all such cases the finest specimens of Human Beauty could now be produced. How important, then, that the science of Electrical Psychology should be thoroughly learned and understood by all, so that, through their assistance, as many as possible may be, by perseverance, brought into the state, and that the great work of producing these sublime impressions may now be understandingly commenced, and some rare specimens of Human Beauty, under the energy of this science, be presented to the world.

We see then, Ladies, the supreme importance of woman being highly educated and accomplished. Colleges should be dedicated to her, and all the great and useful sciences, that strengthen, expand, and elevate the mind, should be laid at her feet. Her mind should be early imbued with political science, and taught the value of liberty, and the deep-toned love of country. She should be taught the history of fallen empires, kingdoms, and republics, and be made acquainted with the hardships, toils, and sufferings of our revolutionary heroes. She should be taught the lofty dignity, honor, and heroism of George Washington, the cradled son of Columbia. She should be educated in every sense equal to the man. It has been generally supposed, in by-gone days, that if woman could barely read and write, it was abundant, as she had nothing to do but attend to her domestic concerns, and to take care of children. But the arrest of her progress in science has but proved to be an arrest of the intellectual, moral, and social advancement of the world. Her station, so far from being insignificant, is indeed a most responsible one. She holds in her silken grasp the destiny of empires, and the weal and woe of our race. She has not only a moulding power over her unborn offspring, but during the first ten years of its existence, as it is almost exclusively confined to her society, so from her it still continues to draw, in a great measure, its cast of character. Hence she should be educated and qualified to breathe to her child the purest thoughts and noblest principles, and to inspire its tender bosom with the deep-toned love of country. She should be qualified to impress upon it a high sense of honor and true greatness, and the most patriotic and exalted sentiments. And, in order to do this successfully, she should be well acquainted with phrenological science and human nature, so as to make her impressions understandingly and forcibly upon the proper organs of the brain. These organs would then be more and more harmoniously developed, and the child would continue to improve in beauty of person, and in intellectual and moral greatness, as he advanced to maturity.

In the light our subject now stands, how lamentable, and how awful is the consideration, that our children should be committed to the care of ignorant, degraded and *too* often of wicked and unprincipled servants, to be almost exclusively reared by them! There the seeds of ignorance, if not of vice, are early sown. How elevated and responsible is the mother's station! How fatal to the character and welfare of her offspring are ignorance and vice! How dreadful, how alarming and fearful, to see her resign her fond charge, and commit its destiny, for weal or woe, to such unskilled hands! She had better resign her child to the silent grave, where, even though her lids are filled with tears, she can yet smile, that its pains are o'er, that its beating pulse is still, its spirit unstained, and its burning brow is cold! Yes, Ladies, the contemplation of this subject is so painful, that I choose to leave you to draw your own conclusions rather than to express my thoughts.

True, the pulpit insists on her social and religious rights, because this is popular. But by neglecting to plead in behalf of her *civil*, her POLITICAL, and INTELLECTUAL RIGHTS it has forgotten her elevated station and high destiny, fallen from heaven to earth, and, by its fall, crushed the dearest hopes of the philanthropist for the speedy, intellectual, and moral advancement of our race. It will not, and dare not speak in a bold, firm, and untrembling voice in defense of these rising sciences and improvements of the age, however useful, against which the current of popular opinion strongly sets. It has ceased to breathe the pure, healthful, and invigorating breezes of Paradise, that inspire an independent and godlike heroism. Woman is thus, in a voice of pretended mercy, oppressed, and it dare not even rebuke oppression and crime, when clothed in gold and sustained by popular impulse.

The pulpit is the great engine of moral power and moral reform. But by neglecting the science of Human Beauty, and the general and extensive education of woman, its energies are in a great degree paralyzed. But it is destined, by the decree of the Ruling Heavens, to be aroused from its dreadful slumberings upon the monster POPULARITY, whose breath is consuming it, and to thunder its energizing and regenerating powers for the accomplishment of this great end which involves the moral elevation and the intellectual grandeur of man. The science of GENETOLOGY, embracing the doctrine of psychological impressions, in connection with the gospel of Jesus Christ, is destined to renovate the world and usher in the millennial morn. Extensive combinations are formed, and the most untiring exertions are constantly made to improve, not only the animal, but even the vegetable race. Fruits and grains, in a few years, have been brought to great perfection, by man simply co-operating with nature so as to enable her to make the most favorable impressions to produce what is beautiful in her vegetable department. So also in the animal kingdom. Horses, sheep, and oxen, and even the race of swine, are annually improving in form and beauty, and premiums are offered for the finest specimens, both as to symmetry and size. But not a single thought is bestowed as to improving and beautifying the godlike lineaments of the human form. To improve these through the educating of woman, and enlightening her how to make a psychological impression upon her embryo-child, is but to improve the morals of our race. The theme is a great one, and it will require future generations to move it on, and to develop and present it perfect to the world. It will be the scroll of Human Beauty unrolled. This is indeed a sublime hope.

> "Eternal hope! when yonder spheres sublime
> Peal'd their first notes to sound the march of time,
> Thy joyous birth began; but not to fade
> When all the sister planets have decayed.
> When wrapt in fire, the realms of ether glow,
> And heaven's last thunder shakes the earth below,
> Thou, undismayed, shalt o'er the ruin smile,
> And light thy torch at nature's funeral pile."

SIX LECTURES

ON THE

PHILOSOPHY OF MESMERISM.

DELIVERED IN THE

Marlboro' Chapel, Boston.

By JOHN BOVEE DODS.

REPORTED BY A HEARER

TWELFTH THOUSAND.

NEW YORK:
PUBLISHED BY SAMUEL R. WELLS,
No. 389 BROADWAY.
1871.

Entered, according to Act of Congress, in the year 1847,

BY FOWLERS & WELLS,

in the Clerk's Office of the District Court of the Southern District of New York.

ADVERTISEMENT

TO THE IMPROVED AND STEREOTYPED EDITION.

WITHIN ONE MONTH after these highly popular lectures were first delivered, an edition of THREE THOUSAND COPIES was published and sold, and a second edition called for, which has also been exhausted, and the demand is still increasing.* Under these circumstances the author was prevailed on to REVISE, ENLARGE, and so IMPROVE the work as to render it, if possible, even much more desirable.

The MERITS of the work may be inferred from this fact: an audience of OVER TWO THOUSAND PEOPLE, composed of the most intelligent citizens of New England, was held six evenings in succession, chained in the most profound silence, listening to these truly philosophical lectures, and

* This work has recently been re-published in England, and has been favorably received by the most scientific men of Europe.

witnessing surgical operations without pain; and other experiments, at once convincing, and full of great practical utility to every human being.

The author, Dr. Dods, is a man of extensive experience and general information. He first qualified himself for the medical profession, then engaged in the study of theology, and has been in the ministry for more than twenty years, and is favorably known as a lecturer on many of the natural sciences.

S. R. WELLS.

CONTENTS

LECTURE I.

ANIMAL MAGNETISM, INTRODUCTORY LECTURE ON . . . . page 7-17

Invitation by Members of the Legislature to lecture on the Science of Animal Magnetism—Wresting the Science from the hands of ignorant and designing Individuals—Skepticism—The cry of Humbug and Collusion supplies the place of sound argument—Galileo, Harvey, Fulton—The Science of Phrenology—Truth can never die—Denouncing before investigation—Mesmerism embraced by men whose names will live always—Animal Magnetism an inappropriate Name—Mind, and its powers—The Law of Equilibrium—The Earth not Eternal—Mountains—Water—Experiments—Electrical Science—Causes of Thunder and Lightning—The Nervo-vital Fluid passing from one Body to another—The Nervous System—Blood—Brain—Insensibility—Who can and who ought to be Mesmerized—Physical Energy—Process of Magnetizing.

LECTURE II.

MENTAL ELECTRICITY, OR SPIRITUALISM 18-29

The Why and Wherefore of Mesmerism—Experiment—Fact—Physical, Mental, and Moral Power—A Lesser Power may Mesmerize a Greater Power—Galvanic Battery—Coloring of the Blood—Voluntary and Involuntary Motion—Power of the Will—Execution of Criminals—Experiments on the Body after death—The Corpse made to move—Attraction and Repulsion—Insanity—Time requisite to produce Insensibility—A Child can Mesmerize its Father—Importance of being Mesmerized.

LECTURE III.

AN APPEAL IN BEHALF OF THE SCIENCE 50-11

The Power of the Creator—The Origin of Matter—John Milton—The World not created out of Nothing—The Eternal Existence of Electricity—Spirit and Matter—The Gradual Creation of Plants—The Sun pure Electricity—Worlds Electrically and Magnetically suspended—Experiments with the Electrifying Machine—The Magnet—The Beauty, Order, and Harmony of all the Laws of Nature.

CONTENTS.

LECTURE IV.

THE PHILOSOPHY OF CLAIRVOYANCE 44-58

Mind—Motion—The Brain—The Expansion and Contraction of Bodies by Heat and Cold—Vision without the Natural Organs—Somnambulism—Dreaming—Catalepsy—Dr. Patterson—Well-authenticated facts—An Appeal to Medical Gentlemen—Great Feats of Climbing and Walking on House-tops in the Dark while in a State of Unconsciousness—Painting in the Dark—A Remarkable Fact—Seeing, Hearing, Tasting, and Smelling—The Transparency of Objects—Magnetic or Galvanic Light—Distinguished Clairvoyants in the United States—Additional Experiments—Philosophy of Hearing—Amputated Limb—Hon. T. G. Greenwood—A Fact.

LECTURE V.

THE NUMBER OF DEGREES IN MESMERISM 60-71

The First Degree—Attraction by the Magnetizer—Second Degree—Third Degree—Fourth Degree—Fifth Degree Clairvoyance—Communication—Experiment—Why is not Magnetism more generally understood—Objections answered—Demosthenes—Cicero—The Methodists—Muscular Power—Concentration—The Dangers and Abuse of Mesmerism—Every blessing abused—Crime—Causes—Magnetizing a part, and not the whole body—A Surgical Operation—A Broken Arm—A Tumor extracted without Pain—Rev. John Pierpont testifies publicly to the Truth and Utility of Mesmerism—The Wonderful Power to Charm all Pain.

LECTURE VI.

OUR SAVIOUR AND THE APOSTLES 72-82

The right to think for ourselves—Restrictions—The Command of Christ to his Apostles to Heal the Sick, as well as to Preach—Miracles—Palsied Arm—The Saviour and the Woman—The Apostolic Power—John the Revelator—Transfiguration—Moses and Elias—The Crucifixion of Christ—His Resurrection, &c.—Dr. Channing on Dying without Pain.

ANIMAL MAGNETISM.

LECTURE I.

LADIES AND GENTLEMEN: It is with much pleasure that I present myself before you this evening, to lecture upon the science of Animal Magnetism. I do this by special invitation from several distinguished members of both branches of our legislature, now in session in this city; and this thronged congregation of more than two thousand hearers speak the interest which is awakened in the bosoms of our citizens in relation to this subject. This dense and anxious crowd too plainly manifest the high expectations which are entertained of the feeble abilities of the speaker to do it justice—expectations which I am fully sensible I shall be unable to answer. Leaning, however, upon the solid grandeur of truth, and believing THAT to be stirring eloquence and living power, I have, therefore, even as things now are, with all your roused expectations crowding upon me, but little to hazard, for I am fully sensible that I am standing before a learned and an intelligent congregation. And when I inform you that I have never written any thing upon this subject, and am, therefore, obliged to speak from the fortuitous suggestions of the moment, I am conscious that you will do me justice, by making every reasonable allowance.

It is not my profession to lecture upon this subject. I have other means for my subsistence, and for that of those who depend upon me. Circumstances have called me into the field. Many, very many ignorant individuals, who know nothing of the human system, nor of the common principles of any science, have gone into the field as lecturers on Animal Magnetism, and by making it a mere puppet-show, have brought it into degradation in the public mind. Such persons are doing the cause, which is one of benevolence and mercy, an irreparable injury. They had better qualify themselves for the work, or else retire from the field. In this state of things, I was urged, by several scientific gentlemen, to step forward in defence of the cause of righteousness and truth, and to lend my aid in raising it from the dust, in wiping off the sneers of men, and in placing it on a foundation where it should command not only the attention, but the respect and admiration which are justly due to it from men of science and talents In this city, I find but one noble spirit laboring and toiling, who is well qualified for the work, and who is deserving a better patronage than he receives.* As these are the circumstances under which I have entered the field, so, of course, I visit those places only where I am invited to lecture upon this science.

I have had the subject of Mesmerism under consideration for about seven years, reading all that came in my way for and against it. Five of these years I remained a stubborn, a most confirmed sceptic, and

---

* Dr Gilbert.

refused even to attend a lecture, or to witness an experiment, until I was persuaded by a particular friend of mine to accompany him, and see and hear for myself. I am, therefore, prepared to make all due allowance for honest sceptics; and, in their opposition to me during this course of lectures, I shall maintain an entire empire over my feelings; and being fully sensible of their condition, I well know how to sympathize with them. But there is yet another class of sceptics, who have witnessed experiments which they cannot resist, and still cry, "HUMBUG AND COLLUSION!" Of these, there are two kinds. First, those who never investigate anything for themselves, and who do not know the definitions of the words, "humbug and collusion;" but who, nevertheless, use them very freely, because they have heard their minister, their doctor, or, perchance, their schoolmaster, use them. They do it by imitation, on the same principle that the parrot imitates the sound of the human voice, and they do it just about as understandingly. Second, those who are talented, and desire to keep on the wings of the popular breeze, and catch the breath of fame. These may be known by the ridicule, wit, and sarcasm they employ, through the press and otherwise. But, "humbug and collusion" have become stereotyped words, and their use costs but little labor; and they answer most admirably to supply the place of sound argument and common sense in the most of minds. If my hearers will please turn their attention to all the talented writers, who have, in various ages, vehemently opposed those now well-established sciences which, in their infancy, appeared incredible, and who assailed them with the bitterest invective and sarcasm, hey will learn that they were men who were always studying what was popular, and who had a large share of self-esteem, and of the love of approbation. This test will hold good from the opposers of the earth's revolution on its axis, discovered by Galileo; from the scoffers at the science of the circulation of the human blood, discovered by Harvey, step by step, down to the scoffers at Fulton's application of steam-power,—yes, even down to the opposers of, and scoffers at, the brilliant science of Phrenology, which is now spreading with a power that can never be successfully resisted, a zeal that cannot be quenched, and a living energy that can never die. True, a candid man, as well as any other, may doubt a new science; yet, however strange or incomprehensible it may appear, he will not denounce till he has given the subject a candid investigation. I am speaking of those only who denounce without investigation, and who can assign no other reason for so doing, but their own willing ignorance, or because the popular voice is against it.

I am, however, proud in the reflection that the science of Mesmerism is embraced by men of the first talents and science in both continents, and whose names will live in the republic of letters, and shine with lustre long after those of fawning sycophants shall have been lost in unremembered nothingness. It is embraced here among us by a Pierpont, the Fowlers, a Gilbert, a Neal, and a Wayland. It is embraced by men who have forgotten more than those who cry "humbug and collusion" ever knew.

I have been in the field as an occasional lecturer ever since October, 1841, and have uniformly advocated the same principles which I am now about to advance and sustain in the course of lectures I am pledged to deliver in this city. This fact, many now present well know who have heard me in other sections, or who have seen the substance of what I have now to offer on Mesmerism, reported by the editor of the Yarmouthport Register, in March, 1842. I shall here contend for the same principles, and endeavor to sustain them by fair experiments, in electricity, galvanism, and common magnetism.

There is one apology, however, to be offered in favor of honest sceptics. It is this: Those who have lectured upon Mesmerism have not pretended to give any cause for the wonderful phenomena produced—have held them in mystery, and perhaps pronounced them inscrutable to the human intellect. Hence, it is not strange that thousands, under such an impression, should refuse to investigate a subject which its advocates held in mystery. That there are mysteries in Mesmerism I readily admit; but that there are more than in any other science, I deny. We may, for instance, tell the chemical properties of earth, water, and air, and the degree of warmth necessary to produce vegetation. But still no one can solve the mystery how an acorn becomes an oak, or a seed becomes a plant. There is no science in the universe, but what has some incomprehensibilities resting upon its face; but this circumstance is considered no objection to the truth of any science. Hence there is no reason why Mesmerism should be rejected on this ground. Yet thousands do reject it, because they contend that it is incomprehensibly strange! They know nothing but what is strange, and yet what is strange they cannot believe! All the operations of nature going on around us are strange, and the only reason we have ceased to wonder is, because they are common. All such objections are therefore futile.

Before I proceed any further, I would remark that I consider "ANIMAL MAGNETISM" a very inappropriate name. It should be called SPIRITUALISM, or MENTAL ELECTRICITY, because it is the direct impulse of mind upon the minds and bodies of others. As it is the science of MIND AND ITS POWERS, so it is the highest and most sublime science in the whole realms of nature, and as far transcends all others as godlike mind transcends matter.

Having made these introductory remarks, I now proceed more directly to the consideration of the subject before me. In presenting before you "the WHY and the WHEREFORE" of these interesting phenomena, and, in order to make them plain to the humblest capacity, it will be necessary to associate the subject with other principles in philosophy which are well understood by all, and thus rise from the consideration of the more gross and dense particles of matter, step by step, up to those which are the most rarified and subtil of which we can form any conception. In doing this, I shall not take into consideration every possible grade or species of matter, but those substances only which belong to the great classifications of nature's empire, and which are the most obvious to every observer.

In the first place, then, I contend that there is but one common LAW pervading the whole universe of God, which is the law of EQUILIBRIUM. In perfect accordance with this law there is kept up a constant ACTION and REACTION throughout every department of nature. It is true there has been much written, and still more said, about the multiplicity and variety of the laws of ture But this is, at least to me, wholly unintelligible. While, however, I contend for but one COMMON LAW, it is still conceded that this law is so varied as to be perfectly adapted to all the variety of substances in being. On this principle the earth is certainly not eternal, for were it so, the hills and mountains would long ago have been washed to a level by the storms of heaven; yes, it would have been done by the gentle descending dews. Indeed, I hazard nothing in saying, that even the mountains of solid granite would have been crumbled into atoms ages ago, by the very operation of the particles of air—" the fingers of Time ;" because every thing in nature is tending to an equilibrium.

Having begun at the grossest particles of matter, let us now rise gradually in our contemplations, step by step, up to those that are the most rarified and subtil of which we can form any conception. WATER is a body lighter than earth. Let a canal be dug of one hundred feet in depth, one hundred in width, and a thousand feet in length. Let a strong lock be constructed across its centre, and one half filled with water. Let the gate be hoisted, and the water in the one division will fall, and in the other rise, until an equilibrium of height is attained. Nature, having gained her end, is then at rest. And the action of this element will be great in proportion as it was thrown out of balance. The rush will be at first tremendous, but continue gradually to lessen until it finds its perfect slumber in equal height.

The same is true in relation to our atmosphere, a substance lighter than water. The air in this room is now arified by heat, and is thus thrown out of balance with the circumambient air which is more cold and dense. Hence, through every key-hole and crevice there is a rush of this element into the room, which will continue until the equilibrium of density is attained. Then, and not before, nature, having gained her end, will be at rest. The air in one section of the globe is more rarified by heat than in another; and hence the gentle zephyrs of heaven are continually fanning the human brow with a touch of delight, and carrying health to human habitations. If this element be thrown still farther out of balance, we witness the stirring gale; and if carried, in this respect, to its extreme, we witness the sweeping hurricane, or the roaring tornado, which prostrates human habitations in its mighty course, and bows the mountain forest to the earth.

The same is true in relation to electricity, a substance more rarified and light than air. If two clouds are equally charged with this subtil fluid, they may pass and repass each other, or mingle into one, yet not a flash of lightning will be seen. But if they are unequally charged, or what is called in electrical science, "positively and negatively charged," then the heavens will stream with forked lightning, till both clouds are equally charged. By long drought and heat, electricity becomes very unequally diffused throughout the atmosphere. One portion of air contains a much greater quantity than another, and when thus thrown out of balance to a certain extreme, nature can hold out no longer. A reaction must take place. Convolving clouds roll the heavens in darkness—the lightnings flash, the thunders roll, and the war of elements continues until the electric fluid is equally diffused throughout the atmosphere and also equalized with the earth.

Nature, having thus gained her end in he equilibrium produced, is at rest—all is calm.

If we pass on from inert matter to animated nature, we shall find that the same law there also holds its empire. If, for instance, a healthy child, three or four years of age, be permitted to sleep every night for a year or two between two very old, decrepit grandparents, it will pine away, and if not removed, perchance it may die. There is, perhaps, not one under the sound of my voice, but what has heard the remark, that "it is very unhealthy for young children to sleep with very old, infirm people." It is even so, and parents should beware. The child is full of animal life, and its nervous system is charged with the vital fluid, secreted by the brain. This gives that suppleness to the limbs, and that buoyancy to the heart which we witness in the young. The grandparents lack the proper quantity of this nervo-vital fluid, which occasions that rigidity of the limbs we witness in the aged. The same common law of equilibrium that pervades the universe, is here also in operation. The nervo-vital fluid passes from this child to the two aged persons in conjunction. The child loses, and they continue to revive, and as this little one can never bring those infirm persons up to an equilibrium with itself, so it must go down to them. Nature will have her equilibrium, if she has it in death.

Once more: there is in the nervous system no blood. By the NERVOUS SYSTEM I mean the brain and all its ramifications. The blood belongs exclusively to the circulating system, which embraces the veins and arteries. I grant that the blood-vessels pass round the convolutions of the brain; but in the nerve itself there is no blood, and the whole mass of brain is but a congeries of nerves. These are charged with a nervo-vital fluid, which is manufactured from electricity. Hence, the circulating system containing the blood, and the nervous system containing the magnetic fluid, are not to be blended, but distinctly considered. Now, as a human being may lack the proper quantity of blood in his circulating system, so he may lack the proper quantum of the nervo-vital fluid in his nervous system. This is certainly rational. And, moreover, it may be easily known when such is the case. When we see persons, who, on hearing suddenly some good or bad news, are thrown into great excitement, tremor, and agitation, we may be certain that their nervous systems lack the due measure of the nervo-vital fluid. Now let a person whose brain is fully charged, come in contact with one whose brain is greatly wanting in its due measure of this fluid, and let the person possessing the full brain gently and unchangeably hold his mind upon the other, and by the action of the WILL, the fluid will pass from the full brain to the other, until the equilibrium between the fluids in the two brains is attained. The sudden change in the receiving brain produces a coolness and a singular state of insensibility. This is MAGNETISM; and it is in perfect accordance with all the principles of philosophy in the known realms of nature. If any one denies the operation of the law of equilibrium in this case, then he here makes a chasm, amidst the immensity of God's works, which he can nowhere else discover I have clearly shown him that, from the grossest matter in the universe, step by step, through every grade, up to electricity, the same law holds its empire, and matter is continually equalizing itself with matter.

On this principle, it will be readily perceived that, if

a person has a great deficiency of the nervo-vital fluid, he can be mesmerized the first sitting, and probably in an hour's time, or a much less period. These we call easy subjects. But if the deficiency be less, it will take a longer period in proportion, and if the brain have nearly its proper quantity of fluid, then the effect produced, at the first sitting, will be small, yet still it will be visible.

From the premises laid down, and in accordance with the law of equilibrium, it will probably be said, that only few persons can be mesmerized. This, however, is not correct. I contend that every person in existence CAN be, and indeed OUGHT to be thrown into the mesmeric state. This, I am well aware, is contrary to the opinion of the advocates of this science. The most liberal calculation I have as yet heard, is that about one in nine of the human family can be mesmerized. But every one can be, and that, too, in perfect accordance with the principles laid down. Let two persons of equal brains, both in size and fluid, sit down. Let one of these individuals remain perfectly passive, and let the other exercise his mental and physical energies according to the true principles of mesmerizing, and he will displace some of the nervo-vital fluid from the passive brain and deposit his own in its stead. The next day let them sit another hour, and so on, day after day, until the acting brain shall have displaced the major part of the nervo-vital fluid from the passive brain and filled up that space with his own nervous force, and the person will yield to the magnetic power, and sweetly slumber in its inexpressible quietude.

LECTURE II.

Ladies and Gentlemen: On the last evening, I had the pleasure to deliver before you my introductory lecture on the science of Spiritualism, and to explain "the why and the wherefore" of the effect produced. I clearly showed that Mesmerism was in perfect accordance with the universal law of nature, which I call the law of Equilibrium; and, as I, in concluding my lecture, contended that every person in the world could be mesmerized, some, as I suspected would be the case, have to-day argued that, according to the principle laid down by the speaker, two brains of equal power can no more mesmerize each other, than one of a less power can mesmerize a greater; and hence, that the arguments of the lecturer are contradictory and irreconcilable. But this objection is by no means valid. It is readily conceded that two brains equally full and healthy cannot affect each other, admitting both persons to be equal in muscular energy, and to make at the same time the same mental and physical effort. But, if one person sit down and passively resign himself, and another even of less power and less nervo-vital fluid exert all his energies, then the law of equilibrium requires that there shall be an effect produced in the PASSIVE object equal to all the power exerted by the ACTIVE agent. Hence, a weaker person can mesmerize one of superior power, and the same persons may alternately throw each other into the mesmeric state. I have known the instance where a small girl, only nine years of age, mesmerized a young man twenty years old, and of uncommon strength. Though it is a well known law, that two bodies of water will seek a level when a communication is made between them, yet it is equally true that, by a pump, water may be thrown from a lower to a higher cistern; and who will deny that it is in perfect accordance with the law of equilibrium? Surely, no one. It is by physical energy that the air is removed from the pump, and the circumambient air pressing upon the water in the cistern, causes it to rise till an equilibrium of height is attained—exactly equal to all the powers employed. But so far as the mesmeric state is concerned, it will be remembered, that man, in acting on his fellow-man, exerts not only a PHYSICAL, but a MENTAL, and MORAL power. These must all be taken into consideration, and duly weighed, in order to form a correct idea of the law of equilibrium in the employment of the magnetic forces. If this common law in nature extended no farther than merely to bring substances that are out of balance down to a common level, then all action in the various elements would soon cease.

It will be remembered that no one kindred element ever disturbs itself, or ever throws itself out of balance. It requires another element to do this. The water would always keep on a perfect level with itself, throughout he globe, if air and heat never disturbed it. By heat it is rarified into vapors, carried over the globe in aerial conductors, condensed by cold into drops, and rained upon the mountains and more elevated portions of the globe, and then again seeks its level with the parent ocean. So there is a power that rarifies the air and the denser portions rush to its aid, and the winds are in action to keep up a perfect balance in its own empire, while air, abstractly, could never disturb itself. Hence it is even the law of equilibrium by which one portion of water is thrown out of balance with itself; and the same is also true in relation to the atmosphere. If heat, which is but the action of electricity, rarifies the water so as to cause it in subtility to approximate itself, then surely it is according to the law of equilibrium that water is thrown out of balance with itself by forcing it into a partial equilibrium with some more rarified substance. Carrying out this principle, and applying it to Mesmerism, it will be readily understood not only how two persons of equal power may mesmerize each other, but even how one of less physical power may mesmerize a greater, and yet the whole be effected in perfect accordance with the law of equilibrium.

Having made these remarks, which the occasion seems to demand, I will now proceed to a direct consideration of the nervo-vital fluid in the human brain.

It is admitted, that the air we breathe is composed of two substances, namely, OXYGEN and NITROGEN. Their relative qualities are about one-fifth oxygen and four-fifths nitrogen. But these are not all. It is evident, that hydrogen and electricity are also component parts of air. Oxygen and electricity are the principles of flame and of animal life, while nitrogen extinguishes both. There is not a single square inch of air but what contains more or less electricity. The air in its compound state is drawn into the lungs. The oxygen and electricity are communicated to the blood, which is charged with iron, while the nitrogen is disengaged and expired. This iron, which gives color to the blood is instantly rendered magnetic under the influence of electricity, analogous to the needles in the galvanic battery which become magnets merely by induction. The blood itself is, at the same time, oxydized by the oxygen of the air, and instantly becomes cherry red. This oxygen generates an acidity in the blood, in some degree answering to the solution of the sulphate of copper in the galvanic battery. The blood, thus magnetically prepared at the lungs, is thrown upon the heart, and forced into the arteries. Hence, arterial blood is red. It is propelled to the extremities, driven into every possible ramification, and is collected and carried back in the veins, through the other ventricle of the heart, to the lungs, for a fresh supply of the electro-magnetic power. Hence, venous blood is dark, and is unfit to be thrown into the arterial system a second time till it has again come in contact with the oxygen and electricity of the air. The blood, thus discharged, is propelled through its living channels, and this friction causes the electro-magnetic power to escape from the circulating system into the nervous system, for which it has a strong affinity, and, being secreted by the brain, it becomes the nervo-vital fluid, or animal galvanism. It is important here to remark, that the blood, in its friction through the arteries, has given off its electro-magnetic power into the nervous system. The blood, thus freed, assumes a dark appearance in the veins, and becomes entirely NEGATIVE. The lungs, being charged with a fresh supply of electricity, become POSITIVE. Hence the blood is drawn from the veins to the lungs on the same principle that the negative and the positive in electricity rush together.

From the above observations, it will be perceived that every muscle of the human body, every organ and gland, is polar, and by the negative and positive principles, as above noticed, animal life is sustained and perpetuated through the action of the lungs and blood.

We thus perceive that the nervo-vital fluid is manufactured out of electricity, taken into the lungs at every inspiration. It completely charges the whole brain, when that organ is in a healthy state. The nerves composing the brain, are of three kinds, namely: the nerves of sensation, the nerves of VOLUNTARY motion, and the nerves of INVOLUNTARY motion. I make these three divisions, so that I may be the more readily understood when speaking of nervous action. I desire you to bear in mind that these three classes of nerves are all charged with the nervo-vital fluid, which is exactly prepared to come in contact with mind.

We put forth a WILL. That WILL stirs the nervo-vital fluid in the voluntary nerves. This fluid causes the voluntary nerves to vibrate. The galvanic vibration of these nerves contracts the muscles. The muscles, contracting, raise the arm, and that arm raises foreign matter. So we perceive that it is through this concatenation, or chain, that the mind comes in contact with the grossest matter in the universe.

It is evident that there is no direct contact between mind and gross matter. There is no direct contact between the length of a thought and the breadth of that door. Nor is there any more direct contact between my mind and hand, than there is between my mind and the stage upon which I stand. Thought cannot touch my hand; yet it must be true that mind can come in contact with matter; otherwise, I could not raise my hand at all by the energies of my will. Hence, it must be true, that the highest and most subtil of inert matter in the universe, being the next step to spirit, can come in contact with the mind. And electricity, changed into nervo-vital fluid, (which is living galvanism,) is certainly the highest and most etherial inert substance of which we can form any conception. Hence, as before remarked, it must be true, that we put forth a will. By the energies of that will this galvanic substance, or nervous fluid, is proudly stirred; that stirring vibrates the nerves; this vibrates and contracts the muscles; the muscles raise the arm, and that arm moves dead matter.

Notwithstanding the plausibility of this argument, it will yet be said that, as physiologists contend that no one can explain through what medium the mind comes in contact with matter, nor even how a muscle is made to contract, and raise the arm, and as the lecturer has undertaken to explain it, we have a right to demand POSITIVE proof. This demand being rational, I will endeavor to meet it. I am, then, to prove that the nervo-vital fluid, (which is perfect galvanism,) is indeed the agent by which we contract the muscles and raise the arm. That being done, my point is gained, and the medium through which mind comes in contact with matter is established.

I would first remark, that it is common when criminals are executed, that their bodies are delivered over to medical men for dissection. Now take a human body, and let it be conveyed from the gallows to the charnel-house, and laid upon the dissecting-table. Let a continuous shock from a strong galvanic battery be given, and the muscles of the dead man will contract, and exhibit many frightful contortions. Many interesting experiments of this character have been published. The dead man has been known to spring upon his knees, jolt them upon the floor, make violent gesticulations with his hands, move his head, roll his eyes, and chatter his teeth. The student, unused to such ghastly exhibitions, has left the room, or fainted away; and even the experienced physician has started back with horror at the frightful contortions which he himself had made. Now, what was it that contracted the muscles of this dead man? There is but one answer to the question. It was galvanism. And what is galvanism, but electricity in a changed form; so that, instead of giving the system a sudden shock, like electricity, it merely produces a singular vibrating sensation upon the nerves, which causes the muscles to contract? It is nothing else. Electricity, galvanism, magnetism, or attraction and repulsion, are but different dispositions of the same common fluid. Now, as galvanism contracts the muscles of a dead man, and is the only power known that, when artificially applied, can contract the muscles of the living, so it must be the agent employed by the will to contract the muscles, and enable us to perform all the voluntary motions of life. Whatever may be the opinions of others, I consider this argument irresistible, and shall hold it as such, until it be fairly refuted.

It must now appear plain to every candid mind, that by the action of the will, and the exercise of all the mental powers, the nervo-vital fluid, this living galvanism, is continually thrown off from the voluntary nerves, and through the respiratory organs is again supplied. There is still, however, a greater waste. The involuntary nerves throw off another large portion through the action of the heart and lungs, and the digestive apparatus. And the nerves of sensation, also, do their part in throwing off this fluid. Let me here particularize. The nerves of sensation are those by which feeling is conveyed to the mind. The voluntary nerves are those through which the mind gives motion to those parts of the body that are under the control of the will. The involuntary nerves are those that give motion to such parts of our system as are not under the control of the will. None but the involuntary nerves pass to the heart, stomach, and liver. So the heart will throb, the stomach digest its food, and the liver secrete its gall, when we are awake or asleep, whether we will it or not. But to the lungs go both the voluntary and involuntary nerves. The involuntary ones are, however, the most numerous, so that though a man may hold his breath and keep the lungs in suspension till he faints, yet the involuntary nerves will get the mastery, and restore him. Through these three sets of nerves the galvanic fluid is continually wasting and passing from the whole system.

That I am correct, as to the nature of this nervous fluid, is certain. Take an animal, and tie off the involuntary nerves that lead to the stomach, and digestion will instantly cease. Then pour a moderate current of galvanism from the battery into the stomach, and digestion will immediately commence. Hence, I have clearly proved that the nervo-vital fluid, secreted by the brain, is of a galvanic nature, and is manufactured from electricity which we breathe into the lungs every inspiration we take. And I have, moreover, proved that this electro-magnetic power is the only matter that can come in contact with mind, and is the only agent by which the will contracts the muscles. Hence, the conclusion is absolutely unavoidable, that, by the concentration of the mind upon an individual, and by the action of the will, this fluid can be thrown upon another person till his nervous system is fully charged. This is Mesmerism.

Having these important facts before us, we perceive that the subject is one of momentous interest. The nervous system, embracing the brain and all its ramifications, when once diseased, seems to baffle all medical aid and skill. Hence, those upon whom fits of derangement are permanently settled, are abandoned as hopeless; and of both of these states, we are all more or less in danger. Those persons, particularly, who, on hearing the least good or bad news, are thrown into tremor and agitation, are in danger. Their brains lack the proper quantity of the nervo-vital fluid. It will be remembered that in the nerves of the brain there is no blood. The blood is exclusively confined to the veins and arteries, while the nerves are charged with this nervo-vital fluid—a galvanic substance. Now if the veins and arteries are filled with blood, and if the nerves are fully charged with the galvanic fluid; in one word, if the circulating system and the nervous system are in perfect balance, health and firmness are the result. But if the circulating system lack its proper quantity of blood, then languor and debility of body are the result. But if, on the other hand, the nervous system lack its proper quantity of galvanic fluid, then nervous excitability is the result, and the person is in danger of fits, derangement, and all the nervous diseases that attend the human race. This is evident from the following facts: Take a person who has a sufficiency of blood in the circulating system, but who, at the same time, has not enough of the galvanic fluid in his nervous system. By some circumstance the blood is suddenly thrown to his head, and the veins and arteries which pass round among the convolutions of the brain are swelled with this pressure. The nerves composing the brain not being sufficiently filled and braced with the galvanic fluid, spasmodically collapse, and a fit is the result. How often do persons, who suppose they are well, suddenly drop down dead in the streets! How often has a father or mother retired to rest, and apparently in health, yet in the morning the children found one or the other a corpse! Here, through eating too much, or some other cause, the blood was suddenly propelled to the brain, and the nerves, not being sufficiently braced with the galvanic fluid, collapsed, and by apoplexy, instant death ensued. Even the bosom companion, slumbering upon the same pillow, never felt a motion.

Now if these persons had been mesmerized, no such calamity would have ensued. Their nervous system, by which I mean the whole brain and all its ramifications, would have been charged from a full and healthy brain, and having been thus charged, it would have stood the war of internal elements, and outrode the rushing storm.

In the light our subject now stands, we perceive how vastly important it is that every person while at ease, or even in health, should be operated upon until the brain is magnetically subdued. As stated in my first lecture, one person can be mesmerized in an hour or less, another in two hours, and so on up to thirty hours. Let a healthy friend of yours sit down, one hour each day, until he subdues your brain. No person should mesmerize more than one hour in twenty-four The exertion is so great, he will injure himself if he do. But here is the glory of this science. Though you may labor an hour each day for twenty or thirty days in succession, yet what you gain, you hold, until the work is accomplished. And not only so, but after the brain is once magnetically subdued, you can then throw the person into the state in five minutes. Yes, a child ten years old can then mesmerize a giant father. Your brain being magnetically subdued, it is worth hundreds of dollars to you. You are then ready for the day of distress Come what may—toothache, headache, tic doloreux, neuralgia, or any pain of which you can conceive; let some one mesmerize you and then wake you up, and the pain is gone. The whole process need not occupy more than ten minutes. Should you fall and break your arm, then let some person mesmerize the arm only, which can be done in one minute. You are free from pain, and though in your wakeful state, yet you can look quietly on, and see the bones put to their places. Your arm can then be kept in the mesmeric state, and thoroughly and rapidly healed without having ever experienced one single throb of pain. Or by simply mesmerizing your arm or leg, you can sit in the wakeful state and see them amputated, and feel no pain. But if you neglect to have your brain magnetically subdued, then when the day of distress comes upon you, as it might require several hours to put you into this state, it will then be too late to avail yourself of the blessings this science is calculated to bestow.

It is not only a preventative of fits, insanity, and of the most frightful nervous diseases, and a safeguard against pain, but it will cure fits, if no congestion of the brain has taken place. It never fails to remove the ague and fever, however long it may have been upon the indiv'dual, and will prevent any fevers prevalent in northern climates, if the individual be mesmerized as soon as taken.

Here, then, are opening before us new fields of ac.ion, where those who have hearts of benevolence may freely roam at large, and find ample scope for the full gratification of all their sympathetic and Christian feelings and those who scoff and sneer at this science, do scoff and sneer at human wo and human pain, and **know not what they do.**

LECTURE III

Ladies and Gentlemen: The two lectures I have had the pleasure to deliver, and the successful experiments I have, during the last two evenings, performed in your presence, have awakened opposition, and the excitement has truly become tremendous. Hundreds cannot gain admittance into this capacious chapel, and the breathless anxiety and stillness of this crowded congregation, show the deep and stirring interest which you feel in the science of Mesmerism, which is the science of mind and its godlike powers. For many ages men have turned their attention to matter, and confined all their investigations to the realms of material philosophy. It is true, that here and there a noble spirit has turned his attention to scan the nature and powers of the human mind itself. But she seemed to close her laboratory against their entrance, and forbid them to lay their hands upon her sacred shrine. In this condition, there was no alternative but to judge of mind itself from its vast and complicated operations, both mental and moral. But that the mind itself could directly produce a physical rsult by its own living energies, seems never to have entered their hearts. But new fields of thought are opened to the human soul, and the mysterious and wonderful powers of the living mind are now seen and felt. Circumstances require me to say that I regard not the opposition or the scepticism of men. I challenge investigation both as to the experiments I perform, or the arguments I offer. stand mailed with immutable truth; and hence, on this subject, am invulnerable to every attack. Truth is immutable, cannot bend to circumstances, and must stand independent of the belief or unbelief of men. It must soar on towering wing far above the reach of scorn, and sooner or later triumph over all opposition.

I now come to speak of mind and its powers. I have clearly shown that the WILL raises the arm through the agency of electricity. Perhaps I should not call it electricity, but NERVO-VITAL FLUID, or GALVANIC FLUID, manufactured from electricity taken in at the lungs The WILL is not an attribute of the mind, but the result of all the attributes brought into council and action. It is the executive of the mind. The question now comes up in proper order before us: Is there any power in mind to produce a result by simply WILLING it? I contend that there is, while the opposers of Mesmerism contend that there is not. Mesmerism, then, must stand or fall on the existence or non-existence of such a power And first, let me appeal to you as Christians. If you deny that mind, or spirit, has any power to produce a physical result, then how does the Creator govern the universe? How can his Spirit come in contact with matter so as to produce any physical results? The creation and government of the world are represented in scripture as the result of the divine will. " He doeth according to his will in the army of heaven, and among the inhabitants of earth." The creation of the world and all its appendages is represented as the effect of his will. " He said, let there be light, and there was light." " He spake, and it was done; He commanded and it stood fast." If, then, the infinite Spirit, by holding his will unchangeably upon all the multifarious objects of creation, moves unnumbered worlds, and governs the universe, then there is also an energy and power in the human spirit proportionate to its greatness. If you grant that the infinite Spirit, by putting forth an infinite will, can produce infinite results, then surely a feeble finite spirit, by putting forth a feeble finite will, can produce a feeble finite result. I only ask you, as Christian philosophers, the admission that the same CAUSE shall produce the same EFFECT.

If, however, you deny the correctness of this conclusion, then I have only to say, that you furnish the atheist with a weapon by which he is sure to defeat you. Argue as long as you please, and even drive the honest atheist from any other ground, he will at last say: "Well, admit there is a God, yet he can do nothing." Your Bible says, "God is a spirit." Hence, he has no hands, feet, nor physical body, as we have. He may therefore, WILL and WILL to all eternity; yet he can do nothing, because spirit, by its mere mental action, cannot come in contact with, nor in the least affect matter We know this, says the atheist, from observation and experience. "And what can we reason but from what we know?" A human being, for instance, may sit down and exercise all his mental energies. He may WILL and WILL to endless ages, yet he can do nothing—cannot produce the least physical result, unless he uses his hands or comes in bodily contact. I now ask those Christians who deny that the mind has such power as we are contending for, how can they answer this argument of the atheist? I contend that they are not able to meet it. There is no human ingenuity beneath these heavens that the Christian opposers of the mesmeric power can summon to their aid adequate to the task

Indeed, it implies a contradiction in terms, and involves them in the following compound dilemma: If the infinite Spirit, by the energies of his will, can produce infinite results, then a finite spirit, by its will, can produce a finite result. But a finite spirit, by its will, cannot produce any result, so an infinite spirit, by its will, cannot produce any result! Of this dilemma, they may take either horn. Now for the consistency of these sapient opposers. They admit that the infinite Spirit, by its will, governs the universe, and produces infinite effects, and yet deny that a finite spirit, by its will, can produce the least physical effect; which is most philosophically absurd! But, if a finite spirit, by its living energies, can produce a finite result, then there is a God, and the heavens do rule. I am willing to meet any intelligent clergyman in controversy who denies the truth of Mesmerism; and before this enlightened congregation, who shall be our jurors, I will either make him acknowledge the mesmeric power, or drive him to atheism. I will leave him no other alternative.

We have, thus far, confined our inquiries to the fact, whether there was ANY power at all in mind to produce results independent of bodily contact. I now take a still higher stand, and deny, in total, that there is any POWER or MOTION whatever, in the whole immeasurable universe, except in mind. There can be no power without motion, nor can there be motion except it originate in mind. I care not through how many concatenations of cause and effect you may trace motion, it is after all but secondary, and must be traced back to mind as its starting point. For instance: suppose a ball should lie at rest upon this floor. It would never stir unless motion were communicated to it by some extraneous power.

If another ball entered that door, and came in contact with the ball at rest, it would communicate motion to it by impulse, losing just as much as it communicated But here is no beginning of motion, and every one would look around for the cause. If, while gazing, you should see another ball enter the door, struck by a bat, you might not yet be satisfied whether that bat was held in a man's hand, or whether it was fastened in some machinery prepared, and put in motion by human ingenuity. But you see a third ball enter the door, and not only discover the bat but the hand that grasps it. You are now satisfied. You know that the hand is connected with a body, and that body with a brain and mind. Now, in these three instances, there is no beginning of motion. The man's hand, the bat, and first ball, are but the three instruments through which motion was communicated to the ball at rest, and the man's mind was sole mover.

As the subject of Mesmerism is directly connected with the powers of mind, and as this is the pivot on which the question between its advocates and opposers must eventually turn, you will permit me to take a wider range in this extensive field. There must be some medium through which the eternal mind comes in contact with gross matter, moves unnumbered worlds accordng to nature's law, and sustains and governs the unbounded universe. That medium must be the finest, the most rarified, and subtil of inert matter in being. It must be the last link in the material chain of inert substances that fastens on the mind. This is electricity. Hence, it is through electricity that the Great Spirit comes in contact with his universe. This is evident, because it is electricity as it exists in the human sysman, through which our spirits come in contact with matter. We are but an epitome of God's universe, and in us is contained every variety of matter and substance in being. " The proper study of mankind is man;" and in this study, the most unbounded fields are opened to the range of human thought.

It may now be asked, if electricity is that substance through which the Creator comes in contact with matter, how then could he act when that splendid substance had no existence? or, in other words, how could he create " all things out of nothing?" I deny the assertion, that God created all things out of nothing, and challenge the proof. Space and duration exist of necessity, and that space was eternally filled with primal matter, which I contend is electricity. The scriptures do not inform us that God created all things out of nothing, and surely philosophy cannot inform us how many nothings it will take to make the least conceivable something! Though it is the commonly received opinion that all things were created out of nothing, yet in all ages of the Christian church, there have been some eminent men of all denominations, who have reected this idea, and contended that all things were created out of some substance. I have not time to refer to those persons this evening, yet permit me to name one. A more orthodox man than John Milton never lived, as all know who have ever read that astonishing production of the human intellect, his " Paradise Lost." He was at war with the idea that all things were created out of nothing. I will present you with an extract from his " Treatise on Christian Doctrine," volume 1 pages 236 and 237. As I quote from memory, I may not be correct in every word.

He says: "It is clear, then, that the world was framed out of matter of some kind or other. For, since action and passion are relative terms, and since, consequently, no agent can act externally, unless there be some patient such as matter, it appears impossible that God could have created this world out of nothing; not from any defect of power on his part, but because it was necessary that something should previously have existed capable of receiving passively the exertion of the divine efficacy. Since, therefore, both scripture and reason concur in pronouncing that all these things were made, not out of nothing, but out of matter, it necessarily follows that matter must always have existed independent of God, or have originated from God at some particular point of time."

So you perceive, Milton contends that both scripture and reason teach that all things were made out of matter. I am under no obligations to prove that all things were not made out of nothing, for no man is bound by the rules of logic to prove a negative. But I will, for a moment, depart from this established rule of schoolmen, and undertake to prove that all things were not made out of nothing. To this end, I will call into my service the following argument:

We raise an axe, and at a single blow cut in two a piece of wood one inch in diameter. Now it is certain that this wood was not severed instantly in all its parts. If it were, then the lower part would have been cut at the same instant that the upper part was, which is perfectly absurd, and therefore impossible. The axe certainly passed gradually through that wood, and progressively separated one grain after another. This you all perceive. By INSTANTLY, we are to understand, that no time shall elapse between the accomplishment of any two objects. It may, however, be said, that there are bodies that move with greater velocity than this axe. I will, then, take another. There is nothing with which we are acquainted, that moves with greater velocity than light; its motion being about twelve million miles in a minute. Hence, the passage of a ray of light from the sun to the earth, would be about eight minutes. It is, therefore, absurd to say that a ray of light could be at the sun and at the earth at the same instant, as it would allow no time for its passage. I will now apply the above argument to the subject before us.

If SOMETHING were created out of NOTHING, it could not, in the nature of things, have been done PROGRESSIVELY or GRADUALLY, because the instant it became the least possible remove from nothing it would be something. It must, in the very nature of things, remain nothing till it becomes something, because there is no possible process by which it can be gradually brought forward into something, for there is no existing medium between something and nothing. Now, if nothing were created into something, it must have been done instantly; and if instantly, then it must have been something and nothing at the same instant, which is the climax of absurdity. It is just as absurd as to contend that the piece of wood before mentioned was severed at the bottom at the same time that it was at the top, or that a ray of light could be at the sun and the earth at the same instant. I shall hold this argument sound until some one is able to refute it.

Hence, I contend for the eternal existence of PRIMAL matter, which is electricity. But even this primal matter does not exist independent of Deity. It *is* the natural atmosphere or substance emanating from Him. It is evident that every substance in being has its atmospheric emanation, by which it may be detected before we arrive at the body. I say ATMOSPHERIC EMANATION because I know of no other more convenient term, by which I can express my ideas. For instance, the rose, and every species of the flower tribe, have their emanations, which like an atmosphere surround them, and by which we detect their existence before we come in contact with them. For the sake of perspicuity, suffer me to call it atmospheric emanation, which in the above cases is detected by smell. The same is true of every species of trees and plants in being. The same is true of every species of earth, and rock, and mineral, in existence. Each substance has an atmospheric emanation peculiar to itself, and by which it can be discovered by man, or by some other living creature. The camel on the desert will detect water twenty miles distant. The same is true in relation to all the races and tribes of animated beings. Each has its own peculiar atmospheric emanation, by which it may be detected by some other creature, by some instinctive sense of which we have little or no conception. As, then, every substance in being has its own peculiar emanation, so the atmospheric emanation of the self-existent Spirit, is electricity, which, proceeding forth from Him, does not therefore exist independent of him.

It will now be said that, on this principle of reasoning, the speaker will make it out that SPIRIT itself is MATTER. If by SPIRIT you mean that which has neither length, breadth, nor thickness, nor occupies any space, then I have only to say that it is a mere chimera of the human brain, a nonentity, a nothing! Does Deity fill all space? Then he is of course a substance, a real, living, acting and thinking being; otherwise, as Christians, we use words without knowledge, when we say that he fills immensity with his presence. But it may be said that MIND IS THOUGHT, REASON, and UNDERSTANDING, and then be asked, whether thought, reason, understanding, etc., occupy any space? But I deny that these are mind. Thought, reason, and understanding are not mind, but the EFFECTS of mind. Mind is something supremely higher than all these. I yet ask what is that which thinks, reasons, and understands? It is the mind. Then mind is something distinct from those effects by which it is made manifest. What, then, it may be asked, is mind? I answer, it is that substance which has innate or living motion; and the result of that motion is thought, reason, understanding, and, therefore, power. As electricity is the highest and most subtil of INERT substances, as it fastens on mind, and is, therefore, more easily moved than any other inert substance in being, so mind is the next step above electricity, is the crowning perfection of all other substances in immensity—is living motion; and the result of that motion is thought and power. It is the living Spirit from whom emanates electricity, and who, out of that electricity, has created all worlds. Hence, the Creator is a real substance or being, possessing personal identity, and is infinite in every perfection of his adorable character.

Electricity, which is an atmospheric emanation from God, and which is moved by his will, is that substance out of which all worlds and their splendid appendages were made. Hence, it will be perceived, that electricity contains all the original properties of all the various substances in being. All the varieties of the universe around us—all the beauties and glories of creation upon which we look with so many thrilling emotions of delight, were produced from electricity, which is the inexhaustible fountain of primal matter. By the living energies of the Divine Mind, electricity was condensed into globes; not instantly, but gradually. The heaviest particles took the lowest point, or common centre, of our globe, and so on, step by step, lighter and lighter, till we reach the surface, which is a vegetable mould. On this we find water, a substance still lighter than earth; next air, which is lighter than water, and so on till we reach the sun, which is the highest point in relation to our system, because it is the common centre. The sun is, therefore, pure electricity. Hence, the twenty-nine globes, belonging to our system, are electrically, geologically, and magnetically made. They are but twenty-nine magnets revolving around our sun as a common centre.

The sun, being pure electricity or primal matter, is but an emanation from the Deity. It is, consequently, in a positive state. Hence, electricity is continually passing from the sun, as a common centre, to the twenty-nine surrounding worlds; on the same principle that it passes from a positive to a negative cloud. Having done its duty in giving light, heat, and vegetation, as well as magnetic power to globes, it is returned by reaction to the sun, and these two motions form the vortices that roll worlds around him. It is impossible that there can be any inherent attraction and repulsion in matter. Attraction and repulsion are but different dispositions of electricity. The best magnets are now made from the galvanic battery. Hence electricity galvanism, and magnetism are but in substance one and the same fluid, and as this is primal matter, an emanation from the Eternal Mind, so all the powers of attraction and repulsion originate in Deity. His will comes in contact with electricity, and through that subtil agent he moves the whole immeasurable universe in accordance with nature's law. All worlds are in motion. They roll rapid as the lightning's blaze, and in the most apparent confusion; yet all is calm, regular, and harmonious. God is, therefore, connected with his universe, and superintends all its multifarious operations. Though he is thus intimately united to inert matter, yet he is distinct from the whole.

> " Thou apart,
> Above, beyond; O tell me, mighty Mind,
> Where art thou? Shall I dive into the deep?
> Call to the sun? or ask the roaring winds
> For their Creator? Shall I question loud
> The thunder, if in that the Almighty dwells?
> Or holds he furious storms in straitened reins,
> And bids fierce whirlwinds wheel his rapid car?
>   The nameless He! whose nod is nature's birth
> And nature's shield the shadow of his hand;
> Her dissolution his suspended smile!
> The great First Last! pavilioned high he sits
> In darkness, from excessive splendor borne,
> By gods unseen, unless through lustre lost.
> His glory, to created glory, bright,
> As that to central horrors; he looks down
> On all that soars, and spans immensity."

Worlds are not only electrically, geologically and magnetically made, but they are electrically and magnetically suspended and moved by the immediate energies of the Divine Mind. Here is an image in paper costume. I will attach it to this electrizing machine and charge it. See! those papers are now all suspended, and being equally charged they repel each other. I will now put my fingers near them. See! how they are attracted by my hand. They touch me, give off their electricity, become equalized with my fingers, and then fall. Here, then, is suspension, attraction, and repulsion, by electricity. It may, however, be said, that if worlds are moved by electricity, that they must necessarily move as quick as lightning. This does not follow. Here is an orrery, with which the most of you are acquainted. I attach it to the electrical machine, and charge. You see it is moved by giving off electricity at its points. But though electrically moved, yet it does not move as quick as lightning. The magnet I hold in my hand was charged from the galvanic battery, and by one single stroke of the battery from the prongs of this magnet towards the bow, I can destroy all its magnetic powers, and by reversing the action, I can just as suddenly restore them.

I have now clearly shown that all motion and power originate in mind, and as the human spirit, through an electro-magnetic medium, comes in contact with matter, so the infinite Spirit does the same, and through this medium he governs the universe. Hence, those who deny the mesmeric power, must, to be consistent with themselves, deny that there is any medium through which mind can come in contact with matter, or else deny that mind, abstractly considered, has any power to produce results. But the denial of either of these is a denial of an all-powerful, self-existent Spirit, the Creator and Governor of the universe. But, on the other hand, how sublime the idea, that God is electrically and magnetically connected with his universe; that, by the energies of his own will, he has condensed and formed worlds from electricity, which is but the atmospheric emanation of his own spirit, and that by electricity he sustains, rolls, and governs them from age to age. And how sublime the idea, that he has " poured spirit from spirit's awful fountain, and kindled into existence a world of rationals." He has poured himself through all his works and stamped upon them BEAUTY, ORDER, and HARMONY, which are but the reflected impressions of his OWN SPLENDOR.

LECTURE IV.

Ladies and Gentlemen: It is a source of gratification to me that public attention, in Boston and vicinity is completely awakened to the interests of Spiritualism, and that they are giving this subject that investigation which its importance demands. We live emphatically in an age of investigation and improvement, when light seems to be pouring in oceans on our world; and he who shuts his eyes, and then scoffs and sneers because others open theirs and see, is not only recreant to duty, but does society an irreparable wrong. But those who remain in scepticism much longer on the subject of Mesmerism, will be suspected either of ignorance or dishonesty. I make this remark, because there is no possible apology that any man of common sense should remain in scepticism another day. He can go home and try it upon his children or friends, and test its power, and know its truth, and this every man is bound to do who desires to mitigate human pain, and assuage human woes. The subject is one of paramount consideration, and is worthy of your best affections, your most ardent zeal, and your warmest hopes.

In my last lecture, I took into consideration MIND AND ITS POWERS, and the medium through which it comes in contact with matter. This medium is electricity, and is that eternal, PRIMAL matter out of which all other substances were made. It fills immensity of space; and worlds are successively and continually formed by the condensation of electricity under the living and ever-acting energies of the Eternal Mind. We are floating in an immensity of space that knows no bounds, like the mote in the sunbeam. This is peopled with swarming worlds, in number beyond an angel's computation; and the residue, which has not yet become the abodes of life, order, and beauty, is filled up with primal matter still in its electrical state. Hence, the work of creation has been going on from eternity, and will continue to progress so long as the throne of the self-existent Jehovah endures, without ever arriving at an end in the sublime career of creation. New brother creations are, therefore, every moment rolling from his omnific hand, and that creating fiat will never, never cease. All this is effected by the energies of mind.

In my last lecture, I stated, and, as I thought, conclusively proved, that thought, reason, understanding, etc., were not mind, but merely the results of mind, and gave what I considered conclusive evidence. I, moreover, stated that mind was a substance that occupied space, that it possessed living motion, and that the result of that motion was thought, reason, and power, and gave what I considered proof. But it seems that both of these positions have been disputed, and hence I will once more touch these two points.

If thought, reason, and understanding are mind, then our minds are annihilated every night in sleep. Because, if all the organs of the brain are wrapped in profound slumber, then there is not a single thought stirring in the whole intellectual realm. It will not answer to parry the force of this argument, by saying that the action of blood upon the brain produces thought, and that this action is suspended in slumber, because the blood flows and acts upon the brain in sleep as well as when we are awake; and hence we should, on this principle, think and reason when asleep nearly as well as when awake. This, however, is not the case. If, then, thought and reason are mind, I must insist that, in profound slumber, the mind is annihilated, for thought is gone. Hence it is plain, that thought, reason, and understanding are not mind, but the effects of mind.

I will now take a different argument from the one offered in my last lecture, to prove that mind is a substance that has innate motion, and that this motion produces thought. It is admitted on all hands, that the mind resides in the brain, not in the blood-vessels, but in the nerves themselves. Now, if the nerves are very much expanded by heat, it is impossible to sleep. By lying perfectly still upon our beds, there is a coolness steals over the brain. The nerves, by coolness, are made to contract. They continue gently to shrink until they press upon the living substance that they contain, and stop its motion. That moment all thought ceases. Recollect, MIND is that substance whose nature is motion. and the result of that motion is thought. By pressure, by FORCE, it is stopped, and thought is gone. The moment our rest is complete, a nervous warmth comes over the brain. The nerves expand, leave the mind disengaged, it resumes its motion, and thought is the result. As cold shrinks, and heat expands the nervous system, so that we alternately sleep and wake under this double action, so the mind is a living, self-moving, and invisible substance, which is capable of being compressed sufficient, at least, to prevent its motion.

Having made these remarks, which the circumstances

of the occasion seemed to require at my hands, I now invite your attention to what is called by sceptics the incomprehensibility and marvellousness of magnetic sleep and who, on this account, openly avow the impossibility and inconsistency of any one being thrown into such a state; and who, whenever they witness experiments to test it, freely use the stereotyped words, "HUMBUG AND COLLUSION," and that, too, with great emphasis, without being able, however, to detect this great, this wonderful imposition on public credulity!

The greatest objection to the truth of the science of Mesmerism arises from the circumstance, that the subject can see in a manner different from the ordinary mode of vision. That any person can see out of the templar region, or out of the top, or back part of the skull, and through solid walls, and in the darkest night they contend is too preposterous to be believed. I deeply regret to say that medical men not only give countenance to such declarations made by the common mass, but are engaged in making the same themselves. But I seriously appeal to them whether they have never seen any patients in a certain state of the nervous system, induced by disease, where they could thus see, and when sensation was so perfectly extinct that amputation might have taken place without pain? Have they never seen a case of catalepsy? If not, have they never seen in medical works well-authenticated cases of this disease reported? Surely they will not deny these things. I further inquire, have they never seen a case nor heard one reported, where patients in a state of catalepsy have been entirely clairvoyant? where they have seen, as no person in the ordinary way of vision can see? I am conscious that they will not hazard their medical reputation by giving these interrogatories an unqualified denial. Of all persons beneath these heavens, medical gentlemen should be he last to sneer at the idea of clairvoyance, or even total insensibility of a person in the magnetic state.

Catalepsy is a sudden suppression of motion and sensation; a kind of apoplexy, in which the patient is in a fixed posture. If the case be an aggravated one, the patient is sometimes senseless and even speechless. To bring this subject directly and plainly before you, I will relate to you an incident which was stated to me about six months ago by Dr. Patterson, an eminent physician of Lynchburg, Virginia. A young lady was taken sick. Her physician, who lived some eight or ten miles distant, was sent for. He found her in a state of catalepsy Though there was no sensation in her body, yet she had occasional fits of talking. He prescribed, stated that he should be there the next evening, and left. The evening came, and a most tremendous storm of rain, with high winds, set in. The darkness was profound. As the family were seated in silence and anxiety in the same room where the patient lay, some one said, " Well, our doctor will not be here to-night." The sick lady answered : " Yes he will; he is coming now ; he is riding on horseback, and is all drenched with rain." the family supposing this to be a mere reverie of the brain, a touch of delirium, made no reply. Nearly an hour passed on ; and the storm continuing with unabating violence, one of the pensive group again broke the silence, and exclaimed with a feeling of regret, " Well, it is certain our doctor will not be here this dark stormy night!" The sufferer again answered, " Yes he will; he is most here now; there he is hitching his horse ; he is coming to the door.' They heard the raps : the door was opened, and in came the doctor I now ask, how did this lady in a state of catalepsy see the physician several miles distant, through the walls of her house, and in so dark a night?

This report was given in a medical journal and well authenticated. And moreover, there are many of a similar character; and of these facts medical men are well aware. Now I appeal to them, who are present on this occasion, that if it is possible to throw the nervous system into a condition by disease, so that the patient can see in a manner entirely distinct from the ordinary mode of vision, THEN, how can they, without presumption, affirm that a person cannot be thrown into a similar state by Mesmerism? It is proved by medical works that such a state of the brain is possible; and who will take upon himself to affirm, that it can be induced by no other means than disease? As a state of catalepsy is thus frequently attended with clairvoyance, and with total insensibility, so that amputation could be performed without pain, then why should we marvel when we see the same identical phenomena clustering around Mesmerism? I have only to say that our surprise is wholly gratuitous.

I appeal to medical gentlemen present. Have you never seen a case of natural somnambulism? There are hundreds of them occur in this city; and, in every town there are those who rise in their sleep, perform labors, and return to their beds without knowing it. In this state they have gone to the top of house-frames, walked on the ridgepoles, and safely descended. They have, in the darkest nights, walked over dangerous and rapid streams on a mere scantling in safety, where a slight loss of balance would have been death, and where it would be impossible for them to have crossed in their wakeful state. Women have arisen, and in this state have done the nicest needle-work. And how did these see? Surely not with the natural organ of vision. A young lady at boarding-school, learning to paint miniatures, and on preparing one for examination-day, found that she could be excelled by the other pupils. It worried her much, and to her suprise she found in the morning, that her picture had greatly advanced under the delicate touch of some experienced hand. She charged the deed upon her teacher, who disclaimed all knowledge of the fact. But on the next morning the picture was nearly finished, but the transgressor could not be found. The Preceptress being strongly suspected, secretly sat up and watched. In the dead of night, when all was still, the young lady arose, and in a dark room arranged her work, mixed her colors, and began to paint. Her Preceptress lit a lamp, entered the room, and saw that lady finish her picture. She then awakened her. How did she see how to mix her colors, and to give the nicest touch with her pencil where no human eye in the wakeful state could discern an object? Such facts as these, and even more wonderful, are well known to medical gentlemen. Now, if persons can by some cause be thrown into somnambulism upon their beds, then reason teaches that they may be thrown into the same state and even a much deeper sleep by the magnetic power.

We will now take into consideration the philosophy of Clairvoyance. It is evident that SEEING, HEARING, FEELING, TASTING, and SMELLING, belong exclusively to the mind. And as we have already clearly proved that electricity is the only substance that can come in contact with mind, so it is through the agency of this fluid that sensations are transmitted to the mind. Hence, it is through the medium of electricity that we see hear feel, taste, and smell.

The power of sight being in the mind, it is evident that we never saw anything out of our eyes. The whole of this congregation, with all their different costumes, their various complexions and different appearances, and all their relative distances from each other, are struck upon the retina of the speaker's eye, on about the bigness of a quarter of an inch. By the agency of electricity, it is conveyed through the optic nerve to the mind where it is seen. Hence, we never saw a piece of matter, but only its shadow, the same as when you look into a mirror, it is not yourself, but your image that you see. Electricity is that substance that passes through all other substances. Air cannot pass through your cranium, nor through these walls, nor metallic substances. But as all these have countless millions of pores, electricity can pass through them. Now if our nervous system could be charged with the nervo-vital fluid, so as to render the brain positive, and thus bring it into an exact equilibrium or balance with external electricity, then we should be clairvoyant. Because the nervous system being duly charged, and even surcharged, the great quantity of this fluid passing in right lines from the mind, as a common centre, and in every direction through the pores of the skull, renders it transparent Uniting with external electricity which passes through these walls and all substances, which are also transparent, the image of the whole universe, as it were, in this transparent form, is thrown upon the mind, and is there seen, and seen, too, independent of the retina. On this principle the whole of those objects which are opaque to natural vision, are rendered transparent to the clairvoyant, and he sees through walls in succession, and takes cognizance of their relative distances, on the same principle that we in a wakeful state could look through said walls if they were thin, transparent glass. On this principle, if the subject be charged too much or too little, he cannot see clearly. Or if the night be rainy, or even damp, and unfavorable to electricity, then experiments in clairvoyance must fail, or be very imperfect. The subject must be magnetically charged exactly to that degree which will bring him into magnetic equilibrium with external electricity. Then, if the night be favorable, the experiments will most likely prove successful.

For the sake of perspicuity, I will take another position. Why can you see through that window? You answer, because the glass is transparent. But why is it transparent? You again answer, because upon every square inch of its surface there are several thousand pores, and the glass is of that chemical property that it will admit the rays of atmospheric light to pass through them. This is philosophically correct. But remember, it is not the WINDOW that SEES, but it is the INHABITANT in the house that looks out of the window. The question now arises, why can you not see through that wall? If you answer, because it is opaque, yet the query arises, why is it opaque? The wall has certainly as many pores upon the square inch as that glass. The answer is, because the wall is of that chemical property that resists the rays of atmospheric light; and where no light passes through the pores of a substance, that substance must be opaque. This is so far philosophically correct.

We are now ready to ask, why can you see through the eye? Because it is formed on the transparent principle, has a certain number of pores upon the square inch, and, by the skill of the Creator, it is so constituted as to chemically receive the rays of atmospheric light. But you will please to bear in mind that it is not those translucent ORBS that see, but it is the INHABITANT in the earthly house that looks out of those windows of the soul. Even the good book says, when speaking of the faded vision of the aged,—" AND THOSE THAT LOOK OUT OF THE WINDOWS SHALL BE DARKENED"—thus calling these eyes but the windows of the soul. It is the spirit only that sees—that alone possesses the inward living eye; for take the spirit from its earthly house, and what can these eyes—these windows of the fleshly tabernacle —see? They can see just as much as the hands or feet, but no more. Let another question be here proposed. Why can you not see through the skull? You will again answer—because it is opaque. But I again ask, why is it opaque? You reply—because it chemically resists the rays of atmospheric light, and will not allow them to pass through its pores, even though they are as numerous as the pores of the eye. This answer is also philosophically correct; and in this wonderful constitution of the human cranium is made manifest the wisdom of the Creator. For were light admitted through it upon every portion of the brain, it would stimulate its organs to such an unnatural degree as to render the mind incapable of manifesting itself through them in a harmonious and rational manner. Indeed, it would be inconsistent with the continuance of life itself.

As the remarks now made are perfectly simple, and can be comprehended by all, I will now ask—if there were a light so much finer than atmospheric light, and of that peculiar property that it could be made to pass through all substances in existence, could you not then see through that wall as easily as through that glass? Certainly; because the wall would be rendered transparent through the action of that light, and wherever light passes, there must exist the possibility to see objects. The question then naturally presents itself to the mind—is there such a light? I answer—there is, and it is MAGNETIC, or GALVANIC LIGHT. It exists not only around, but within us. Go into a dungeon of total darkness, and strike your head a sudden blow, and you will see a flash of light. From whence comes that light? It is within you: it is the nervous fluid—the living light of the brain, which is of a galvanic nature. By this concussion it was thrown into confusion, forced from its accustomed channels, and laid suddenly at the footstool of the living mind; and the mind saw the flash. Hence, it is electrically that we SEE, and HEAR, and FEEL, and TASTE, and SMELL. All mesmeric subjects cannot, however, see with the same brilliancy in clairvoyance, when the brain is surcharged with this light. The most distinguished clairvoyants now in the United States, are Jackson Davis, Lucius E. Burkmar, and Walter S. Tarbox, who have astonished thousands; and by their examinations of the diseased, and saving the lives of many, have rendered themselves the benefactors of suffering humanity This galvanic light can be conveyed to the brain independent of the natural eye—the outward organ of vision.

That the above principles are correct, and that TASTE, SEEING, etc., are electrically conveyed to the mind, try the following experiments. Take a half dollar, and a piece of zinc of the same size: touch them separately to the tongue, and you will not perceive any taste; but put the tongue between them, and, in this position, touch the edges of the two pieces together over the end of the tongue, and you will taste a pungent acid. This taste is produced electrically. Zinc contains a greater portion of electricity than the silver, and when they come in contact it gives it off to the silver, and conveys the sensation of taste through the glands to the mind. In further proof of this being electricity, put the half dollar against the gums under the upper lip; open the mouth, and lay the zinc upon the tongue. by moving the tongue up and down, you will touch the pieces together, and every time they come in contact you will not only perceive the same taste before described, but you will see a flash of lightning. Now that this lightning is seen directly by the mind, and independent of the natural organ of the eye, you may enter a dark room, and in the darkest night—close your eyes, and even bandage them,—and yet when you touch those pieces, as described, you will see the flash, even when one from the heavens could not be seen. This flash is conveyed through the nervous system directly to the mind, where alone exists the power of vision. This is not only proof that taste and sight are electrically conveyed to the mind, but also that electricity is that substance which alone comes in contact with mind.

It is the same in relation to the other senses. Even HEARING is not produced by the concussion of the particles of our air, but by the vibration of the particles of electricity conveyed to the mind, and in that tremulous manner through the organ of the ear coming in direct contact with mind. It is impossible, in the nature of things, hat so gross a substance as air can pass the barriers of the ear and enter the brain to produce any sound But it may be said, that though the particles of air do not enter the brain, yet with a vibrating motion they strike the drum of the ear and convey sound to the mind. This cannot be, because there is no air in the brain itself; and hence, there is no internal aerial medium through which sound could be transmitted to the mind, even if we admit that the concussion of the particles of external air conveyed it to the drum. I yet ask, what is the internal medium beyond, through which that sound is conveyed to the mind? There is no air there; and if it be a vacuum, then no sound whatever can be conveyed. The truth is, that the same substance in tremulous motion, which conveys sound to the drum of the ear, also passes through it into the nervous system, and conveys its oracle to the very throne of the living mind. This is electricity, which is the only correspondent or mediator between mind and matter, laying its brilliant hand upon both parties, and bringing them into communication.

The sense of smell exists in the mind, and from surrounding substances the sensation is electrically conveyed to it. But as smell is so nearly related to taste, the same argument may be applied to both. I will therefore proceed to notice the sense of feeling.

It is generally said that the sense of feeling is in the nerves. But I contend that it belongs exclusively to the mind, the nerves being the mere medium through which it is electrically conveyed to the mind. Indeed, all our sensations, whether of seeing, hearing, feeling, tasting, or smelling, are conveyed to the mind, through the nervous system, from their correspondent organs, which are but the mere starting points, or inlets of sensation And as the nervo-vital fluid, which is of an electric nature, is the only substance that acts through the nerves, so electricity is the agent which conveys all our sensations to the mind. Though it is said that feeling is diffused over the whole system, yet, strictly speaking, this is not true. All feeling is in the mind It is evident that the mind resides in the brain. It is not diffused over the whole nervous system, for when we might be as sensible that thought proceeded from the hand or foot, as from the head. In this case, the loss of a hand or foot would be the loss of some portion of our minds. The spinal marrow is but a continuation of the brain. Branches shoot out, and from these, other branches in infinite variety, until they are spread out over the whole system ten thousand times finer than the finest hair-sieve,—so fine that you cannot put down the point of a cambric needle without feeling it, and you cannot feel unless you touch a nerve. Hence you perceive how very fine the nervous system must be! Of this system, the brain is the fountain, and is the local habitation of the mind.

Now touch the finger to any object, and that touch produces a corresponding action upon the brain, and through the agency of the electro-magnetic fluid, that sensation is conveyed to the mind. It is the mind that feels it, and by habit we associate the feeling with the end of the finger. But amputate the arm, and then touch the correspondent nerve at the end of the stump and he will yet associate the feeling with the end of the finger. But the feeling is not even in the end of the stump. It is in the mind which has its residence in the brain.

I knew a blacksmith who had his leg amputated above the knee. When healed, he put on a wooden leg and resumed his labors in the shop. He could feel his leg and toes as usual, and many times in a lay, he would, without reflection, put down his hand to scratch his wooden leg. Being unlearned and superstitious, he supposed that his leg was buried in an uncomfortable position, and therefore, haunted its wooden substitute. He dug it up, placed under it a soft cotton bed, and re-buried it; but all to no purpose. He made the circumstance known to his physician, who told him to find the corresponding nerve on the stump, and he could cause the itching sensation to cease. He did so, and the difficulties were at once overcome.

A gentleman called upon me, in October, 1842, at the house of the Hon. T. J. Greenwood, in Marlboro'. He stated, that he injured his arm, the cords contracted and drew up his fingers, so as perfectly to clench the hand. It gave him great pain, and the arm was amputated just above the elbow. And though three years had passed away, he said there was yet a constant pain as though the fingers were drawn up; and from that contraction the pain seemed to proceed. Now the whole of this difficulty was felt in the brain. If I may be allowed the expression, the brain has its legs and arms, and toes, and fingers. Or allow me to go entirely back. It is the mind which has its limbs and all its lineaments of form, and from which all form, proportion, and beauty emanate.

I observed a moment ago, that the spinal cord was but the brain continued. Now let a knife be inserted between the joints of the spine, and let this cord be severed, and all the parts of the body, below the incision, will be paralyzed. You may now cut or burn the legs, but all feeling is gone; neither can they be moved by the will. The will cannot come in contact with flesh and blood, only through the electro-magnetic fluid. The mind is in the brain, and as the spinal marrow is severed, so the lower parts are separated from the fountain of feeling. The communication of the electrical influence is destroyed between the extremities and the mind, and hence, the extremities can convey sensations to the mind no more.

I might continue the argument to an indefinite extent to prove that all our senses (seeing, hearing, feeling, tasting, and smelling) are in the mind, and that these sensations, through their corresponding organs, are electrically conveyed to the mind, through the nervous system, but I forbear, aud proceed, as usual, to the anticipated experiments of the evening.

LECTURE V.

Ladies and Gentlemen: We are again assembled to take into consideration the subject of Mesmerism. Its growing interest in the public mind is manifest, by the increasing throngs that assemble in this chapel, to investigate its claims to truth and science, and the multitudes that are obliged to retire, unable to gain admittance. As several notes, since my entrance into this house, have been handed me, I shall be obliged to omit introductory remarks, and attend to two or three important requests.

An inquiry is made as to the number of degrees or states into which a subject may be thrown. In reply to this, I would say, that there are but FIVE degrees which have, as yet, come under my observation. The FIRST degree is, when the hands or even the whole body of the subject can be attracted by the conjoint action of the mental and physical energies of the magnetizer. The SECOND degree is, when the hands, or body of the subject, can be attracted by the mental energies alone, or by the physical energies independent of any mental effort. The THIRD degree is, when the subject can neither hear nor answer any person but the magnetizer and those who are in communication. The FOURTH degree is, when the subject can taste what the magnetizer tastes, and smell what he smells. The FIFTH degree is clairvoyance. I would not be understood that these five degrees always occur in the order I have now stated them; but I mean that there are these five different degrees. Some never seem to go further than the third degree, and no surgical operation should be performed, unless the subject be put completely into this third state, so that no voice but the magnetizer's can be heard. It can then be performed without any pain.

Another inquiry is made, whether any person can put himself into communication with the subject without the magnetizer's consent? I answer, yes. Any person may put himself into communication by ardently fixing his attention upon the subject while another is magnetizing him, especially if he sits near him. Or he may do it by touching, or too freely handling him. He may do it by violently throwing his hands towards him, and within a foot of his body. Or, lastly, he may take two or three electric shocks from a charged Leyden jar, within eight or ten feet of the subject, being careful to fix his eyes firmly upon him while taking the shock. The second or third shock, the subject will start with him who receives it—and when he starts he is in communication.

A third inquiry is made, whether any one but the magnetizer can awaken the subject? Certainly, any person who is put in communication with him can take him out of the state. Or by a firm determination, he can awaken himself. In fact, he may be put in bed, and in a few hours, say from eight to fourteen, he will come out of it the natural way.

A fourth, and last inquiry is made, if magnetism be true, why has not more of it been seen, at least in some small degree, in different ages? I answer, that its history dates back to a very early age which I cannot now pursue, but would refer to "Fascination, or the Philosophy of Charming, illustrating the principles of life in connection with spirit and matter," published in New York city by Fowlers & Wells; also to the American Phrenological Journal. They are conducted with great ability, and should be in possession of every family. But the inquirer asks, "why has not more of it been seen, at least in some small degree, in different ages?" I answer, it has been seen and felt. Have you never read the bold, lofty, and full-gushing eloquence of Demosthenes, whose thunders roused Greece into action, and moved her sons as the wind in its rushing majesty moves the sublime magnificence of ten thousand forests? This was but the magnetic principle, the lightning of the mind, by which they were electrified, and made to act as one man against the powers of Philip. The same is true of Cicero, who shook the Roman senate with his voice, and beneath the electric glance of whose awful eye, even Cataline quailed. I am well aware that you will call this sympathy. But what is sympathy? It is the nervo-vital fluid thrown from a full, energetic brain, upon another of kindred feeling. That brain being roused affects another, and that still another, till the whole assembly are brought into magnetic sympathy with the speaker, and by him are moved as the soul of one man.

As a further answer to this question, I will notice one fact more; and in doing this, I shall remove what has long been considered as a stigma on a large and respectable denomination. I mean the Methodists. Ever since that class of Christians had a religious existence in the United States, persons have fallen down into a species of trance. Other denominations call this delusion, and many call it deception, because such things never occur in their meetings. But there is no deception in this—it is really the magnetic state—or more properly the spiritual state. Every preacher cannot do it, and as it is done without contact, comparatively few are subjects of it.

But take a preacher of strong muscular powers; one who has large concentrativeness, and eye of lightning, and a warm, a sincere, and ardent soul. He enters a tent at camp-meeting, where there are fifteen or twenty persons. He kneels down and prays most fervently; he rises and sings most devotionally. He is in close contact with his little group. He begins to exhort most sincerely; and soon the deep fountains of his soul are broken up. A female, perchance, is moved to tears. His concentration being large, he keeps his eye steadily fixed upon her, and he wills and desires, that she shall feel as he feels, and be converted to God. At length she falls into this singular state. She has gone there in the preacher's feelings, and in his feelings she will come out of it. Now, if he would follow my directions, he could restore her in two minutes. I will pledge myself to arouse any one from this magnetic state in five minutes. Dr. Cannon, of this city, took a lady out of this state a few weeks ago, in Provincetown, who was thrown into it in a religious meeting, and who appeared nearly lifeless. A report of this was published in the "Christian Freeman." Now all these are really magnetic effects that we have seen, and for many years in succession. So the inquiries are all answered, and I hope, to the satisfaction of the inquirers and the congregation.

I must now proceed to notice the dangers and abuses of Mesmerism. It is often said by its opposers, that even if it be true yet it is dangerous, because it can be abused, and therefore ought not to be practised. But do you know of any blessing beneath these heavens but what has been, and still continues to be abused? No you do not. Do you know of a more common blessing than taste? yet to gratify their taste, millions on millions have gone down to a drunkard's tomb! Mothers have been more than widowed, and children more than orphanized. They have been beaten and abused, and suffered cold, and hunger, and nakedness. Under it, crimes have been committed, and the state prisons filled with wretched men. Human beings have also by millions gone down to their graves through excess in eating. But is taste a curse because men abuse it? and must it, therefore, be struck from the catalogue of Heaven's mercies? All answer, no. Acquisitiveness, benevolence, and combativeness can be abused, and so can all the organs of the human brain. But ought they not on that account to be indulged?

Once more: there is not a greater blessing than the Gospel of Christ. It teaches us to love and forgive our enemies; to resist not evil, and to do unto others as we would that they should do unto us. It is calculated to moderate our feelings in prosperity—to comfort us in the day of adversity—and to sustain us under all the troubles and disappointments incident to mortal life. When our parents, friends and children are on their dying bed, we can shake the farewell hand of mortal separation, with the hope of meeting them again in future realms. And not only so, but when we lie down upon the bed of death, and the embers of life feebly glimmer in the socket of existence, then the Gospel of Christ points us to brighter scenes—scenes beyond the tomb.

Yet men have abused that gospel, and one denomination has risen up against another, and doomed each other to the stake. Rivers of human blood have flowed in the holy wars. But is the gospel a curse, and should it be struck from existence merely because men abuse it? No, is the answer of every Christian heart. Then the objection fails. One thing must settle this point. There is nothing that God has established as a law in our nature, but what was designed to be a blessing to his creatures. The magnetic principle is not of man, but one the Creator has established, and is, therefore, a blessing. And if it could not be abused, it would differ from all other blessings he has bestowed on man.

But it is said, that a man upon the high-way may be thrown into the state and robbed. But I deny that any person can be thrown into the state against his will, if he will at the same time use physical resistance. And when in the magnetic state, he has twice the strength to resist, and defend himself, that he has when out of it. We generally know with whom we have to deal, and surely we would not suffer an enemy, nor the unprincipled, to put us into the mesmeric slumber. But if you wish to be safe, and are really fearful of consequences, I will give you a rule of action. It is this: never allow any one to magnetize you unless it be in the presence of a third person. Observe this rule, and no danger arising from this source will ever cross your path.

Having answered these objections, I will now show you where there are real dangers. In the first place, though every person can be mesmerized, yet there are but few who can be easily thrown into this state. The greater proportion, by far, would require several hours of hard labor. Hence, when one is found who is easy to mesmerize, curiosity is awakened, and every one wishes to make the trial of his power and skill. One mesmerizes this individual in the morning, another in the evening, and a new set of operators perform the same task on the next day, and so on. Now, in such cases, there is that mixing and crossing of all these different fluids in the subject's brain, which, if persisted in too long, will prove injurious, even if all these magnetizers are healthy persons. If you mesmerize a person, and thoroughly wake him, yet the whole of that fluid does not completely pass from his brain short of a week. Select one healthy magnetizer, and continue him. If you change to another, then wait a fortnight before you allow him to operate. Too much care in this respect cannot be taken. But I point out to you a still more serious danger.

There are persons who undertake to mesmerize others, who have some local disease, or are in feeble health. By so doing, they injure themselves, and also the subject. Such persons have no nervo-vital fluid to spare, and what little they have is in a diseased state, and unfit to be thrown upon the nervous system of another. I care not what the disease may be, by long persisting in mesmerizing a person, that disease will be, at length, communicated to the subject. Great caution, in this respect, should be observed by both parties, if they would not impair their health. Weakness of lungs, and even consumption, may be, by thirty or forty magnetizings, brought upon an individual, and send him to his grave. I therefore seriously admonish you to beware of this common danger. Never allow any person of a poor constitution to put you into this state; and I also warn those who are diseased, or even in delicate health, never to mesmerize others, for they will, by so doing, inflict upon themselves a serious injury

But, on the other hand, there is no danger in a healthy person magnetizing those who are diseased. As the operator imparts the nervo-vital fluid, and does not receive any in return, he is in no danger of taking the disease of his patient. Caution is, however, to be observed in taking the patient out of this state. He should not make the upward passes in such a manner as to throw the fluid on himself. If he do, he is in some danger of contracting the disease. An experienced magnetizer will understand how to avail himself of this caution.

Once more: there are persons who undertake to mag netize others who are entirely ignorant as to the mode of operation, and frequently bring persons into serious difficulty by getting alarmed, or otherwise thrown out of bias in their feelings. Several cases of this kind I have been called to attend to, in various sections, and some of a very serious character. No persons should undertake to mesmerize others until they shall have learned of some experienced magnetizer how to perform it, and made themselves acquainted with all the difficulties that may cluster around it.

Having attended to these important points, I will now turn your attention to local magnetism. By local magnetism, I mean the magnetizing of some part of the human body without charging the whole brain. Hence, the finger, the hand, the arm, the leg, yes, even the eyelid, the lip, or the tongue, may be mesmerized while the person is in the wakeful state, and so may be any of the phrenological organs. It is true, that this cannot be so easily done on persons who have never been mesmerized at all, as on those who have been thrown into the state.

If the brain has been once magnetically subdued, then there is no occasion, even if the amputation of a limb is to be performed, to magnetize any other part than the one to be subjected to the operation. If a person be very hard to mesmerize, then it will be proportionally difficult to mesmerize any limb. But it will be borne in mind, that however long it may take in successive sittings to magnetically subdue the brain, yet after that is once accomplished, then the person can, in future, be wholly mesmerized at any time in five minutes, and locally so in a much less period. Hence, should an arm be broken or mutilated, it will only be necessary to put that limb into the magnetic state, and it can be set or amputated without pain; and thus, by occasionally renewing the mesmeric action, it can be kept in this state and healed, without ever experiencing any suffering whatever.

I perceive that some smile in view of these statements. They are truly so wonderful, that incredulity adjures us to reject them. But they are, nevertheless, Heaven's unchanging truths, which cannot bend to circumstances, nor shape themselves to the belief or scepticism of men. They stand out in bold relief, and bid defiance to the sneers and scorns of mankind. A surgical operation has just been performed in Lowell on a lady while in the mesmeric state. A tumor was extracted from the shoulder, where it was necessary to cut to the depth of two inches. Dr. Shattuck was the magnetizer; and in the presence of several medical men of Lowell, one of whom was the operator, this tumor was removed without the slightest sensation of pain. This was not done in a corner, but publicly, and in the presence of several hundred spectators. It is too late in the day to cry "HUMBUG AND COLLUSION," for the battle is fought, and the victory is won, and the scale has turned in favor of truth, and turned with most preponderating weight, and on the stereotyped argument "HUMBUG AND COLLUSION," is written "TEKEL."

Well authenticated facts, and medical reports of operations in surgery and dentistry, performed under the energies of Mesmerism, in both continents, and without pain, are continually reaching us. And with this flood of light pouring upon the world, and when men of the first talents and science in the republic of letters, and out of all the various professions and denominations, are among its advocates, scepticism is not only waning, but justly losing its popularity. Those men have seriously investigated and weighed the matter, and they severally declare, as did the Rev. Mr. Pierpont, on the last evening, before two thousand hearers, in this house, "I have NO BELIEF nor UNBELIEF on this subject. I KNOW, I KNOW it to be so!" And now I ask, what ought the MERE OPINION, or the expressed UNBELIEF of even an honest sceptic, to weigh against the absolute and certain KNOWLEDGE of an equally honest, intelligent, and scientific man, whose character is above suspicion? I leave the candid to judge, and have only to say, that in the face of modesty, they have no right to call this science "HUMBUG AND COLLUSION."

Others pretend that the science of Animal Magnetism was condemned by the French Committee in Paris, among whom our illustrious Franklin was numbered. And as it received its condemnation under the scrutiny of such minds, therefore they conclude that it has no foundation in truth. There always have been, and still are, men who dare not think for themselves, but wholly lean upon the opinions of others. Their father, their doctor, their lawyer, and their minister, thought thus and so, and they think just so, too. Their fathers put down a central stake, gave them their length of line, and bid them travel round in that circle of revolving thought till the day of their death! All beyond that circle is darkness! Their field of thought is as exactly measured off to them, and just as legally bequeathed to them, as their farms. They received them both by inheritance. For the one they never LABORED, and for the other they never THOUGHT! And they never questioned the TRUTH of the one, any more than they did their title to the other!

But surely the French Committee did not deny the truth of the experiments produced, nor pronounce them "HUMBUG AND COLLUSION." They simply decided that the evidence adduced was not sufficient to prove that the magnetic state was caused by a FLUID proceeding from the magnetizer. They attributed the singular effects they witnessed to the power of the imagination. But it will also be remembered, that this committee were not all agreed, and hence appeared the remonstrance of the minority, which it would be well for modern sceptics to read, side by side with the report.

Many sceptics have been obliged, like the French Committee, to admit certain results as being truly wonderful, and, like them, attribute it to the force of the imagination. But to believe that the imagination can bring human beings into a state where limbs can be amputated, tumors cut out, teeth extracted, and broken bones set, and the whole healed without experiencing one throb of pain—to believe, I say, that the imagination can do all these wonders, in giving such boundless trifling pain, requires a far greater stretch of credulity to believe in the magnetic power! And surely if the imagination possesses the wonderful charm to bring the nervous system into a condition where we can bid defiance to pain, and gain a complete victory over the whole frightful army of human woes, then surely the science is equally important, possesses the same transcendent claims upon our benevolence, and the man who discovered that the imagination possessed this charm is worthy of the united thanks of all human-kind; and being dead, his bones are worthy to repose with the great men of the universe. In this case it will only be necessary to change its name, and call it—THE SCIENCE OF THE WONDERFUL POWER OF THE HUMAN IMAGINATION TO CHARM ALL PAIN.

Sorry:
The defect on the previous page was that way in the original book we reproduced.

LECTURE VI.

LADIES AND GENTLEMEN: In the first four lectures I delivered of the present course, I brought forward the philosophy of Mesmerism, and flatter myself that I have not only succeeded in establishing it as a science, but have shown it to be one of transcendent interest to the human race. Here love and benevolence stretch out a healing hand over a world groaning and travailing in pain. Those groans, by that silken hand, shall be hushed, and those pains be removed. There is a power basined up in the fountains of the soul, that has long been dormant. But it is rousing up and stirring itself for some mighty action, and is already beginning to gush forth in healing streams on the world. This science is in its infancy, is imperfectly understood, but yet it breathes the breath of mercy as a sovereign cure for all human woes.

In my last lecture, I answered several notes of inquiry, pointed out the dangers of Magnetism, refuted several common objections in re ation to its abuses, noticed the utility of the science in performing painful surgical operations, and took a friendly glance at the conduct of men in justifying their scepticism by pleading the general issue of the Report of the French Committee, and concluded by touching lightly upon the power of the human imagination.

I now stand before you in the confident conviction

that much good will result from my labors to the cause of benevolence and mercy. I am urged to repeat my course of lectures next week, but it will be out of my power to comply with this request at that time, but have consented to do so, week after next. As this will be my closing lecture for the present, I can render you no greater service than to show what connection this subject has with divine revelation. I am well aware that many will call me an enthusiast, and sneer at, and condemn me for thinking independently. But when the path of duty is plain, and when I am once satisfied of truth, I then go on, and reason, fearless of all consequences. Under such circumstances, I have nothing to do with the inquiry, what will men think of me? I care not what they think, and much less do I care what they say. I suffer no man to invade the sanctuary of my civil and religious rights, and dictate to me how I shall think, or what I shall believe, or what I shall proclaim. I therefore hold no one responsible for what I shall advance in this lecture, nor do I know as there is one, with whom I am connected, who will endorse my ideas.

I believe the doctrine of our Saviour to be a perfect doctrine, and exactly adapted to the bodies as well as to the souls of men. I believe that he is our example to follow, and as he went about doing good, healing sickness, and relieving distress of body, as well as preaching the gospel to heal the moral maladies of the soul, so it is our duty to do the same. It is, moreover, most evident that his doctrine, to the full extent he commanded his apostles to preach it, was to go down to all subsequent ages, so long as human beings should have a habitation on earth. And our Saviour just as much commanded his apostles to heal the sick, as he did to preach the gospel. Now I cannot believe that one half of the power and mercy of his doctrine should cease with the ministry of his apostles, and the other half continue. I cannot believe that its healing efficacy, so far as the body is concerned, should cease, and what was applicable to the soul should continue. If this be so, then what a favored generation of Christians existed in that day, so far, at least, as healing the body was concerned. It was said, in the apostolic age, "Is any man sick, let him send for the elders of the church, and let them lay their hands upon him and pray, and the sick shall recover." I believe this now, and so far as we have power and faith, it can be accomplished now as well as ever.

There is a difference between a miracle and a gift of healing. If an arm be palsied, we know that the difficulty exists in the brain, and that nothing more is necessary than to throw upon it a sufficient quantity of the nervous fluid to bring it into healthy action. The moment this is accomplished, the difficulty existing in the arm, which is but secondary, will be relieved. To restore this, would be a gift of healing, but not a miracle. What, then, would be a miracle? Answer: amputate an arm, and then cause a new one to grow out. Though healing diseases is sometimes called a miracle, yet when speaking of them specifically, they are not so denominated. Paul says, "God hath set some in the church; first, apostles; secondarily, prophets; thirdly, teachers; after that, miracles, then gifts of healings, helps, governments," etc. And there is not a scrap of evidence that these things were ever to cease while the generations of men endured.

Now if our Saviour restored a palsied arm, then there must something have passed from him to the person healed, in perfect accordance with the principles f animal life. It must, therefore, in this case, have been the nervous fluid, as this was the only substance that could have restored this arm.

It is undeniably true, that there was always something passed from our Saviour, when he exercised the gift of healing, to the person whom he restored. In evidence of this, you will recollect, that on one occasion, when he was called to visit a sick person, a multitude followed after, and thronged him. As he passed by, a woman, who had been afflicted with an issue of blood for twelve years, touched the hem of his garment, and was made whole. He turned himself around, and said, " Who touched me?" His disciples exclaimed, " Master, the multitude throng thee, and sayest thou, 'Who touched me?' But he perceived that virtue had gone out of him." The word VIRTUE, in this instance, does not mean moral goodness. It means FORCE, POWER, EFFICACY; the same as when we say a medicine has great VIRTUE in it.

Our Saviour so lived, and breathed, and moved in the divine Being, that he became one in communication with him; so that when the Father WILLED, he felt that will—He himself then willed, and it was accomplished. So, if any one bowed in reconciliation to God, he became one with the Saviour, so that the Redeemer also, felt that one's will. Such was the case of this woman. She willed in faith to be healed. The Saviour felt that will—He willed, and it was done. Now every being has power in proportion to the energy of his own will; but the energy of the will, depends upon the intrinsic greatness of that being's mind. And as a miracle is a thing performed by the energy of the will

SO THAT mind must be great in power and goodness, that is capable of performing a miracle. We sit down, and put forth the energy of a thousand wills, and at last produce but a small result.

The apostolic power was far greater, and in the same ratio, their results were more splendid and glorious. But still they had not the power of Christ. The leper said, "Lord, if thou WILT, thou canst make me clean. Jesus stretched forth his hand, and touched him, and said, I WILL, be thou clean, and his leprosy was cleansed." By a word, he put to right disabled limbs, and drew back life and warm gushing health to their abode. He put forth a greater energy—and said to the winds and waves, Peace! be still! His will fastened upon electricity in the heavens, equalized that fluid, hushed the winds, and calmed the waves. He opened the blind eye to the splendor of the noon-tide blaze, and instantly penciled on its retina, the universe. He opened the deaf ear, and poured into its once silent, but now vocal chambers, the harmony of rejoicing nature. He spoke, and the dead stirred in their graves, and rose up from their icy beds before him, and walked. That same dread voice shall speak with a living energy, that the very heavens shall hear, and the dead shall rise to die no more, and turn their eyes from the dark, ruinable tomb on the scenes of eternity! Mind and will in the Creator, still more increased, move unnumbered worlds. That same will, now infinite and immutable, puts forth creative energy. He spake, and it was done; He commanded, and it stood fast; laid the measures thereof, and stretched the line upon it when the morning stars sang together, and all the sons of God shouted for joy. Hence, every grade of mind, from the humblest up to apostolic greatness; up to angel and archangel, cherubim and seraphim; up to Jesus Christ, till it reach the infinite Jehovah, has power proportionate to its greatness and goodness. Hence, it will be readily understood, that a miracle is nothing more than a result produced by mind itself, independent of all physical energy, except that one substance which is put into motion by the living mind.

It may perhaps be said, that the apostles were inspired to heal, and as we are not inspired, therefore we do not possess the gift to heal. On this principle I might reply, that the apostles were inspired to preach, and as we are not inspired, therefore, we have no gift to preach! I grant that the apostles were inspired to preach and to heal, because it was not possible, that at the starting point, they had any other means for preparation. But now men preach, not by inspiration, but because they feel it to be their duty. So men must now heal because they feel it to be their duty.

It is by no means to be expected that we can come up, at once, to apostolic power. No; our faith is too weak. But let us bring up our children in the faith as we ought, and they will learn to mesmerize as naturally as they learn to walk. Their concentrativeness will become largely developed. Their children will be born with more favorably developed heads, and become greater in goodness, until at length the whole apostolic power will return to the earth in all its primitive splendor. It is SPIRITUALISM, because it is the innate power of the living mind, executed through the agency of the will. It is that power which created worlds, for this was done by the will of God. It is that power by which worlds are governed, and creatures ruled, for this is also done by the will of God. It is that power by which we make impressions reciprocally upon each other, for this is done by the will of man. And lastly, it is "that power which shall awake the dead from dreamless slumber into thoughts of heaven," for this will be done by the will of God, and there is no medium, only electricity, through which he can come in contact with his creatures.

I will now bring forward a few cases from Scripture, to show that the living have been thrown into a singular slumber by the very presence of immortal beings. Indeed, there is scarcely an instance where angels have appeared to men, but what it has had this effect. I will bring forward those that first strike my mind, regardless of their arrangement.

It will be remembered, that when John the Revelator was in the isle of Patmos, he had this vision: "And being turned, I saw seven golden candlesticks, and in the midst of the seven candlesticks, one like unto the Son of man, clothed with a garment down to the foot and girt about the paps with a golden girdle. His head and his hair were white like wool; as white as snow, and his eyes were as a flame of fire; and his feet like unto fine brass as if they had been burned in a furnace, and his voice as the sound of many waters. And he had in his right hand seven stars, and out of his mouth went a sharp two-edged sword, and his countenance was as the sun shineth in his strength. And when I saw him I fell down at his feet as one that is dead." Here then, is a singular slumber approximating death.

Our Saviour, when he was transfigured on Mount Tabor, took Peter, James, and John with him. For a moment he was changed into his resurrection splendor and met Moses and Elias in glory. The sacred historian, in describing the scene, says, " And his face did shine as the sun, and his raiment became shining, exceeding white as snow, white as the light, so as no fuller on earth can white them, and there appeared unto them Moses and Elias talking with him. And Peter and them that were with him were heavy with sleep; and Peter said, Lord, it is good for us to be here. Let us build here three tabernacles; one for thee, one for Moses, and one for Elias; not knowing what he said." That is, when he came out of this sleep he did not recollect what he had said. They were thrown into this state by the very presence of these minds.

Do you remember that after our Lord had eaten his valedictory supper with his disciples, he went into the garden of Gethsemane, and commanded them to watch? He went a few steps from them and prayed in agony, and sweat as it were drops of blood falling to the ground. The guardian angel of Jesus Christ appeared from heaven strengthening him. The apostles fell into a deep sleep. Though this was a scene of great interest to them, yet it seems that the presence of this ange thus affected them.

He was nailed to the cross between two malefactors, to darken his glory and blot his name. The Jews were nis accusers, and the Romans his executioners. Hence, the world was combined against him, while his own disciples forsook him in that dark hour of peril. The universe thus combined against him, mocking and deriding him, and covering him with disgrace, even nature herself stepped forward as it were, and with a mighty hand wiped off that disgrace, and sustained him in his majesty. The sun w'thdrew his light, rolled back his chariot, midnight darkness spread her robe of sackcloth upon his brilliant disc, and hung the world in the dark shroud of mourning. Earthquakes awoke from their tartarean dens and thundered. The earth shook, the rocks rent, the graves opened, all nature roused up and there brought to a centre all that is grand, awful, and sublime in her realms, as the magnanimous sufferer expired! He was conveyed to his tomb, and Roman soldiers were there stationed to guard it. Soldiers whose business it was to die,—who had been brought up in tented fields of war, and who had from childhood encountered hardships and toils, fatigues and dangers. They were men, who had often bared their bosoms to the shafts of battle, and undismayed listened to its stormy voice, and who knew not what it was to quail beneath the glance of a mortal eye. Such men as these, were stationed to guard that tomb, and hold the Prince of Life in death. But—

"An angel's arm can't snatch him from the grave;
Legions of angels can't confine him there."

On the morning of the third day, the last grand scene in this interesting drama was opened. The guardian angel of Jesus Christ was once more dispatched from the eternal throne. He descended from heaven, and an earthquake shook creation. He approached the tomb of the Holy Sleeper, and stood before it. "He rolled back the stone from the door of the sepulchre and sat upon it. His countenance was like the lightning, and his raiment white as snow; and for fear of him, the keepers did shake, and become as dead men!"

What, I ask, was it that threw them into this slumber, with feelings of a cold shuddering fear, so nigh approaching the dead? I answer, it was the WILL of this angel, whose countenance was like the lightning, that sunk them into a motionless sleep. It was his WILL which struck the vibrations of terror through the dark chambers of their souls, and withered them to the earth.

I should like to notice the circumstance of Paul being caught up into the third heavens—whether out of the body or in the body, he could not tell—of Peter falling into a trance when he went upon the house-top to pray, and of Zacharias being struck dumb in the temple; but time will not permit.

I close, by returning my sincere thanks to the Moderators, for the good order they have preserved; to the various Committees, for their patient examinations and impartial reports of the experiments performed; and to the ladies and gentlemen, for their faithful attendance and respectful attention, and also for the good feelings they have uniformly manifested towards the lecturer during the entire course, which is now brought to a termination.

NOTE.—FROM CHANNING.

"We are created with a susceptibility of pain, and severe pain. This is a part of our nature, as truly as our susceptibility of enjoyment. God has implanted it, and has thus opened in the very centre of our being a fountain of suffering. We carry it within us, and can no more escape it than we can our power of thought. We are apt to throw our pains on outward things as their causes. It is the fire, the sea, the sword, or human enmity, which gives us pain. But there is no pain in the fire or the sword, which passes thence into our souls. The pain begins and ends in the soul itself. Outward things are only the occasions. Even the body has no pain in it, which it infuses into the mind. Of itself, it is incapable of suffering. This hand may be cracked, crushed in the rack of the inquisitor, and that burnt in a slow fire; but in these cases it is not the fibres, the blood-vessels, the bones of the hand which endure pain. These are merely connected, by the will of the Creator, with the springs of pain in the soul. Here, here is the only origin and seat of suffering. If God so willed, the gashing of the flesh with a knife, the piercing of the heart with a dagger, might be the occasion of exquisite delight. We know that, in the heat of battle, a wound is not felt, and that men, dying for their faith by instruments of torture, have expired with triumph on their lips. In these cases, the spring of suffering in the mind is not touched by the lacerations of the body, in consequence of the absorbing action of other principles of the soul. All suffering is to be traced to the susceptibility, the capacity of pain, which belongs to our nature, and which the Creator has implanted ineradicably within us."

PSYCHOLOGY;

OR THE

SCIENCE OF THE SOUL,

CONSIDERED

PHYSIOLOGICALLY AND PHILOSOPHICALLY.

WITH AN APPENDIX, CONTAINING NOTES OF MESMERIC AND PSYCHICAL EXPERIENCE.

BY JOSEPH HADDOCK, M.D..

WITH ENGRAVINGS OF THE NERVOUS SYSTEM.

NEW YORK:
PUBLISHED BY SAMUEL R. WELLS,
No. 389 BROADWAY.
1871.

Entered, according to act of Congress, in the year 1869, by
FOWLERS AND WELLS,
in the Clerk's Office of the District Court for the Southern District of New York

PREFACE.

This work was recently published in LONDON under the following title: "SOMNOLISM AND PSYCHEISM, otherwise VITAL MAGNETISM or MESMERISM: considered Physiologically and Philosophically: being the substance of lectures delivered under the auspices of the Bolton Mechanics' Institution; with an Appendix, containing notes of Mesmeric and Psychical experience."

We have taken the liberty to omit, in our title, such terms as may not be fully understood by all readers; taking care, however, to make it equally appropriate.

The subject on which this work treats, is fast becoming of the most absorbing interest to our people, and it gives us pleasure to place before the American public the conclusions of those who have penetrated most deeply into these supposed mysteries of nature.

We look forward, hopefully, for the time when we may KNOW those things which the world have always "believed" to be truths. Nor is it POSSIBLE for ANY influence to LIMIT the desires of the human mind to in-

PREFACE.

vestigate, until it has penetrated every subject which comes within the range of its comprehension.

May this work go forth to "open the eyes of the (spiritually) blind," and excite to further investigation and reflection those minds best capacitated to evolve "new light" on intellectual and spiritual vision.

This is a progressive age, not only in moral and physical development, but in spiritual science.

AMERICAN PUBLISHERS.

CLINTON HALL,
131 NASSAU ST., NEW YORK.

TABLE OF CONTENTS.

                                               PAGE.

INTRODUCTION TO PSYCHOLOGY.   8–12

Characteristics of the age.—Chemistry a new science.—Geology.—A new world without and a new world within man.—Knowledge not confined to superstitions, assumptions, barren negations, nor skeptical philosophy, but something real—the nature, powers, and capabilities of his being.—Assistance afforded us by a knowledge of magnetism, or psycheism.—Discoveries and doctrines of an enlightened physiology.—Laws and developments of the world of mind capable of being displayed before our physical sight.—The curious and interesting phenomena displayed by mesmerism too often neglected.—Authority too often no aid in eliciting truth.—The most astounding statements of mesmeric experiments not more wonderful than universally admitted facts.—Wonder-working telegraph.—A dreaming theory or enthusiastic vision a reality.—Mesmerism the discovery of a new method of working an old medium.—A spiritual and a natural body.—The blessing of sight a fact that all philosophers have been heretofore unable to explain.—Our present standard of knowledge should not be the measure of future acquirements.—Psycheism a means of acquainting ourselves with the distinctive qualities of mind.

ORIGIN OF MESMERISM, ... 12–17

In records of past ages extraordinary cures ascribed to miracle, or magic.—Magnetism discovered toward the close of the last century.—Brief history of Mesmer and his discovery, and method of applying it.

PHENOMENA AND PHYSIOLOGY OF MESMERISM, . 17–60

Stages or degrees of mesmeric influence.—How they are to be understood and accounted for.—The brain and nervous system the medium through which the mind acts upon the body.—Illustrations and descriptions of the brain, etc. (see list of illustrations).—Methods of inducing the somnolent state.—Remarkable facts.—Catalepsy.—Phantasy.—Transfer of Feeling.—Phreno-mesmerism.—Cerebral lucidity, or clairvoyance.

PHILOSOPHY AND PSYCHOLOGY OF MESMERISM, 60–78

Clairvoyance the internal sight of the soul.—Sight without the aid of the eye not more difficult of explanation, when thoroughly examined, than ordinary vision.—Description of the human eye.—Clairvoyance and ordinary vision assume the same basis.—Mind and matter, soul and body, psyche or animus.—The external of the spirit.—Psycheism, or the science of the soul as manifested in nature.—Psychological change induced by mesmerism.—The superior state.—Independent clairvoyance.—The general power of the sensorium to form images within itself of objects that are without itself.—Are all persons subject to mesmeric influence? and why all cannot be made clairvoyant.

TABLE OF CONTENTS.

APPENDIX.

PAGE.

MESMERIC AND PSYCHICAL EXPERIENCE, . . 78–95

Case of E. L.—Injury of the knee.—Treatment.—The vapor of ether.—Its effects.—Hypnotism.—Phreno-magnetic developments.—Catalepsy.—Rigidity.—Attraction.—Delusion.—Susceptibility without the mesmeric sleep.—Personal influence.—Mesmerism without contact.—Tooth extraction.—Discovery of lucidity and clairvoyance.—Reading in a mesmeric state.—Pictures a reality.—Description of absent persons and objects.—Picture of the cat.—Emma's visit to the queen.—To the planets.—Omnipresent vision.—The cash-box stolen.—Successful clairvoyant search for it, and interview with the thief.—Tracing the route and circumstances of a traveler.

CLAIRVOYANCE AS APPLIED TO PHYSIOLOGY AND MEDICINE, ... 95–100

Description of man's internal structure.—The application of this power one of the most legitimate uses of clairvoyance.—Discovery of disease by the handwriting of a person at a distance, also by a lock of hair.—Remarkable cure of insanity by the aid of clairvoyant prescriptions.—Tasting medicines through bottles.—The exalted sense.

SPONTANEOUS EXTASIS, OR TRANCE, . . . 101–106

A higher and more interior character.—Scenery and nature of the spirit-world.—Recollections, predictions, and verifications.—Rigidity and insensibility to pain during a trance.—Communications with the spirits of the dead.—Finding a Bible and a particular place in it.—Man represented as a spiritual being after death, and his sensational perception.—The male and female sexes retained.—Growth of infants.—The living influenced by the spirits of the dead.—Spirits not subject to the laws of time or space.—The body only the "*shell*" of the spirit.

PRACTICE AND USE OF MESMERISM, . . . 106–109

A simple process.—Depends more on peculiar constitution of the subject than power of the operator.—Modes of operating.—Curative influence of mesmerism.—Necessity of Mesmerisers.—Mesmeric institutions.

ILLUSTRATIONS.

1. Cerebro-Spinal Axis.
2. The Nerves of the Brain.
3. View of the Top of the Brain.
4. Side View of the Brain.
5. Front View of a Section of the Spinal Cord and Nerve.
6. View of the Structure of the Brain
7. The Right Hemisphere of the Brain
8. The Cerebellum.
9. Horizontal Section of the Brain.
10. The Cerebellum, etc.
11. Parts about the Base of the Brain.
12. Right Hemisphere of the Brain.
13. Vertical Section of the Brain.
14. Perpendicular Section of the Brain
15. Right Hemisphere of the Brain.
16. Ganglionic System of Vegetable Life
17. Spinal Cord, etc.

INTRODUCTION.

1. One of the striking characteristics of the present age, is the vast amount of knowledge respecting external objects, which has been accumulated in a comparatively short period. For within the compass of human life, so extensive has been the discovery of the physical properties of natural substances, that Chemistry, although of ancient date, may be considered as a new science; and Geology has opened a new world to human enquiry. While man has thus been permitted to increase his knowledge of the world without him, we might reasonably expect that some additional knowledge would be acquired of the world within him. That his knowledge would not be confined to the superstitions of the dark ages, or to the assumptions of self-constituted authority on the one hand; nor to the barren negations of a sceptical philosophy on the other hand; but that something real, positive, and satisfactory, should be learnt respecting his own constitution. For what knowledge can be so interesting to man, as a knowledge of himself? of the nature, powers, and capabilities of his own being.

2. To every calm, and well-informed enquirer, it will, I think, be evident, that the remarkable phenomena of what is called Mesmerism—or, as it is con-

sidered that it may more properly be called—PSYCHE-ISM, *rightly interpreted*, do afford us the means of acquiring a knowledge of the laws and nature of the psychical, or mental part of our being, as much transcending what is commonly known, as the recent discoveries in magnetism and electricity exceed the ancient ideas of those natural powers; and at the same time, they afford us the means of becoming better acquainted with the more abstruse points in our bodily organization also.

3. The discoveries and doctrines of an enlightened physiology, teach us, that all the forms and forces of the entire universe are found in their highest perfection in the bodily form of man; and that in him, as the *Microcosm*, or little world, is to be found all that exists in the *Macrocosm*, or great world of the universe. And as in the great world without us, the most astonishing and transforming powers are displayed by those subtle, imponderable, and invisible elements, which elude the most acute physical senses, even when aided by the highest artificial means; so in the world within us, the most wonderful and unexpected powers are manifested by those psychical or mental operations, by which the laws and developments of the world of mind are capable of openly being displayed before our physical sight.

4. But the curious and interesting phenomena displayed by Mesmerism, instead of being calmly and carefully investigated by all enquiring minds, especially by those whose profession or pursuits ought to have interested them in the enquiry, have, in too many instances, been scornfully and contemptuously neglected.

Authority, instead of lending its aid to elicit the **truth**, has rather scowled upon the attempt which has been made to lift the veil under which truth has been concealed; and in some cases, has misrepresented the character and intentions of those, who, at any cost, were determined to seek her for themselves. It is possible indeed, that the very remarkable results said to flow from the enquiry—results, so different to the expectations and ideas of a materializing age, and in some respects, disclosing matters which seem to clash with established opinions—may have been the reason, for this unfair, and certainly unphilosophical mode of proceeding. But, granting that the most astounding statements made by mesmeric experiments are true, they are not, when properly considered, more wonderful than things now universally admitted as facts. Look at the wonder-working electric telegraph! The elements on which that invention rests, must be as old as the present order of things; yet if any one in the middle of the last century had ventured to assert that, by human ingenuity, electricity or magnetism could be made to transmit *human thought* with mathematical precision, and yet with the velocity of light, he would have been set down by the practical authorities of that age as a dreaming theorist, or an enthusiastic visionary. To *us*, however, the visionary theory has become a reality; and yet what magnetism or electricity *really are*, is no more known to us than it was to our great-grandfathers. The truth is, the mode has been elicited, by which certain comparative unknown mediums may be practically applied to subserve the purposes of social life; and herein, and for all practical purposes, consists the *useful discovery*. If we shall never know what magnetism and electricity in themselves really are, we certainly do know much of the mode by which their laws and powers may be developed and manifested: we have discovered a mode of working mediums altogether unknown to our ancestors.

5. Just so, I apprehend, it is with the discoveries of Mesmerism. Here is, in fact, a discovery of a new mode of working an old medium. That mind and matter are both necessary to form the peculiar organism we call man, is no new doctrine; but the true nature of the body, as the mind's medium or instrument, and of the *necessary organization* of that superior indwelling power—the soul or mind, which directs and controls the outward form, has been somewhat overlooked. Metaphysicians have studied mind irrespective of form or matter; and some philosophers would resolve all things into material operation, irrespective of mind. I believe that fact and demonstrative evidence will prove both classes of philosophers to be wrong. From Divine Revelation we know that there is both spirit or mind, and matter; both a spiritual body and a natural body. These cardinal truths will be found to lie at the bottom of all mesmeric experience, and from that experience, the *a priori* statements of the Scriptures will receive abundant confirmation. And we shall see that in our present state of existence, if we wish to study mind or spirit, we must study it as manifested in its divinely appointed, and true correspondent instrument, the material bodily organization.

6. With some of the mind's operations, and the bodily functions and sensations thence ensuing, we have

become so familiar, that we scarcely ever stop to think of the perpetual miracles involved in our daily experience. Thus the great blessing of sight involves, as we shall point out presently, a fact which all the philosophers that have ever lived have been unable to explain! Yet when some manifestation of mind or spirit, which has hitherto eluded general notice, is brought before us, although it may not be more inexplicable than natural sight, yet we are apt to deny the possibility of the declared manifestation, simply because we were not previously acquainted with it—apt to make our present standard of knowledge the measure by which all future acquisitions are to be estimated. Sometimes too, we are told authoritatively, that it is impossible for us to know any thing of mind or spirit. What, I ask, do we know of matter? Simply some of its *laws* and *properties;* and from these we predicate its *qualities*. So it is with mind or spirit; Mesmerism, or more truly Psycheism, furnishes us with a means of acquiring an experimental acquaintance with some of its most distinctive qualities—distinctive I mean with respect to the qualities of inert matter. Whether we shall ever know what spirit or what matter really is, remains for a higher stage of existence to determine. It is privilege enough to be enabled to know something of the laws and properties of that higher and imperishable organism, to which our outward bodily organism is subservient.

SOMNOLISM AND PSYCHEISM

ORIGIN OF MESMERISM.

7. In the records of past ages, we have many statements of remarkable mental or psychical manifestations, and also of the performance of extraordinary cures, by mental or moral agency, which ignorance and superstition have ascribed to *miracle* or *magic*. And hence, cases resting on the best historical authority, have been doubted, and even denied in later times. Toward the close of the last century, the existence of some of these powers was discovered, partly from accident and partly from research; and to the agency by which they were accomplished, the name of Animal Magnetism was applied by its modern discoverer—Mesmer. This individual has been represented in works of authority as an impostor and cheat, and as owing his celebrity entirely to the silly credulity of imaginative people. Few persons who have really taken the trouble to enquire into the matter, would now hazard such an assertion; yet, whether from ignorance of the true cause of the phenomena he witnessed, or from a desire to mystify the subject, it must be admitted that he both did and said many things which justified suspicion.

8. Anton Mesmer was born in 1734, at Mersburg, in the shores of the Lake of Constance; and died in his native place in 1815, at the advanced age of eighty-one. At the age of forty-two he took the degree of Doctor of Medicine, in the University of Vienna. He appears to have been a man of an imaginative cast of mind; for the inaugural Thesis he published on obtaining his degree, was "On the influence of the Planets on the Human Body." Such a mind, if likely to fall into many errors, was still open for the reception of any new ideas which might present themselves; and was not prone, as men of a more sceptical cast, to reject any new truth, because it did not harmonize with preconceived opinions. The then Professor of Astronomy, at Vienna, believed in the efficacy of the loadstone as a remedy in human disease; and he had invented a peculiar form of magnetized steel plates, which, it is said, he applied to the cure of disease with much success. Mesmer obtained from the Astronomer, who was his personal friend, these magnets, and applied them in his own way; and it is said, with such striking results, that he communicated them to the Astronomer, who published an account of them, but attributed the cures performed to the *form of the plates*, and merely represented Mesmer as a physician employed by him to use them. Mesmer, who had discovered the peculiar mode of using them to insure success—that was, in fact, by *manipulations*, now called Passes—was indignant at this, and accused his friend of a violation of the confidence placed in him. The result was a controversy between the parties; each accusing the other. Notwithstanding this quarrel,

Mesmer proceeded in his own way, and acquired considerable popularity. But, whether from indiscretion on his part, or jealousy on the part of others, he was opposed by the scientific authorities of Vienna, and was ultimately obliged to quit that city.

9. In the year 1778, two years after obtaining his degree, he arrived at Paris, whither his popularity appears to have preceded him; for we are told, even by his enemies, that upon his opening public apartments in that gay metropolis, for the reception of patients, they were speedily crowded by the numbers who daily resorted to them, including all classes, from the peer to the peasant; and that hundreds were ready to testify to the cures wrought upon their own persons by the Great Magnetizer. Now, making every allowance for *imagination* or *fancy*, striking results must have followed his treatment, or no such enthusiasm could have been raised in his behalf. A French physician became a disciple of Mesmer, and is said speedily to have acquired the best practice in Paris. So great, in fact, was Mesmer's success, that the French Government took up the matter, and offered him a large annual income, if he would communicate his secret, and they appear to have thought so highly of the USE to which this new agent might be applied, that they actually proposed to guarantee him a large sum, even if a commission appointed to examine the subject should make an unfavorable report! Mesmer, however, did not accede to the government proposal. After some time, and divers vicissitudes, the sum of £14,000 was raised by his disciples, whom he had instructed in his art, but whom he did not consider entitled to practice

it publicly—a right which they considered themselves to possess. Mesmer then returned to his native place; and this has been represented as " running away from his dupes;" but it appears that he retained faith in his views, and in his last illness sought relief from his own discovery.

10. As Mesmer's discoveries arose out of the use of magnets, it is not surprising that he should consider Magnetism as the agent by which the effects he witnessed were produced. He therefore taught that there was a fluid, or gas, universally diffused, which influenced the earth, and planets, and all animated bodies, and this fluid he called " Animal Magnetism." He considered that it was capable of healing diseases of the nerves immediately, and other diseases mediately; that it perfected the action of medicines, and tended to promote favorable crises in disease; and that in Animal Magnetism, nature presented a universal method of healing the diseases, and preserving the health of mankind. The great end of Mesmer's proceedings, appears, therefore, to have been USE—the application of a remedy for human suffering; and he does not appear to have been aware of the more curious, and distinctly psychical phenomena elicited by later enquirers. To the Marquis de Puysegur, a French nobleman, one of Mesmer's disciples, is attributed the discovery of the faculty called Clairvoyance, in the year 1784.

11. For the sake of brevity, I omit describing Mesmer's mode of operating, save that among other means for acting on his patients, he had a sort of box, filled with iron filings and pounded glass, placed in the centre of the room where they assembled; and that they each

were placed in connection with it, by means of polished metal rods, which they held in their hands; and the patients were further united and connected by means of a chain encircling them. When the French Commissioners applied to this box the usual tests for *terrestrial* magnetism, and found no indication of ordinary magnetic influence, they reported that the whole was the work of *imagination*, meaning *fancy;* yet admitting that cures were effected. This Commission seems to have been both a prejudiced and unfair one. The name of Dr. Franklin occurs among the Commissioners, but he was at the time unwell, and incapable of attending to the enquiry; and while the public report condemned Mesmer and his proceedings, one of the Commissioners, who had paid the greatest attention to the proceedings, published a private or individual report favorable to him. But in the year 1826, the French Government appointed a second Commission, and their Report, published in 1831, fully admits the truth of all the phenomena usually ascribed to Animal Magnetism. However, our business is not so much with the opinions of Mesmer, or that of his friends or enemies, as with that of the facts and phenomena associated with his name. It was soon discovered that the steel rods had but little if any thing to do with the phenomena produced; but the name of Animal Magnetism continued to be used, and is still used on the Continent, and by this name the practice was introduced into England a few years ago. But the English enquirers into this remarkable human faculty, finding that the use of a name, which implied the existence of a fluid which could not be demonstrated to the senses, was frequently turned into an argument against facts which admitted of complete demonstration, adopted out of respect to the memory of Mesmer, and to avoid the appearance of the adoption of any theory of their own, the name of MESMERISM; just as Magnetism is applied to the properties of the loadstone, from Magnes, the ancient reputed discoverer of its powers, or Galvanism, to the discoveries of Galvani. We therefore proceed to notice the facts and phenomena associated with the names of Mesmerism, or Animal Magnetism, and shall endeavor to ascertain the Laws and Causes to which these phenomena may be referred.

PHENOMENA AND PHYSIOLOGY OF MESMERISM.

12. There are several stages or degrees of what is called Mesmeric Influence; or, in other words, the Mesmeric or Psychic State, involves *a variety of states*, having one common character, but presenting widely differing phenomena. Thus, there is *simple Mesmeric* DROWSINESS or SLEEP; COMA, or more profound sleep; INSENSIBILITY TO PAIN; this, I believe, only occurs when the Mesmeric Coma is fully established, and most of the external senses, together with the proper consciousness of external objects is rendered dormant; and the internal faculty of imagination is called into activity, without the guidance of true reason. PHANTASY, or that state in which the Mesmerised

person takes the mere suggestions of the mind of the operator to be realities. PHRENO-MESMERISM, or the manifestation of the Phrenological sentiments and feelings, which is but another form of simple imaginative action; TRANSFER OF STATE AND FEELING, or that Imaginative action which causes the patient to feel what is done to the Mesmeriser, as if it were done to him; MENTAL ATTRACTION, or apparent Magnetic drawing of the person of the patient, even contrary to his inclination. CEREBRAL LUCIDITY, or apparent illumination of the Brain; with other forms of what is called CLAIRVOYANCE; but which I think would be better called INNER VISION, or INTERNAL, or SPIRITUAL SIGHT. Assuming, therefore, for the present, that these phenomena exhibit a series of great and important facts, which cannot be set aside, neither by reason nor ridicule, I proceed at once to enquire—How we are to understand them? In what way to account for the curious and interesting manifestations thus cast upon our notice?

13. We must now therefore examine the *medium* by which the mind acts upon the bodily organization—namely, the BRAIN and NERVOUS SYSTEM. It is common to speak of the nervous system, as consisting of the brain, the spinal marrow, and the nerves springing from them. This arrangement is true enough as far as it goes; but it is not sufficiently particular for our purpose. For upon examining the interior of a human head, it will be found that every individual *has two distinct brains*. These two brains are very different in size as well as form and convolution. The upper and very much larger portion, and which in fact

CEREBRO-SPINAL AXIS.

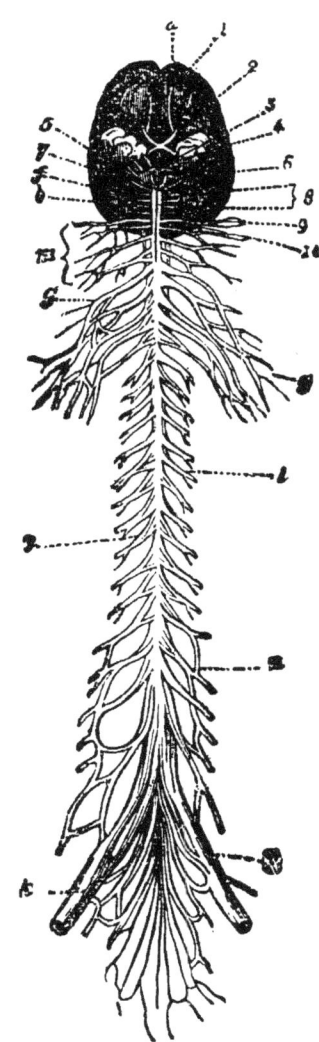

a, The brain.
b, Cerebellum.
f, Medulla oblongata.
g g, Nerves distributed to the arms.
h h, Great sciatic nerve distributed to the lower extremities.
l, Dorsal, and n, Lumber nerves.
m, Plexus of cervical nerves.
1, Olfactory nerve.
2, Optic nerve.
3, 4, 5, 6, The third, fourth, fifth, and sixth nerves
7, Portio dura of the seventh nerve
8, Auditory nerve and par vagum.
9, Hypoglossal nerve.
10. Sub-occipital nerve.

THE NERVES OF THE BRAIN.

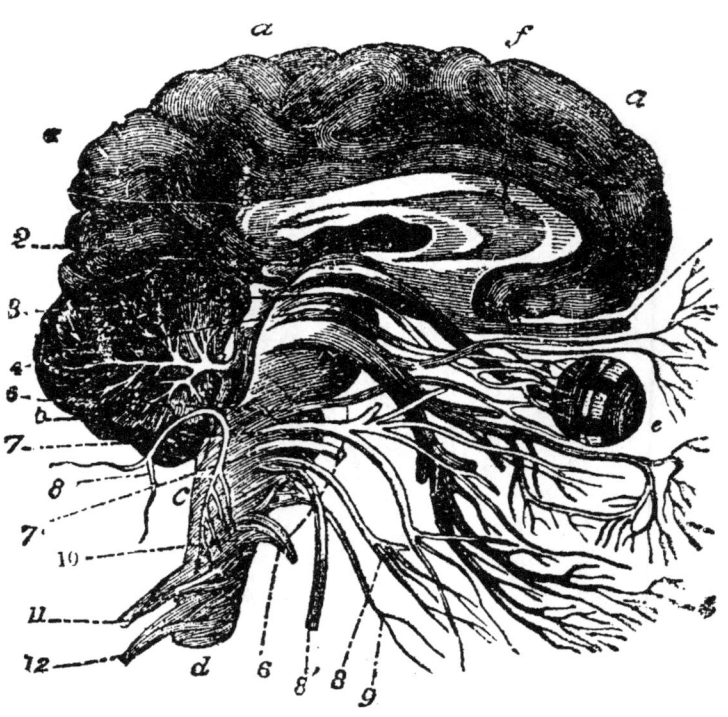

a a a, Convolutions of the brain.
b, Cerebellum and arbor vitæ, or tree of life.
c, Medulla oblongata.
d, Upper part of the spinal cord.
e, Eye.
f, Lateral ventricle.
o, Corpus callosum.
n, Pineal gland.
s, Quadrigeminal bodies.
1, Olfactory nerve.
2, Optic nerve.
3, 4, 5, 6, Third, fourth, fifth, and sixth nerves.
5', 5'', Branches of the fifth nerve.
7, Portio dura of the seventh nerve.
7', Auditory nerve.
8, Glossopharyngeal nerve.
8', Par vagum.
8'', Spinal accessory nerve.
9, Hypoglossal nerve.
10, Sub-occipital nerve.
11, 12, First and second cervical nerves.

VIEW OF THE TOP OF THE BRAIN.

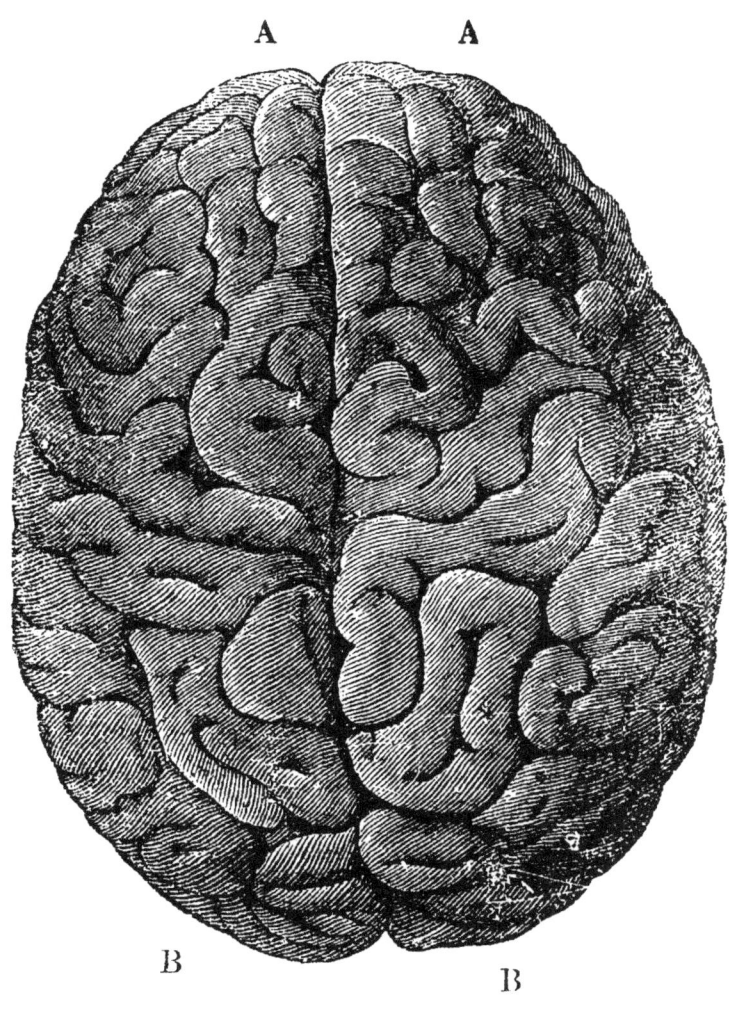

AA, Front part of the brain.
AA, BB, Right and left hemispheres.

SIDE VIEW OF THE BRAIN.

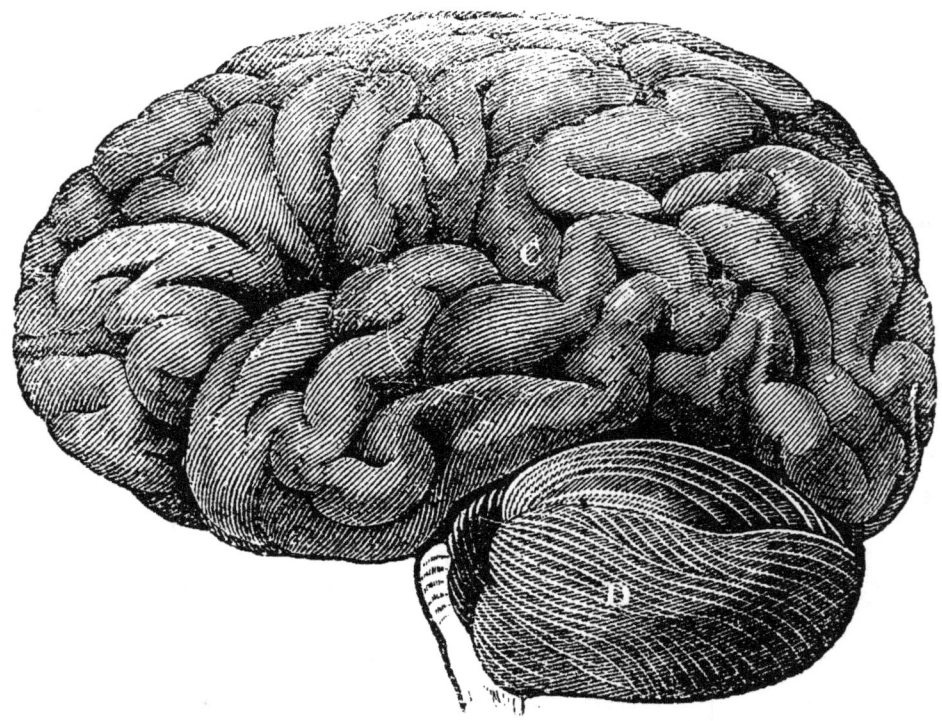

C—Cerebrum. D—Cerebellum. E—Medulla oblongata.

FRONT VIEW OF A SECTION OF THE SPINAL CORD AND NERVES

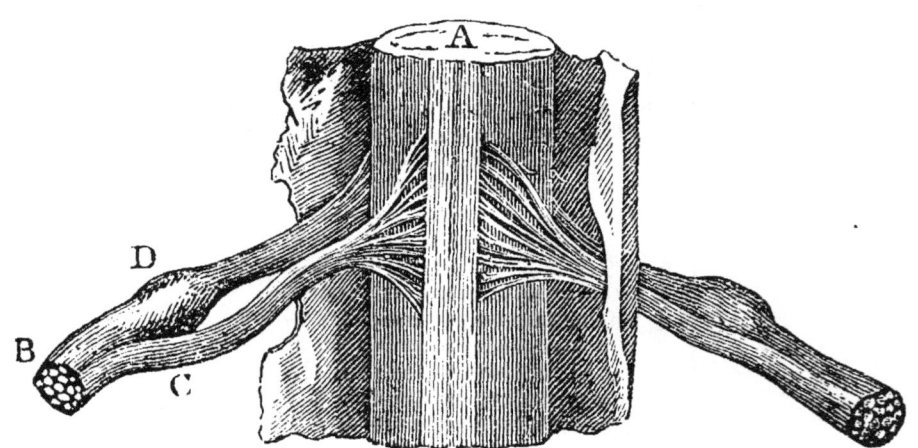

A—Spinal cord. B—Spinal Nerve. C—Motor branch of spinal nerve. D—Ganglion of posterior branch of spinal nerve.

VIEW OF THE STRUCTURE OF THE BRAIN.

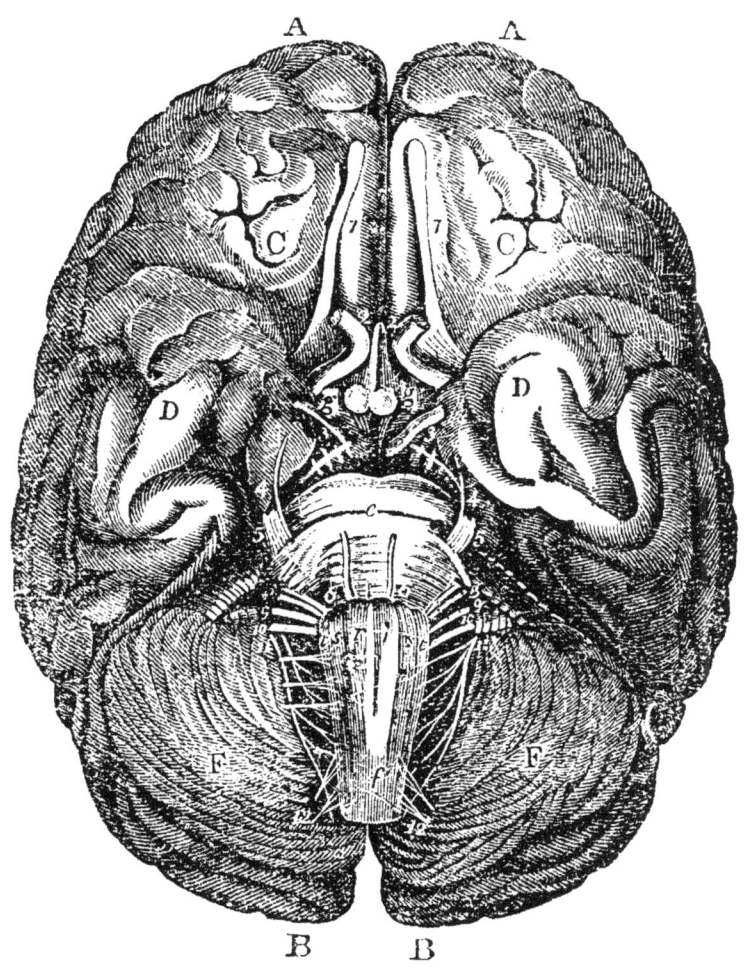

AB, AB, Are the right and left hemispheres of the brain.
FF, The cerebellum.
AA, The anterior lobe.
e e, The line which denotes the separation between the anterior lobe and the middle lobe
DD, The middle lobe.
BB, The posterior lobe.
e, The *pons Varolii*, which brings the two sides of the cerebellum into communication. It is also named the *Tuber annulare*.
f, The *Medulla oblongata*.
r r, The *Corpora pyramidalia*.
s s, The *Corpora olivaria*.
t t, The *Corpora restiformia* are on the opposite side of the corpora pyramidalia.

1. First pair, or olfactory nerves, arise by three origins. These unite and proceed forward and inward in a groove in the inferior surface of the anterior lobes of the brain, and form a greyish swelling or ganglion. From this ganglion a great number of filaments proceed through the cribriform plate of the ethmoid bone, and are distributed upon the mucous membrane of the nose. It is the nerve of the sense of smell.

2. Second pair, or optic, arise principally from the anterior *corpora quadrigemina*. Each nerve passes outward through the optic foramen of the sphenoid bone, and is expanded upon the retina. It is the nerve of the sense of sight.

3. Third pair, or *motores oculorum*, originate from the motor tract of the spinal cord, immediately after they have passed through the *pons Varolii*. Each nerve escapes through the sphenoidal fissure, and supplies five of the muscles within the orbit with motor filaments.

4. Fourth pair, or *trochleares*, originate from the *processus e cerebello ad testes* and *valvula* of Vieussens. Each nerve passes out from the cranium at the sphenoidal fissure, and is entirely distributed upon the superior oblique muscles of the eyeball. It is a motor nerve.

5. Fifth pair. These nerves issue from the surface of the brain, near the junction of the *pons Varolii* and *crus cerebelli*, but actually arise from the restiform bodies. Each nerve escapes from the cranium by three separate openings, and is extensively distributed upon the orbit and other parts of the face. Part of the filaments of this nerve are *sensitive*, and part *motor*.

6. Sixth pair originate from the pyramidal bodies, as they are about to enter the *pons Varolii*. Each nerve escapes through the sphenoidal fissure, and is entirely distributed upon the external rectus muscle of the eyeball. It is a motor nerve.

7. *Portio dura* of the seventh pair originate from the restiform bodies. Each nerve is extensively distributed in the muscles of the face and external ear. It is the motor nerve of the muscles of expression of the face.

8. *Portio mollis* of the seventh pair, or auditory nerves, (eighth pair of some authors), arise principally from a small grey swelling on the upper surface of the restiform bodies at the side of the fourth ventricle. Each nerve is distributed upon the internal ear, and is the nerve of the sense of hearing.

9. Glossopharyngeal nerves, or upper division of the eighth pair, (ninth pair of some authors), arise from the restiform bodies near the sulcus which separates them from the olivary, and are distributed upon the pharynx and mucous membrane at the back part of the tongue. It is a sensitive nerve.

10. *Par vagum*, or pneumogastric nerves, or principal division of the eighth pair, (tenth pair of some authors), originate in the same line with, and close upon, the glossopharyngeal. These nerves are extensively distributed upon the larynx, pharynx, trachea, œsophagus, heart, lungs, and stomach. Part of the filaments of this nerve are sensitive, and part are motor.

11. Spinal accessory nerves, or lower division of the eighth pair, (eleventh pair of some authors), originate from the upper part of the spinal cord, in the same line with the two preceding nerves. They enter the cranium by the foramen magnum, and pass out again from the cranium through the foramen lacerum, along with the other two divisions of the eighth pair. It is principally, if not entirely, a motor nerve.

12. Hypoglossal or ninth pair, (twelfth pair of some authors). Each originates from the sulcus between the pyramidal and olivary bodies, and escapes from the base of the cranium through the anterior condyloid foramen, and is distributed upon the muscles of the tongue. It is the motor nerve of the tongue.

THE RIGHT HEMISPHERE OF THE BRAIN.

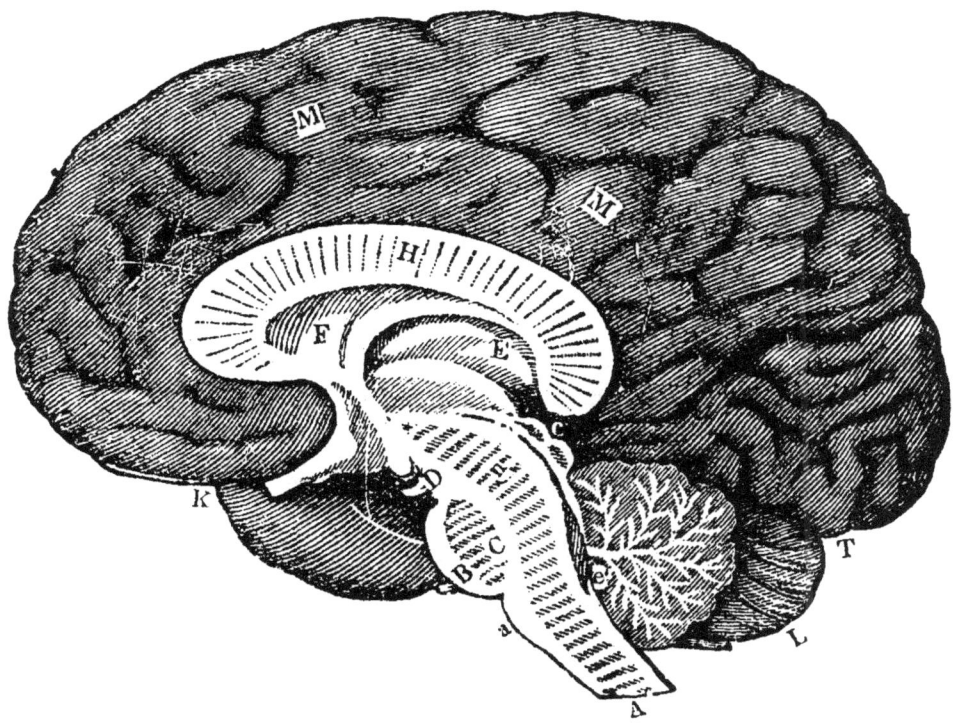

MM, Convolutions, flat—color, reddish grey.

A, Medulla oblongata cut through the medium line. Color—outer portion, bluish white; inner portion, reddish grey.

a, Pyramidal body.

B, Pons Varolii, or tuber annulare. Color—white outside; inside, reddish grey.

c, Tubercula quadrigemina.

D, Crus cerebri.

f, The great inferior ganglion—posterior striated body (thalamus)—color, bluish white.

c, The great superior ganglion—anterior striated body—color, reddish grey.

i, Annular ganglion.

A, Corpus callosum—color, bluish white.

K, Fissura Silvii.

L, The cerebellum.

e, The arbor vitæ—color, white, in the reddish grey ground of the incised cerebellum.

T, The tentorum, separating the cerebellum from the brain.

s, Locus niger.

THE CEREBELLUM.

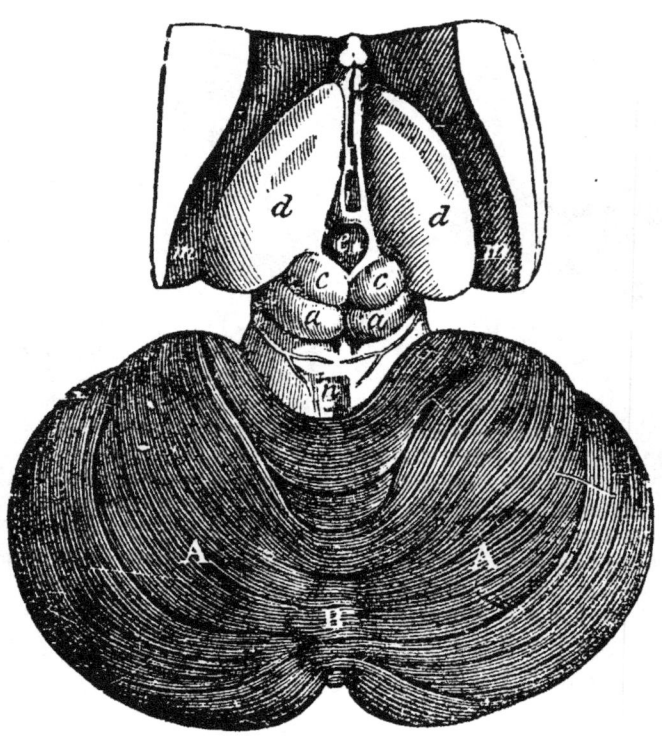

A A, The cerebellum—color, reddish grey
B, Processus vermiculares.
a, Processus e cerebello ad testes—semi-transparent—color, bluish white.
a a, The posterior corpora quadrigemina—color, bluish white.
c c, The anterior corpora quadrigemina—color, bluish white.
d d, The great inferior ganglions—posterior striated bodies (thalamus)—color, bluish white.
m m, Posterior part of the great superior ganglions—anterior striated bodies—color, reddish grey
e, Pineal gland—color, reddish grey
l, Third ventricle.

HORIZONTAL SECTION OF THE BRAIN.

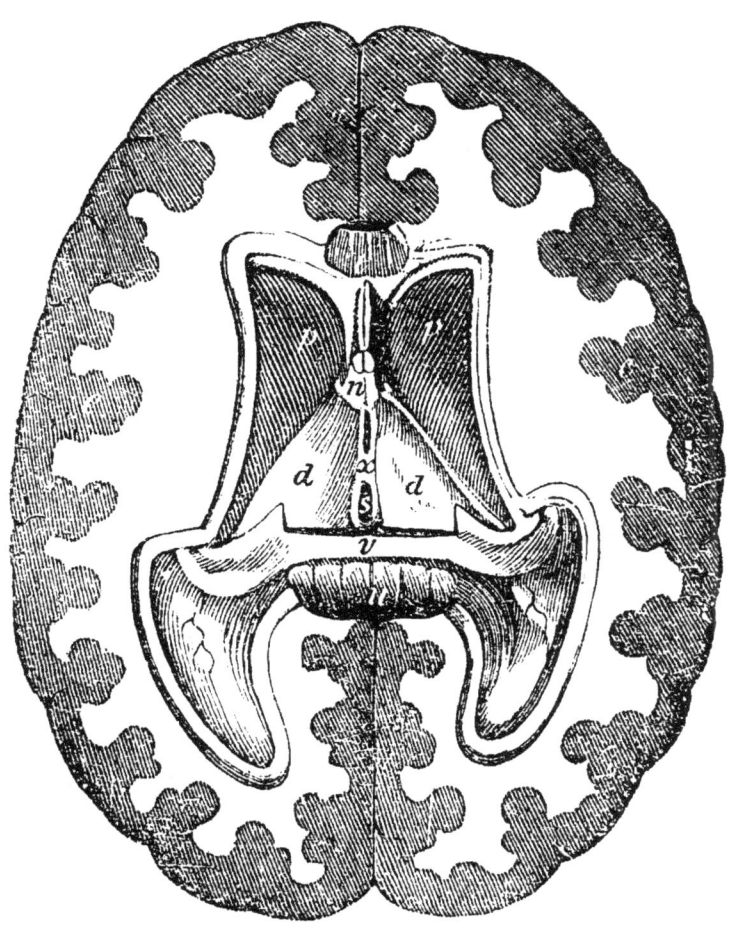

  s e, Convolutions, or cortical part of the brain; color, reddish grey
  t, Fourth ventricle.
  r, Posterior commissure; color, white.
  s, Third ventricle, or separation between the great ganglions.
  d d, Great inferior ganglions; color, bluish white.
  x, Middle commissure.
  n, Anterior commissure.
  p p, Great superior ganglions—striated; color, reddish grey.
  t, Anterior opening into the lateral ventricles.

THE CEREBELLUM, ETC.

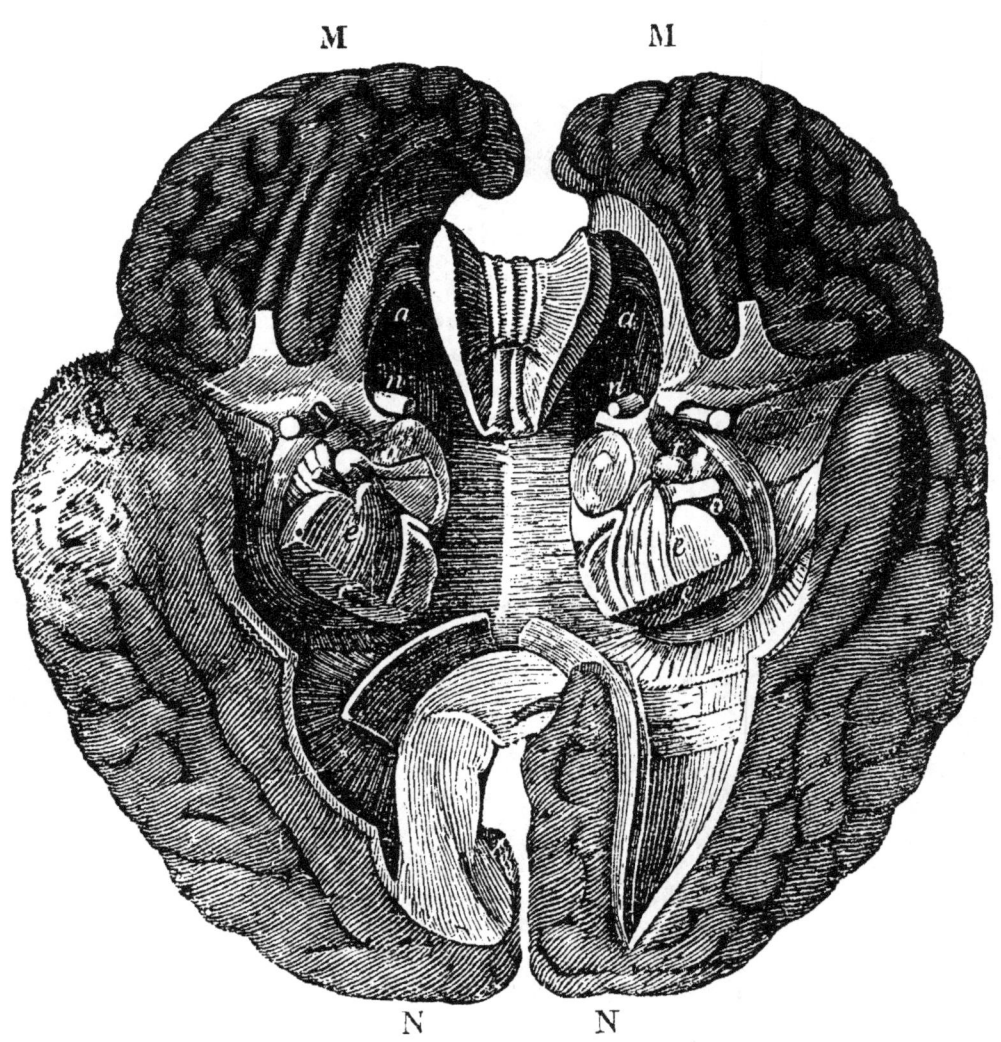

M M The anterior part of the brain.
N N Posterior part of the brain.
e e, Vertical sections of the great inferior ganglions; color, bluish white.
c   The black substance in the centre of the great inferior ganglions.
b b The cords of the mammary bodies which plunge into the interior of the great inferior ganglions
    Mammary body of the right side, the left being cut away.
r r, Optic nerves.
n n. Olfactory nerves.
a a. Great superior ganglions; color, reddish grey.

VARIOUS PARTS ABOUT THE BASE OF THE BRAIN.

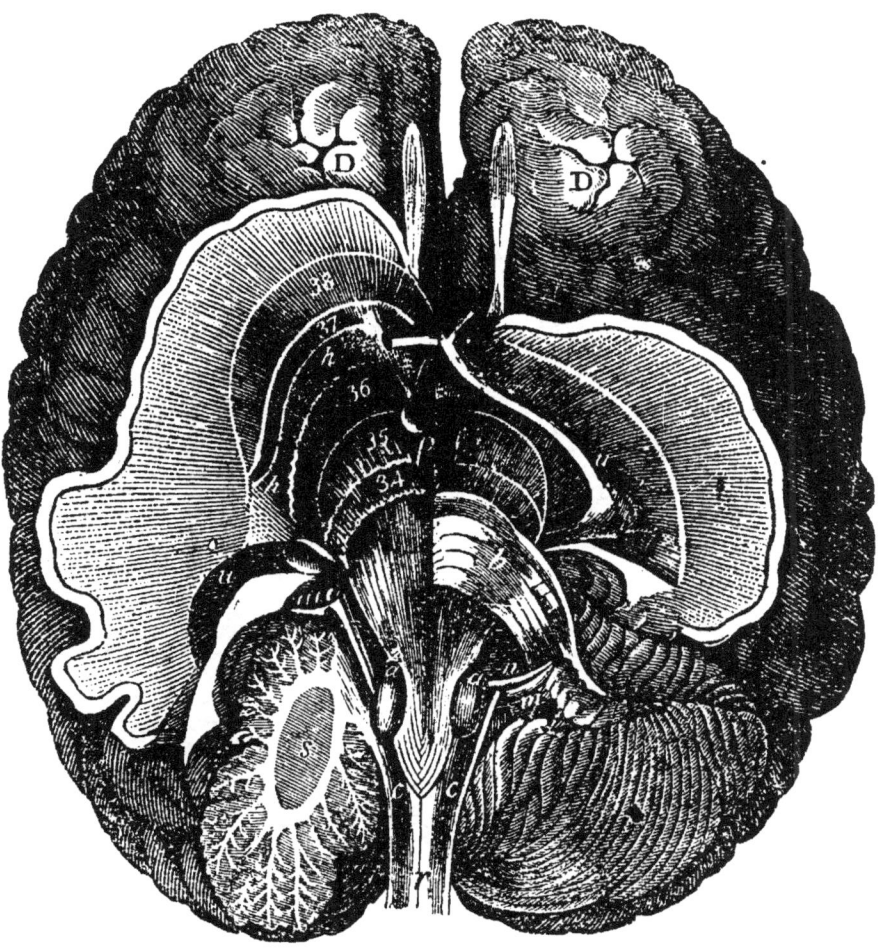

r, Medulla oblongata.

c c, Decussation of the fibres of the pyramidal bodies, which explains the influence of the lateral cerebral parts of the brain upon the opposite sides of the body. These fibres cross the mesial line of the body one above another from below, upward, like plaited straw. Those of the right side come from the left pyramidal body, and those of the left side from the right pyramidal body, and is a constant peculiarity, modified only by the number of decussating fibres. They are contracted in their course in passing the olivary bodies a a, and then diverge as seen in the figure.

m, Auditory nerve.

n, Facial nerve. The primary bundle of fibres of the cerebellum are here seen to plunge into it between these nerves.

l Part of the annular protuberance, or pons Varolii, plunging into the cerebellum.

s Cerebellar ganglion.

p, Mammary bodies, with the diverging cords to which they are attached.

u, Optic nerve. "The optic nerves decussate partially, and is the cause why the eye is frequently deranged on the same side as that on which the brain is diseased."—*Spurzheim.*

h h, "Nervous fibres that expand in the convolutions and contribute to their formation."—*Spurzheim.*

i i, Olfactory nerves.

v, Side of the great lateral ventricle.

34, 35, 36, 37, 38, The fibres which pass through the great cerebral ganglions, and ultimately expand into the convolutions of the brain.

DD, Converging convolutions.

RIGHT HEMISPHERE OF THE BRAIN.

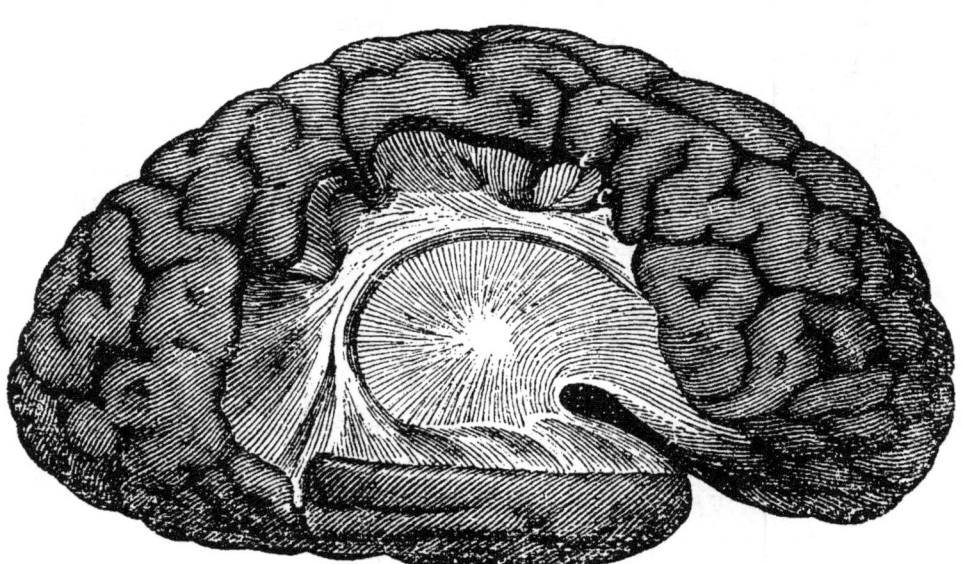

c, Internal structure of the convolutions.

o, Fibres of the convolutions agglutinated by a very delicate neurilema.

This engraving represents the right hemisphere of the brain, in which the convolutions are cut away to the depth of about three quarters of an inch, to show the fibres radiating from the centre of the outer surface of the great inferior ganglion into the convolutions.

The white spot in the centre of the figure represents the outer surface of the great inferior ganglion, over which the fibres are drawn with great accuracy from the original.

VERTICAL SECTION OF THE BRAIN

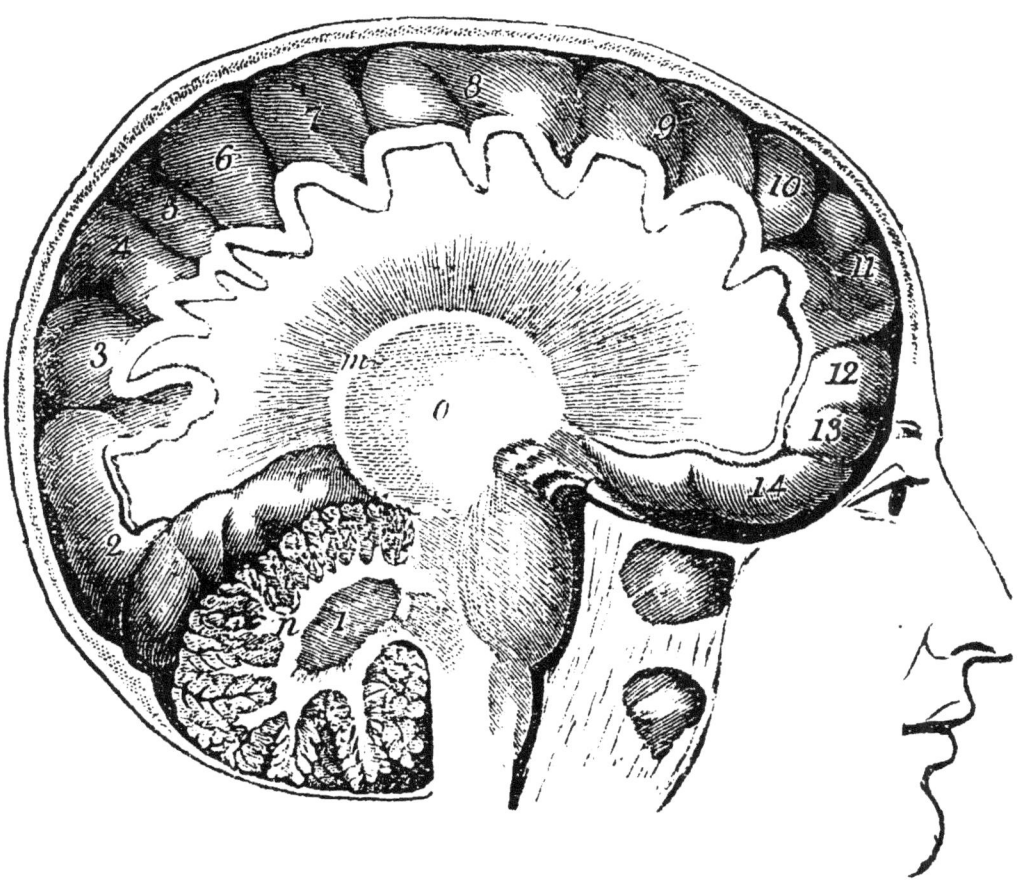

A fine view of a vertical section of the brain through the convolutions, the white substance, the great inferior ganglion, and the cerebellum.

This section is made through the ganglion to the depth of about the quarter of an inch from its outer surface, and through the middle of the cerebellar ganglion.

o, Great inferior ganglion.
m, Fibres radiating from the surface of the ganglion.
l, Cerebellar ganglion (corpus dentatum).
n, Arbor vitæ.

Some of the principal organs formed by the convolutions of the brain are numbered thus.

1, Amativeness, or sexual love.
2, Philoprogenitiveness, or love of offspring.
3, Inhabitiveness, or attachment to home.
4, Concentrativeness, or power of mental concentration.
5, Approbativeness, or love of approbation.
6, Self esteem.

7, Firmness
8, Reverence.
9, Benevolence
10, Imitation.
11, Comparison, or power of comparing one thing with another.
12, Eventuality, or power of observing action.
13, Individuality, or power of observing existence.
14, Language, or power of learning or using verbal signs

PERPENDICULAR SECTION OF THE BRAIN.

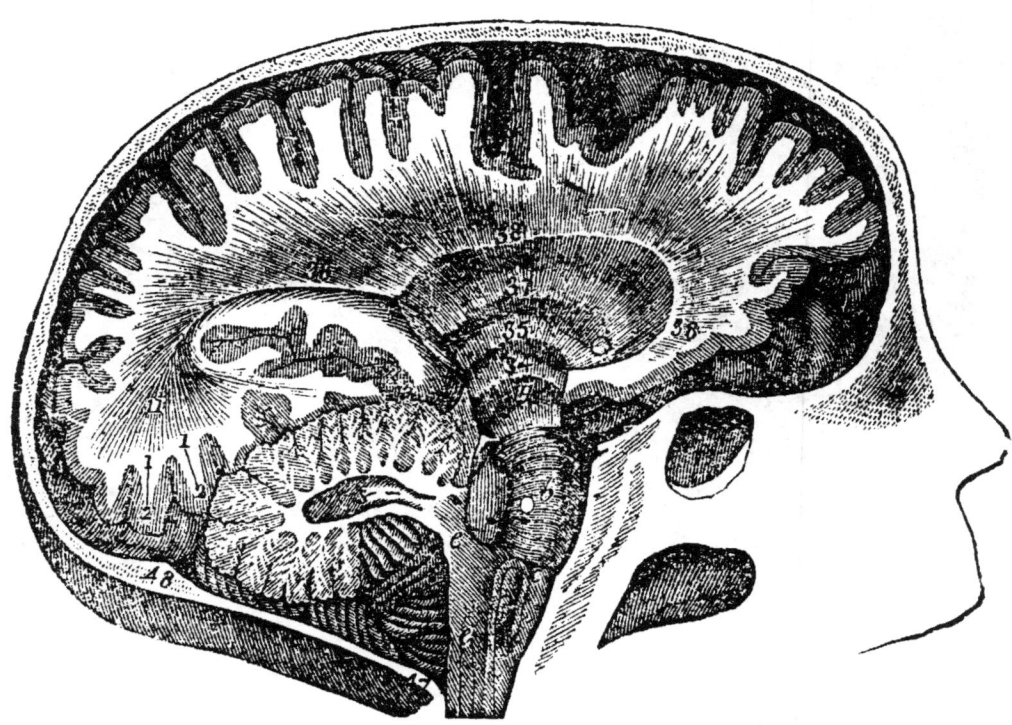

The fibres of the white or medullary substance radiate, as seen in the figure, from the base of the brain into the convolutions, the folds of which are plunged into the white substance, generally from a line to an inch deep.

e e, is a section of one of the *corpora restiforma*.

f, Is a section of one of the *corpora pyramidalia*.

b, Is the *pons Varolii*.

g, Is one of the *crura* of the brain.

a, Is the cerebellar ganglion, surrounded by the arbor vitæ.

34, 35, 37, 38, and 11, Are the cerebral fibres, which, originating in the *medulla oblongata*, pass under the *pons Varolii*, through the *crura*, and *corpora striata*, and great *inferior ganglions*, and ultimately expand into the convolutions of the brain.

47, 48, Situation of the cerebellum within the skull.

These crura contain cineriterous matter in their interior, from which additional fibres are continually sent off as they advance to join and strengthen those that have come from below.

The cerebral crura are besides divided into two parts, viz.: an anterior and external, and a posterior and internal mass, the limits of which are marked by two superficial furrows. They are the roots of the primary bundles of fibres of the brain, which *diverge* as they advance to form the immense mass of the hemispheres.

A great portion of these fibres pass to and through the ganglions in their course to the convolutions, from which another set of fibres *converge* through the white substance, and corpus callosum to the same ganglions in the centre of the brain.

RIGHT HEMISPHERE OF THE BRAIN.

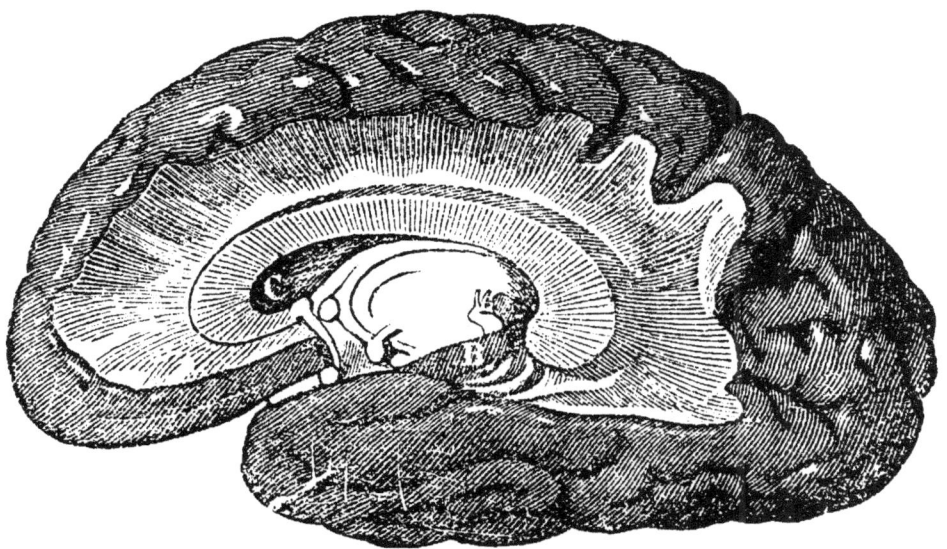

A, Front part of the right hemisphere of the brain.
B, Great inferior ganglion.
C, Great superior ganglion.

84 SOMNOLISM AND PSYCHEISM.

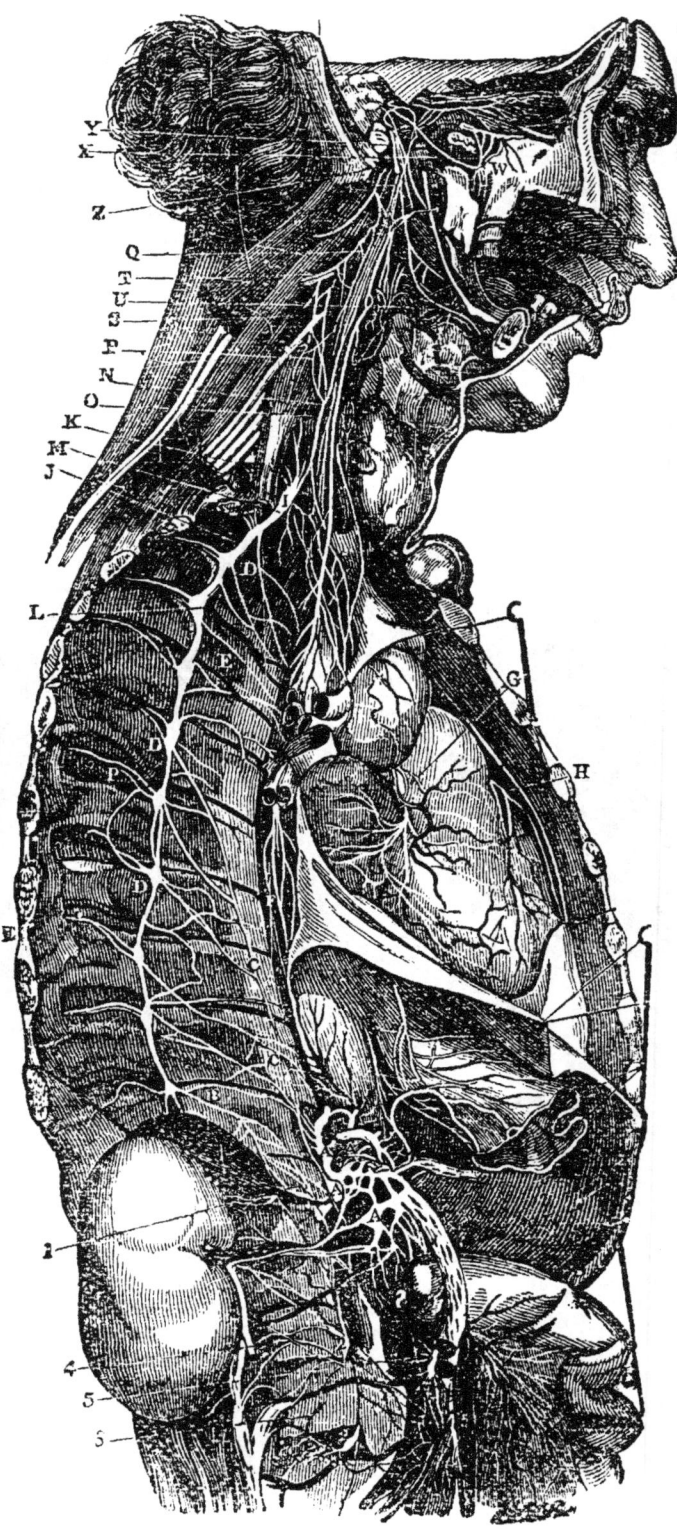

GANGLIONIC SYSTEM OF VEGETABLE LIFE.

ILLUSTRATIONS.

GANGLIONIC SYSTEM OF VEGETATIVE LIFE.

A view of the ganglions of the organs of the body, and other structures, connected with the great sympathetic nerve, reduced from Manec's grand plate, by John Harrison Curtis, Esq., London.

AAAA, Semilunar ganglion and solar plexus. The ganglion is placed upon the base of the two pillars of the diaphragm, one being on each side, and the right generally larger than the left.

B, Small splanchnic nerve. Consists in the union of two or three twigs, furnished by the last thoracic ganglia.

C, Great splanchnic nerve. Formed by the junction of three, four, five, or eight twigs, coming from as many thoracic ganglia.

DDD, Thoracic ganglia. Ten or eleven in number, corresponding with the posterior part of the lateral side of the body of the dorsal vertebræ; most of them rest on the head of the ribs; others correspond with the level of the intercostal space.

E, Internal branches. All of them are attached upon the body of the vertebræ, and advance, ramifying and communicating with each other, toward the medium line, where they are distributed over the œsophagus and the aorta.

F, External branches. Two for each ganglion, very different from each other; one large, red, pulpous, and going to the intercostal nerve; the other much smaller, white, giving off no twigs, and passing from the intercostal to the ganglion.

G, Right coronary plexus. Passes between the pulmonary artery and the aorta, and accompanies the anterior coronary artery.

H, Left coronary plexus. Passes before the left branch of the pulmonary artery, goes to the posterior side of the heart, and accompanies the left coronary artery.

I, Inferior cervical ganglion. Placed behind the vertebral artery.

J, Inferior twigs. Commonly a single branch communicating with the first thoracic ganglion.

K, External threads. Very slender, and communicating with the last cervical and the last two dorsal pairs; some filaments pass round the subclavian artery.

L, Internal twigs. Very minute, and distributed to the longus colli, upon the anterior part of the spine; some of them descend to the pulmonary plexus.

M, Anterior threads. Two or three in number, constituting the inferior cardiac nerves.

N, Middle cervical ganglion. Placed on a level with the body of the fifth or sixth cervical vertebræ, and covered by the internal jugular vein.

O, Interior twigs. Three or four in number, all passing over the inferior cervical ganglion.

P, External twigs. Vary much in number, and give off ramifications communicating with the cervical pairs and the phrenic nerve.

Q, Superior cervical ganglion. Situated on the anterior and lateral part of the second, third, and fourth cervical vertebræ.

R, Superior branches. Two in number, and placed behind the internal carotid artery.

S, Inferior branch. Rarely double, and descends upon the great rectus muscle as far as the middle cervical ganglion.

T, External branches. Their number very variable; they communicate with the first, second, and third cervical pair.

U, Submaxillary ganglion. Situated upon the internal side of the submaxillary gland, a little below the styloglossal muscle.

V, Vidian nerve. A branch springing from the posterior side of the spheno-palatine ganglion.

W, Naso-palatine branch. One of the internal branches of the spheno-palatine ganglion, entering the nasal fossæ by the spheno-palatine foramen.

X, Spheno-palatine ganglion. Placed in the summit of the zygomatic fossa.

Y, Opthalmic ganglion. Situated in the orbit, and occupies the external side of the optic nerve.

Z, Auditory nerve and membrane of the tympanum, containing, within its cavity, four small bones, viz: the stapes, the incus, the malleus, and the os orbiculare.

1, Renal plexuses. Furnished by threads coming from the solar and cœliac plexuses, and from the last dorsal ganglion, the first lumbar, and the small splanchnic nerve.

2 2, Lumbar ganglia. Commonly four or five; the first corresponds with the body of the first lumbar vertebræ, the last with the fifth.

3, Internal branches. Numerous; go downward and inward, to the aorta, where they are lost in the aortic plexus.

4, External branches. Two of these, at least, arise from each ganglion; they follow a course more or less flexuous toward the anterior branches of the lumbar nerves.

5, Aortic flexus. Formed by threads from the solar plexus, superior mesenteric, renal, small splanchnic nerve and internal branches of the lumbar ganglia.

ILLUSTRATIONS.

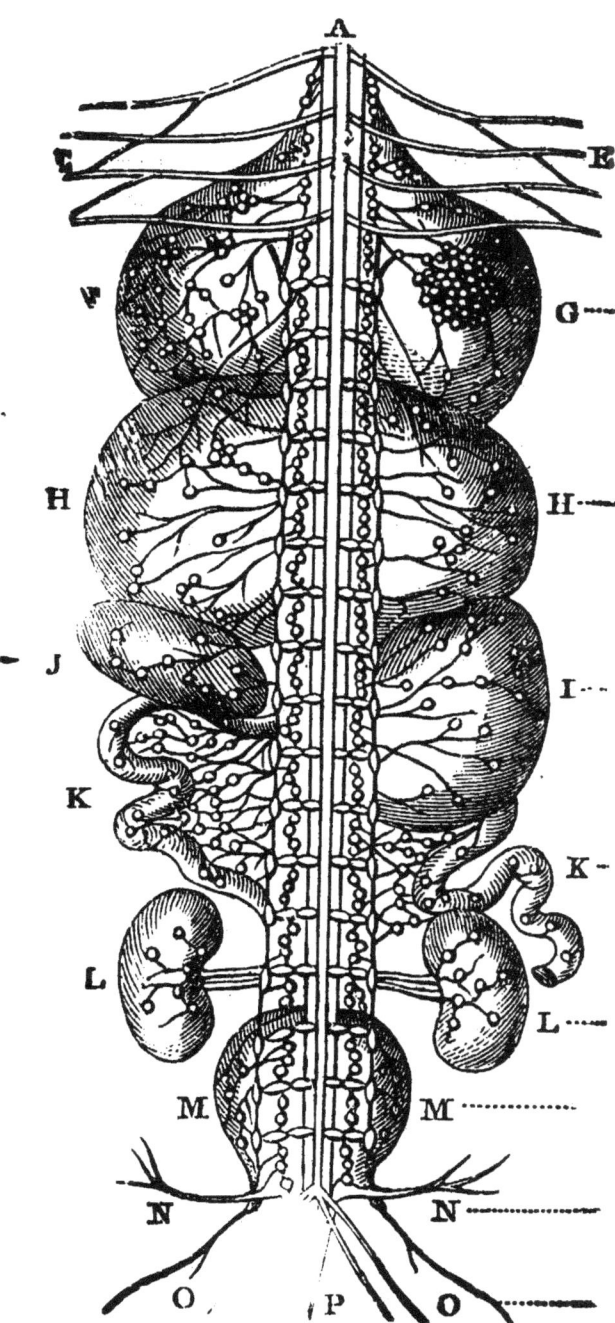

A, Spinal cord.
EE, Spinal nerves connected with the right and left arms.
FG, Lungs. HH, Stomach. I, Liver. J, Spleen.
K, Small intestines and mesentary. L, Kidneys. MM Uterus
NN, Spinal nerves connected with the sacrum.
OPO, Spinal nerves distributed to the lower limbs

occupies the greater part of the cranium, or skull, is called the CEREBRUM. The smaller portion is situated in the hinder part of the head, just above the spinal marrow, and is called the CEREBELLUM—a word meaning "the little brain." The cerebrum is laterally divided into halves, called *hemispheres*, and also into smaller divisions, called *lobes*. The interior portion is made up of various cavities, and delicately-arranged *minute fibres*, which commence in extremely minute bodies, called *cortical glands*, which every where occupy the surface of the Cerebrum; some of these fibres afterwards converge to form the spinal marrow. The surface of the cerebrum is also every where disposed in wavy furrows, not unlike the folds of the intestines. But the cerebellum, not only differs in size and situation, but also, in exterior and interior form; for the exterior, instead of the wavy folds, is arranged in what are called *lamina*, or plates; and the interior has an arborescent or tree-like appearance—so much so, that it is called arbor vitæ, the tree of life. Now, viewing man as formed according to the Infinite Wisdom and perfect order of a Divine Creator, we must expect to find consummate order and design within him, and that every organ of his body should be formed for some specific and determinate *Use;* for USE is the great end of all the Creator's operations. Hence we may conclude that each of these brains has its own specific use, and such we find to be the case; and I will endeavor to point out such of those uses as bear upon the subject we are now considering—my object at present being, not to present you with a full view of the physiology of the human brain, but only so much as is indispensably necessary to be known in order to comprehend the phenomena of Mesmerism.

14. On the base, or lower part of the cerebrum, are found various nerves, which may be easily seen in any good anatomical engraving. Thus in front are found the bulbs of the olfactory nerves, or nerves of smell, which, to use a familiar phrase, *grow out* of the base of the cerebrum, and expand towards the forehead, and from these bulbs a multitude of filaments depend, which are spread out on the delicate membrane in the upper part of the nose. The optic nerves, or nerves of sight, also issue from the under part of the cerebrum, then approach each other and form a union, called the commissure; they then separate, and proceed in the form of a round white cord to the ball of each eye, which they enter behind, and then spread out to form the delicate nervous expansion called the retina. The nerves which *move* the eyes and eyelids, also issue from the base of the cerebrum. There are also other nerves arising from different portions of the cerebrum; but except those by which sensation is experienced, they have no particular reference to the phenomena of Mesmerism. There are other important nerves which arise within the cranium, but not from the cerebrum, and in respect to mesmeric phenomena, the chief are the seventh and eighth pairs, which arise from the cerebellum, and the great sympathetic nerves, which, by means of the eighth pair of nerves, are also connected with the lesser brain. It is also worthy of notice, that *all* the nerves of the cerebrum issue from its *base*, thus leaving the fibrous and cortical portions free; and by this means the General Sensorium is placed in a re-

gion above the ministering nerves, and thus, as it were, *midway* between the mind and outward nature.

15. Now it is essentially necessary to be known, in order to form any correct idea of the physiological phenomena of Mesmerism, that all the nerves of the body, innumerable as they may appear to be, arise either *directly* or *indirectly* from the cerebrum or cerebellum; but in speaking of the *origin* of the nerves, my remarks have no reference to *their development* in the embryo, but to their situation and *use* in the perfect organism. And also, that whatever may be the *parental character*, so to speak, of any nerve, that character it preserves to its termination, however circuitous its course may be, and however its filament may be mixed up with filaments of nerves of another order, so as to form a *compound nerve*. This is one of those traits of Divine simplicity which are so manifest in the Animal Economy. Now all the nerves by which we *feel* or *act*—that is, all what are called the voluntary and sensory nerves, may be said to arise, either *directly* from this larger portion of the entire brain, called the cerebrum, or *indirectly* from it, by means of the *spinal marrow*—which may be considered as *a continuation of the cerebrum in the body*. The SPINAL MARROW is composed of three distinct columns—the anterior, or front column, being formed of what are styled *motor nerves;* that is, nerves that are concerned in voluntary motion. The posterior column, or hinder part, of *nerves of sensation;* and the middle part of the column contains the roots of the *nerves of respiration*. If the brain is attentively examined, portions of nervous fibres may be seen passing by and

through other nervous portions, and yet having no connection with them. Thus, portions of the motor fibres of the cerebrum, may be traced under the arch of the optic nerves, and through that appendage of the cerebellum called the Bridge of Varolius; and yet they are uninfluenced by the cerebellum, but preserve their cerebral character, and pass intact and directly into the *fore part* of the spinal marrow; and portions of *sensory fibres* may be traced in the same manner going by and through nervous substances of another character without losing their own specific character, and then passing into the *hinder* part of the spinal column. Now it is by this mode of arrangement, that the true character of the nerves at their origin is preserved to their extremities; and so carefully is this distinction preserved, that even if filaments of *motor* or *sensory* nerves appear to be united in one cord, yet each order of filaments retains its original character. If I raise my arm, I do so by muscular power, communicated by nerves having their true origin in the cerebrum; the same may be said of walking, or of any other action under the control of the will. All these voluntary and external actions, are done by and through the medium of the cerebrum. Thus one great use of the cerebrum, is to originate and control the *voluntary* and *sensory* nerves; it is thus the soul's medium for external knowledge and voluntary action—the great organ of what is called *Animal Life*. Hence pressure on the cerebrum, by paralyzing its action, instantly suspends all sensation and capability of motion.

16. But the office of the CEREBELLUM, the smaller, and curiously organized portion of the entire brain is

of another kind. This is the great organ or fountain of organic life; that is, of the life of the internal organs of the body, and of the *involuntary* motions: the pulsations of the heart; the circulation of the blood; the digestive actions of the stomach and bowels; the action of the reproductive organs; in a word, of the thousand functions performing *within us*, and over which our will has no control. All these *internal* functions are under the direction and control of nerves proceeding directly or indirectly from the cerebellum or its appendages; and this chiefly, by the aid of the great sympathetic nerves, and the eighth pair already alluded to.

17. The eighth pair of cranial nerves, called also the par vagum, arises from the cerebellum, and its connections, and gives off numerous branches which ramify plentifully on the stomach and lungs, and in fact are continued to nearly all the viscera. The *great sympathetic nerves* differ from all the other nerves in the body, both in their arrangement and form: they are studded with small kernels called *ganglia*, or knots, into which, and out of which, numberless nervous twigs have their entrance and exit; and in the neck, by some of these branches they are connected with the par vagum, and thus with the cerebellum. These two pairs of important nerves may be considered as forming *the trunk of the system of the cerebellum*, just as the spinal marrow forms the trunk of the system of the cerebrum. And to perfect the operation of the animal economy, twigs from each are united with each other; and from the great sympathetic with all the nerves of the body. Now the existence, and **dis-**

tinct functions of these two brains, and the systems of nerves depending on them, must be carefully remembered, if we would understand the phenomena of Somnolism, or ordinary Mesmerism. And to enable you to comprehend the *physiology* of this wonderful discovery, I will, as the first step, point out the principal difference between a state of wakefulness and sleep, and the immediate *physical* cause of this difference.

18. During wakefulness, both brains are more or less in a state of activity; but of the action of the larger portion—that is of the cerebrum—we are conscious, so that *our will* bears rule in the animal economy, and the sensory nerves convey to the sensorium within the cerebrum, the various impressions made by outward objects. But when sleep seals up the eyelids the activity of the cerebrum ceases, and hence we become insensible to outward things; and then nature, or the involuntary portion of our nervous centre—that is *the Cerebellum*, with its derivatives— has the entire control and direction of the animal kingdom. It is well known that "balmy sleep" is "tired nature's kind restorer," but it is not so generally known that one great reason for the refreshing and restorative nature of sleep consists in the complete suspension of the faculties of the cerebrum, and the operations of nature being carried on by the cerebellum, without any of those manifold disturbing causes which arise from our voluntary and conscious activities. The cerebrum is composed, as I have already observed, of innumerable fibres, originating in little lobules or glands. In the *active* state of this portion of the entire brain, or in other words, in the *wakeful* state, these fibres are *erect*

and, with their lobules or glands, point towards the circumference of the cranium, and there is a capability of moving them either *singly*, or in *greater* or *lesser groups;* and hence arises the power of the will to exercise such an immense variety of muscular actions, and the rapidity and delicacy with which the behests of the will are transmitted by the nerves. In a state of inactivity or sleep, the fibres collapse, or fall together, and hence the capability of this individual action ceases, and a more general or combined action only remains possible. This *general* or *combined* action is similar to the true natural action of the cerebellum, which, from its peculiar organization, is incapable of the *individual* action which distinguishes the cerebrum. But with the cessation of *individual* or separate action in the cerebrum, all ordinary sensation ceases; and hence the unconsciousness of a state of sound sleep.

19. Another physical cause for the state of insensibility in sleep is, that by the collapse, or falling together of the fibres of the cerebrum, the blood is prevented from entering the finer channels of the brain, but courses along the *pia mater*, or membrane investing the brain. This is occasioned by a law generally overlooked, namely, *that the brain has an automatic movement of its own*, synchronous, not with the action of the heart, but with the respiration of the lungs; and on this account the brain has the control of the blood circulating within its substance, independant of the action of the heart. Hence the vertebral and carotid arteries which supply the blood to the brain, have a peculiar erratic course, more so than any other

arterial trunks; and every mechanical precaution is taken to impede the propulsive force of the heart, so that the brain may imbibe or reject the vital and stimulating fluid just according to the state induced upon it. Whatever, therefore, induces a change in the state of the fibres and cortical glands of the cerebrum, changes the state of its automatic action, and thence produces either somnolency or wakefulness.

20. Now let us apply these anatomical and physiological facts to the illustration of mesmeric phenomena, and I think we shall be able to understand something of the mode by which they are produced, that we shall find ourselves in possession of the *true key* to unlock these generally considered mysteries. But first I will briefly describe the most usual manifestations.

21. The simplest *visible* state is that called mesmeric sleep. This I have induced both by the ordinary method, and also by Dr. Braid's mode of making the patient steadfastly gaze upon some small fixed object, called by him Hypnotizing; but I consider the mesmeric mode the best way, where the patient is susceptible of its influence, and by it, and, as far as my present experience goes, by it only, can the *higher* developments be produced. Whatever the mode of operating employed, the primary effect is on the *state of the cerebrum*, which, by modifying the circulation of its blood, collapses in various degrees, and thus assumes the somnolent state. But in using the ordinary mesmeric mode, I altogether discard those formal and mystic modes of proceeding sometimes practised and recommended by some writers on Animal Magnetism. I have reason to believe, as I shall point out in the

sequel, that *mind* is the grand agent in all really mesmeric phenomena, and the manipulations are merely so many means of fixing mental action. My usual mode of proceeding is simply to place the subjects or patients in a sitting posture, and take both their hands in my left hand, and then place my right hand on their head. Where there is any degree of mesmeric sensibility, this is the best and most gentle mode of proceeding; but in more difficult cases, the desired effect may be sooner produced by gentle passes, made from the crown of the head over the forehead downwards, or, in some cases, by making the passes over the entire head *backwards*. In this simple mesmeric sleep, just as in ordinary sleep, we find different degrees of soundness. Some persons merely feel a little drowsiness; others find it impossible to open the eyelids, and yet are perfectly conscious, and, in other respects, awake. Other persons of greater susceptibility, either the result of continued experiment, or peculiar nervous temperament, proceed quickly into a sound sleep, or, as I propose to call it, SOMNOLISM. This state may quickly pass into one having all the characteristics of *somnambulism*, or what is commonly called sleep-walking; in fact, I can see no difference between this state and natural somnambulism, except that the latter is the result of spontaneous natural causes, while the former is the direct result of human agency. I have also reason to believe that natural somnambulists will make the best mesmeric subjects.

22. The induction of the true somnolent state, is all that is required to produce the curious and manifold phenomena of mesmerism, save and except the higher

stages of cerebral lucidity and clairvoyance. Some of these states I will now proceed to notice; and, first, INSENSIBILITY TO LIGHT AND PAIN. If the eye of a patient in the somnolent state is examined, it will be generally found drawn *upwards* and *inwards*, and this, perhaps, in proportion to the complete development of the state; but it will exhibit little, if any, susceptibility to the influence of light. In fact, I have satisfied myself, by repeated and careful observation, that all external vision is withdrawn. There is the perfect visual organ, but the party sees not. There is also the healthy skin, with its infinitude of nervous papillæ, but it exhibits no sign of feeling. The most sensitive parts may be pinched, or pricked with needles or pins, but the patient will exhibit no consciousness of suffering, or, in fact, of any kind of feeling, but will continue to converse with the mesmeriser or the experimenter without noticing in the least degree the apparently painful experiment to which he is being subjected. Nay, more, it is an undoubted fact, that the most severe surgical operations have been performed, both in this country and on the continent, without the patient evincing any susceptibility. I will mention one only, recorded in the French medical journals, and also in the *Penny Cyclopædia*, under the article Somnambulism. An elderly French lady was the subject of cancer in the breast. Her physician was a practiser of mesmerism, and he had frequently employed that agency, in conjunction with other means, to abate, and, if possible, cure that dreadful malady. But he found that although he could always allay pain, and put the lady into a state of complete ease by mesmerising her, yet the disease continued its ravages, and the only hope was in an operation—that is, by amputating the breast. When this only alternative was proposed to her in the wakeful or normal state, it produced the most intense anguish and apprehension; but in the abnormal mesmeric state, she would calmly discuss the matter with her physician and friends. At last the operation was determined on, and Jules Colquet, the eminent Parisian surgeon, was chosen for the operator. The surgeon, in his narrative of the case, says that he found the lady seated in a chair, her eyes closed as if in sleep, yet conversing with her physician, who had, in fact, put her into the mesmeric or somnolent state some short time before. She spoke calmly of the intended proceedings, removed her own dress to expose her bosom to the surgeon's knife, and during the operation, which lasted about a quarter of an hour, she conversed cheerfully both with the surgeon and physician who was seated by her, and supported the arm on the diseased side, without exhibiting the slightest pain or consciousness of what was going on. The lady was then put to bed and carefully attended to, without being awaked from the mesmeric state. On the next day but one the first dressings were removed—usually a most painful trial to the patient—the wound dressed again, and then, after the lapse of some hours, she was aroused, having been kept for more than two days in the somnolent state. When awakened she was unconscious of all that had transpired since she was put into the sleep, more than two days before! When she found that her breast had been removed, that the wound had again been dressed, and found herself surrounded by anxious and sympathising relatives, her feelings may be better imagined than described! But I will here make a cautionary remark. It must not be supposed that because persons in a state of somnolency feel no pain, that, therefore, they will be unconscious of any injury inflicted on them in that state when they return to the normal condition; on the contrary, when they are aroused they will feel the effect of any injury just in proportion to its severity. Common humanity therefore requires, that *experiments* made to ascertain the state of the sensibility, should be such as only to occasion transient pain.

23. CATALEPSY, or rigidity of the muscles; PHANTASY; TRANSFER OF FEELING from the operator to the patient; and what is called MAGNETIC ATTRACTION.—These are all interesting displays of mesmeric, or rather *psychic* states, and will be better understood when we come to the consideration of the psychological part of our subject. The facility with which these states can be produced depends entirely on the susceptibility of the subject. In the majority of cases, manipulations, actual contact, or audibly spoken words are necessary to produce the desired result; but in some cases the mere volition of the operator is sufficient. Thus in case of catalepsy, by merely drawing the hand over the patient's arm, that is, in mesmeric language, *making passes* from the shoulder towards the tips of the fingers, the muscles of the arms may be rendered perfectly rigid, so that by no effort of the patient could they be put down, nor could a stranger render them flexible; by the application of great force the shoulder joint may be moved, but as soon as the pressure is removed

the arm will instantly resume the position in which it had been placed by the operator. If the hand of a person of about the same physical strength as the mesmerised subject is placed in the hand of the subject, and the fingers made to clasp it, it will be found almost impossible to withdraw it, so tight will be the grasp; and yet, notwithstanding this great apparent exertion of muscular power, the mesmerised subjects will continue to converse on various topics, and evince neither mental nor physical consciousness of the power they are displaying! This peculiar characteristic of the somnolent state can be most beneficially employed as a curative agent in the restoration to strength of palsied or weakened limbs, provided the somnolent state can be induced on the diseased person.

24. But the phenomena above alluded to are among the simplest of these displays. By a single touch the mouth of the patient may be closed, so instantaneously, as to leave a word half pronounced; and by a single *pass*, as speedily set at liberty. Even the nostrils may, by a single pinch, be partially closed, so as instantly to produce the *nasal twang* common upon stoppage of the nasal passages by cold or otherwise; and then as quickly, by a wave of the hand, be restored to perfect freedom. Some patients, while putting themselves into various postures, may be instantly rendered immovable and statue-like in any posture. If a rod, or any other suitable article, be put into the hand, and the hand closed by the operator, by no effort can the patient let it go, although he may be so far demesmerised as to be fully conscious of his state and of all around him. On the other hand, by a mere pass of the hand of the mes-

meriser, or it may be, by a motion of his *will*, the mesmerised party finds it equally impossible to retain his hold. By a single pass or pressure, an individual may be rooted, as it were, by his feet to the floor, fixed immovable in his chair, or his hands fixed firmly to a wall or bench, or any other object. Some of these experiments are highly interesting and amusing, but the most wonderful, and apparently inexplicable, are but varied manifestations of the simplest forms of catalepsy, and are, as we shall see, explainable by the same simple law which also explains other phenomena.

25. PHANTASY.—By this is meant such an action on the mind of the mesmerised party, that the mere suggestions of the mesmeriser—sometimes not audibly expressed, but merely silently willed—are taken for realities. Thus a handkerchief may be thrown into the lap and silently willed to be a rabbit, a guinea-pig, a child, or even any disagreeable object, as a snake, or other reptile; and upon directing the attention to the object, as by simply asking " What have you got in your lap?" the action and language soon evince that it is considered to be just the object the operator *wills* it to be; nor can the subject conceive it to be anything else, or divest himself of the Phantasy. The effects of this mere *imaginative action* will generally be more strikingly displayed by touching such of the phrenological organs as have an affinity with the sentiment or feeling intended to be produced. Thus philoprogenitiveness and benevolence, in case an infant or an inoffensive animal is suggested; and cautiousness, in suggesting the idea of a snake, or other disagreeable objects. Again, an empty glass may be offered, and

by stating it to contain strong hot brandy and water, the same coughing and difficulty of swallowing will be produced as would follow the attempt to swallow such a liquid by a child, or a person wholly unaccustomed to it. Then, by taking the glass away and immediately presenting it again, saying that it contains cold water, but care must be taken lest it cause toothache, immediately all the effects of an intense cold draught will be manifested. Once a mesmeric subject asked me for a particular drink; I presented an empty glass and silently willed it to be castor oil. No sooner had the glass touched the lips than it was dashed away and broken to atoms, at the same time the party exclaiming, "Ah, it's so nasty!" Many more striking and interesting experiments may be exhibited, but they may be all referred to the same primary causes.

26. TRANSFER OF STATE.—By this is meant that remarkable phenomena exhibited by good mesmeric subjects, in feeling whatever may be done to the mesmeriser as done to themselves. This I have witnessed so often, and under such a variety of circumstances as to admit of no doubt as to its correctness. Thus, on one occasion, while lecturing, one of the audience, to test the matter, came unawares and pricked my leg. I looked round for a moment with surprise and some little indignation, but by the time I comprehended the motive of the seeming offender, the mesmerised subject felt it, and screamed out loudly "that some one had pricked her leg," and pointing at the same time to the corresponding portion on her own leg which had been pricked in mine. At the same time a pin might have been thrust *really* into her leg without her evincing

any consciousness. I have got individuals to tread on my toes, pull my hair, or pinch different parts of the body, and I have invariably found that with this subject not many seconds would elapse before she would complain of exactly similar treatment, and refer the pain to the exact corresponding part; and sometimes I have experienced considerable difficulty in dispelling the illusion. These undoubted facts shed much light on what may be called the highly spiritualized, or purely mental origin of some diseases, and will afford some clue to the *apparently* miraculous manner in which some peculiar diseases have been removed.

27. PHRENO-MESMERISM.—This is the name usually applied to the manifestation of the phrenological sentiments and feelings of a mesmeric subject. It has been considered as affording a triumph to the materializing class of phrenologists, and hence has been decried and attempted to be set aside by the metaphysical spiritualists. Possibly both classes of reasoners may be wrong. Certainly the mere placing of the finger of the operator on any part of the head, and it being followed by the manifestation of a sentiment or feeling proper to the organ said to be situated in the part touched, is no proof that such organ is really there; because the *idea* of the feeling or sentiment is in the operator's mind, and the fact may be accounted for by mesmeric imaginative action and the transfer of feelings. Again, anatomy reveals nothing within the cranium analogous to the arbitrary divisions marked on phrenological busts. Besides, when we touch the head, the skull prevents us acting directly on the brain; we only

excite the extremities of those cranial nerves which ramify in the scalp. On the other hand, the opportunities I have had for acquiring experience enables me positively to assert, that contact with at least certain parts of the head will produce those feelings phrenologically ascribed to those particular portions. Thus, for example, I have seen *alimentiveness* powerfully excited in a mesmerised subject who, when left alone for a little while, accidentally reclined, so that a portion of the head where "alimentiveness" is situated was brought into contact with the edge of a table. Again, I have seen philoprogenitiveness excited by a subject accidentally rubbing the occipital portion of the head against a high-backed chair—not to mention other instances. But this apparent proof of the material view of the question is not the whole one; for I have seen some of the phrenological sentiments excited without touching the head! Thus, upon simply taking the hand and silently thinking reverently of the Deity, the mesmerised subject has fallen down on the knees and manifested the most profound veneration. On other occasions, when more than one subject had been mesmerised, on touching the "organs" on the head of one, the other, without any touch or connection, or any knowledge of any action, would instantly manifest the sentiment. Upon the whole, I think the real evidence afforded by mesmerism is favorable to phrenology; but I am far from thinking that the evidence *properly interpreted* necessarily leads to that sort of materialism which is, by many persons, associated with phrenological doctrines. The brain is undoubtedly the mind's organ;

this position remains, whether we suppose the mind uses the whole brain in every mental action or only an appropriate part.

28. It has been said that phreno-mesmerism is the result of electrical action, and that, in fact, all mesmeric action is but an electrical phenomena—the operator being *positively* electrified, the patient *negatively* so. For this, I believe, there is no evidence whatever. It is true that electricity may be made to *stimulate* certain vital actions, but it is admitted by the best physiologists that there is no *identity* between them. I have carefully experimented, and cannot find that there is any perceptible difference between the electrical and magnetic state of the mesmerised subject and that of the operator, where, according to electrical theory, the greatest difference ought to be manifested. Whatever *name* or *cause* may be assigned to mesmeric agency, it is undoubtedly a vital one. It is true, as I observed at the outset, that within the living organism are collated all the powers of the universe; but they are in the organism in its own peculiar manner. The magnetism and chemistry, the attractions and repulsions, and the other internal operations of the body, are *not* the magnetism and chemistry, the attractions and repulsions of outward nature; but they are *living actions*, analogous to outward cosmical and terrestrial activities, but perfectly distinct from them, and existing in a degree altogether above them. They are, in fact, the antitypes of which the types are found in outward nature.

29. With the exception of CEREBRAL LUCIDITY, magnetic vision, as it is sometimes called, and CLAIR-

VOYANCE, the foregoing classification may be made to embrace all ordinary mesmeric or somnolent phenomena; lucid and clairvoyant manifestations are so evidently of a psychical nature, that before noticing them, let us apply ourselves to the solution of the *physiology* of the states we have briefly described.

30. We have seen that within the skull there are, in reality, two distinct brains, although popularly called the brain; that there are two distinct systems of nerves connected with these two brains; that by the larger brain, or cerebrum, and its nerves, we feel, think, and act; and that it is thus the soul's medium of conscious intercourse with the external world. That by the cerebellum, or little brain and its nerves, are directed and controlled all the involuntary and vegetative functions of our bodies; that the brain has an automatic, or in other words, an independent action of its own, by which it has the control of the blood circulating within it, and that in the state of sleep the fibres of the cerebrum collapse or fall together, and the blood is prevented entering the finer channels and thereby stimulating the brain to activity, and that from this state of collapse and altered circulation of the blood arises the unconsciousness and insensibility of profound sleep.

31. The true mesmeric action is, as will be presently shown, primarily and fundamentally of a *psychological* character, but it induces a peculiar *physiological* state. The direct effect of the passes, or whatever means are employed, is to produce a somnolent state of the brain, in some respects resembling common sleep, but in others widely differing from it. When the true

mesmeric, or rather psychical, relation between the operator and his subject is established, *the cerebrum of the latter is rendered dormant*, the cerebellum and its dependencies alone preserving their normal state. In the first place *all* consciousness appears to be suspended, but by degrees an *inner consciousness*, similar to the consciousness of dreaming is awakened, and from this inner consciousness the somnolized person speaks and acts. The optic nerves and the other nerves of the eye belong to the cerebrum, hence one of the first *visible* effects of mesmeric influence is an inability to open the eyelids, although the eyeball may be as yet uninfluenced; but as the somnolent state continues, the optic nerves, or nerves of sight contract, and the ball of the eye rolls upwards, and all power and perception of vision is withdrawn. Then, as observed, with the increase of the somnolency the fountain-head of all the other sensory nerves becomes dormant, and that of the motory too, in a partial degree. The *sensorium* being by this *change in the internal state of the cerebrum* removed from its connection with the external world, all sense of pain is of course absent; and hence the seeming mysterious phenomenon of a person conversing with another and yet being unconscious of feeling, is at once solved by a knowledge of the simple fact, that the *state of the cerebrum* is changed by the somnolent influence, and an *inner consciousness* awakened.

32. Another physiological state, arising also primarily from a psychological cause, is now perceptible; for although the operator and his subject or subjects are of course two or more persons, yet, in respect to *cerebral* action, or more distinctly, in respect to the

action of the cerebrum, *they are* one. In each person the *cerebellum* and its system of nerves is in the normal condition, but there is only *one* normal and active *cerebrum*, namely, that of the mesmeriser or operator. Hence, however many may be the subjects, if they have all been mesmerised by the same operator, and are all fully susceptible of the somnolent influence, they are all so intimately, interiorly blended with him, that the absence of their own external cerebral consciousness causes them to feel his cerebral consciousness as their own. Here then we discover the *physiological* reason for the strange and anomalous states exhibited. Thus, in cases of phantasy, the idea existing externally in the cerebrum of the mesmeriser is, when willed by him, perceived by the subject as if existing in his or her cerebrum. So also in cases of catalepsy, the somnolency of the subject's cerebrum permits those muscles which are influenced by the voluntary nerves to be actuated by the will of the operator's cerebrum. Hence, in the best cases, the silent operation of the mesmeriser's will, that is, of the power of his cerebrum, is sufficient to throw the subject into a state of statue-like rigidity; but generally it requires the aid of *passes*, which determine more efficaciously the downward nervous currents. Hence, also, any pain inflicted on the operator, which, of course, he feels in the sensorium connected with the origin of the sensory nerves, is felt as if the impression was made on the cerebrum of the subject.

33. But we shall generally find that although sight and feeling are withdrawn the subject retains a perfect capability of Hearing. He may sometimes be so indrawn as to evince no perception of sound, similar, in

this respect, to a person engaged in deep thought; but by patiently persevering until the attention is excited, or the *desire* of the operator is felt, we shall generally be able to demonstrate that the sense of hearing remains. Yet by no means can *sight* and *feeling* be restored except by partially or wholly demesmerising the subject. This fact may be thought to militate against the theory of cerebral action I am endeavoring to inculcate, but it in reality tends to confirm it—for the nerve of hearing, which is a portion of the seventh pair of cranial nerves, has its roots in what is called the *corpora restiformia*, which is directly connected with the *cerebellum*. Sight is solely under the direction of the cerebrum, and we can exert that faculty or not at our pleasure, but we cannot help hearing if we are within the influence of sound, that is, by no organism connected with our ears can we shut out sound. The ears of a person in deep sleep are still open to the modulations of the air, on which sound depends; but the dormant state of the cerebrum prevents the conscious perception of sound, unless it is so loud as to produce that state of partial wakefulness on which dreaming depends; and the mesmerised party is conscious of sound, because, as we have already observed, the state of inner consciousness is in some respects analogous to the state of dreaming. But hearing is not so entirely dependent on the cerebellum as the *internal* involuntary functions, but is somewhat of a mixed nature, like the functions of respiration.

34. Here then is the *whole physiology* of the mesmeric or somnolent state, and *the reason* for the seeming mystery and contrariety to our *usual* feelings and

common experience. The cerebrum of the subject is *dormant*, the cerebellum continues its normal state of activity, while, from the peculiar relationship of the parties, to which we shall presently allude, the cerebrum of the operator dominates over his subject, and is, in a degree, the common cerebrum of both parties.

PHILOSOPHY AND PSYCHOLOGY OF MESMERISM.

35. CLAIRVOYANCE.—Of all the extraordinary phenomena of mesmerism, none appear to stagger the general belief more than the different manifestations of clairvoyance or magnetic vision, or to speak more truly and plainly, the internal sight of the soul. To say that a person can see without the aid of the eye, or by any other means than light entering into the pupil of the eye in the usual manner, seems like uttering an absurdity, or declaring the possibility of an impossibility. Yet, strange as it may sound to those who have had no experience in this matter, there is no mesmeric phenomena more capable of *positive proof*, provided the necessary care be taken in making the experiment, and the subject be placed in proper circumstances; and I trust this evening to afford you ocular demonstration of the fact.

36. But before proceeding further, I wish that it may be distinctly impressed upon you, that when we carefully examine the eye and the brain, we shall see

reason to acknowledge that an internal function of sight, although remarkable and unexpected, and generally unknown, is not more difficult to explain than ordinary vision when thoroughly examined. On referring to the human eye, or any correct representation of it, we shall find that it is a hollow ball, filled with three different kinds of fluids arranged in a determinate order. In front is a horny transparent lens, something like a small watch-glass, to admit the rays of light; behind it is the small chamber containing the aqueous humor, then a hole, called the *pupil*, through the iris, to allow the rays of light from different objects to pass into the interior parts of the eye, first passing through the crystalline lens and through the vitreous humor, and then forming an image of the objects on the delicate membrane called the retina, which is spread out on the back of the eye. Now up to this point ordinary vision may be explained on optical principles, and the eye shown to be the most perfect optical instrument. But the moment we attempt to pass beyond the retina, science is at fault; no natural philosopher has been able to explain *how* the optic nerve conveys the image to the brain; we know that the mind is conscious of the images formed on the retina—or, in more familiar language, of the things seen by the eyes—but in what manner an opaque nervous cord, differing in no essential particulars from other nervous cords, conveys that impression to the mind, we are entirely ignorant. Ordinary sight has, therefore, *a psychological basis*— and this is admitted by the best physiologists.

37. Clairvoyance, or internal sight, assumes the same BASIS necessary to perfect ordinary vision; but as it

acts independently of the external visual organs, so it is not trammelled by those natural laws to which they are necessarily subject. Thus by this internal sight, and by light issuing from within, and not from without, as in common sight, things may be seen which are out of the range of natural sight, and altogether above its nature. For instance, our physical sight can see the remote starry orbs, placed at the distance of perhaps thousands of millions of miles, because the undulations of light proceeding from them in straight lines can impinge, or strike upon the retina of our eyes. Yet the intervention of any opaque body immediately shuts out the vision of the object, even if placed in close connection with us; so that if our *penetrating* powers of sight were immensely increased, whether naturally or artificially, still the rotundity and opacity of the earth would prevent us seeing beyond a certain distance. But opacity is no barrier to internal sight; objects to which the mind is directed, either designedly or spontaneously, will be equally visible through doors and walls as if placed directly before the face. Nay, to the higher stages of clairvoyance there seems, comparatively speaking, no bounds; for whether the object sought be in the same house, or town, or country, or across the broad Atlantic, or still remoter Pacific oceans, it appears to be found and seen with equal facility, and to be equally near to the internal perception of the truly clairvoyant individual. The human body is seen as clearly, and its living actions described as plainly, as if the external and internal parts were alike as transparent as glass, and this also, without any bodily connection, such as by bringing the clairvoyant and the person to be described together; but, as I have proved, when more than one hundred miles have intervened between them.

38. But we have now arrived at a stage in our enquiry where physiology ceases to afford us light; for physiology as such, that is, as the science of our outward living organism, knows nothing of an internal or supersolar light, or of sight that can penetrate alike through *opaque* and *transparent* substances. To psychology and philosophy we must therefore look for aid in our endeavor to investigate the apparent mystery of this interesting subject. And I regret that the abstruse nature of the enquiry, the little that is *generally* known in this branch of knowledge, together with the necessary brevity of popular lectures, will only permit me to present you with a sketch of the views opened to the eye of rational research.

39. It is usual to represent man as composed of *mind* and *matter*—Soul and *body*. This is correct. And as we find that the body is not a mere simple uncompounded substance, but a collection of innumerable parts and organs, so, by parity of reasoning, we may conclude, that the mind, or spiritual body, as the parent and director of the natural body, cannot be that simple entity, that *abstract nothingness* so generally represented by metaphysical writers; but rather that, the controller of the animal organism must be itself organized according to the laws of its own peculiar nature, and capable of manifesting those laws, under certain circumstances, through those organs of the body, that is, of the brain and nervous system, which are united with it by the law of correspondent activity and con-

nection. St. Paul, therefore, spoke the language of the profoundest philosophy, when he declared that there were spiritual bodies and natural bodies, and that the natural body was the first in its development, and *afterwards* the spiritual body; and when, on another occasion, he defined the entire human organism, as existing here, to be a compound of " spirit, soul, and body," in this respect giving his apostolic sanction to the doctrine of the ancient sages of Greece. The two first terms used by the apostle to describe the spiritual part of man, are, in the original Greek, *Pneuma* and *Psyche*, and the latter term, which in our version of the Scriptures is, in the passage alluded to, translated *soul*, is, by the Latin writers called the " *animus ;*" and this term is always used to signify the *animal soul*, as distinguished from the pneuma, or more interior human spirit.

40. And here it will be as well to observe, that no truth is more evident to sound rational enquiry than that the Creator has given to every department of his " handy-work" *a specific* character, and that from the Creator to the lowest inert matter, there exists a *chain* of DEGREES—and that each object of creation can only be well and truly studied by viewing it in its *own degree*, and comparing it with objects in *another degree*. But if we confound this distinction of degrees, we shall never arrive at a clear and satisfactory solution of many important facts. Each degree will be found to have laws or properties peculiar to itself, and if we transcend the degree of the object of our enquiry, by applying to it qualities or properties belonging to another distinct degree, we may expect nothing but confusion and mys

tery. Now, in our investigation of the nature of man, it is especially necessary not to overlook these distinctions. By no process can matter be sublimed into spirit; and spirit having, according to apostolic authority, and the general *law of analogy* observable in all things, its distinctions and degrees, the properties of the *lower* degree may not apply to a *higher* one. True philosophy also teaches, that if spirit in no degree is material, that is, does not possess those properties which we apply to ponderable matter, still it is no less on that account a truly real and substantial existence—more truly substantial than the granite rock, because more unchanging and more enduring.

41. Now viewing the spiritual organism of man as consisting of two distinct degrees, called by the apostle the pneuma and psyche, or as possessing both a spiritual internal and external, together forming, while in this mortal life, the *common internal* of the natural organism, the PSYCHE or ANIMUS will be the connecting medium between the pure human spirit and the nervous system of the natural body. By its connection, through correspondence and vital affinity, with the body, it is placed in relation with outward nature, while as a spiritual entity, and by its indissoluble union with the higher spiritual principle, it has, at the same time, immediate connection with the spirit-world; and because it is a subject of the laws, and possesses the properties of that world which have nothing in common with *time, space,* or *common matter,* it displays those powers which can be explained by no merely natural or physiological knowledge, but which receive an easy, rational, and satisfactory solution, when man is really

seen to be that which revelation, philosophy, and the statements of true clairvoyants declare that he is—namely, a compound of spiritual and natural organisms intimately united by the exactest correspondence or analogy. And that although the lower, or natural organism, cannot act without the continued influence of the higher, or spiritual organism, nor can the spiritual organism be developed without the medium of the natural one, yet, when developed, the higher organism can act, not only by and through the lower organism, but even independently and when disconnected from it.

42. It is this psyche or animus—the *external of the spirit*—that, from all that I have yet learned on the subject, I take to be the true seat of what is called mesmeric influence; the psyche, or animal soul of the operator, influences the same external spiritual organic principle in the subject, and from the animus the influence flows *downwards*, to use analogous natural terms, and thence affects the brain and nervous system—and hence I propose to call that part of mesmerism, which manifests mental and super-sensual phenomena, by the name of PSYCHEISM, or, *the Science of the Soul as manifested in nature*—while to the lower and physical stages, the name of SOMNOLISM may be applied, as indicative of its sleep-like and dream-like character.

43. Now as to the *psychological change* induced by mesmerism.—It is a common law of our being that conscious perception should have its apparent seat in the *ultimate*, or *extreme*, of every development. Thus, although it is a well-established fact, that the sensorium is within the brain, and that if a sensory nerve be divided no sensation will be experienced, yet it is as well

known that if we prick a finger, the pain will be felt where the wound is inflicted. So, notwithstanding the body feels and acts by and through the spirit, our conscious perception, in the usual normal condition, is confined to the bodily organization—because, while in the present state, *the body is the ultimate development of the spirit.* When death severs the connection between mind and body, the *ultimate* of the immortal man is the psyche or animus, and *to it* is transferred all conscious perceptions and sensations. It is from this differing seat of the conscious perceptions that, in our ordinary state, we have no *sensational* knowledge of the spirit-world, or of its laws. But psycheism, or the higher stage of mesmerism, may aptly be compared to partial death—for it is a *closing* of the common external of our being, a *transfer* of the *sensational* perceptions from the *ultimate of the body* to the *ultimate of the spirit*—and thence, and simply from this transfer of ultimates, arises an awakening of the conscious sensational perception of the inner man, or spirit. All those apparently miraculous powers which we sometimes see displayed by good mesmeric subjects, are, in fact, but the result of the psyche or animus being so far set free from the bodily ultimate as to enable the spiritual body to act nearly, if not quite independently of the sensual organs, and by perception, and in light from an inner world; but the connection of the mind and body is yet sufficient to enable the soul's sight and feeling to be manifested to our physical senses by and through the natural organization of a clairvoyant.

44. From this transfer of consciousness and sensational perception, we may also account for the anoma

lous, and often incongruous, statements and descriptions of clairvoyants. They forget much of that mode of speaking of things which is common to our external condition, but which, in itself, is often purely arbitrary and conventional; and they speak according to their newly-awakened and uninformed consciousness. As we have to learn to talk, and even to see, or rather rightly to interpret what the eye reveals, so do clairvoyants require a continued exercise of their peculiar power to familiarize them with its use.

45. We now proceed to explain the manner by which the influence of the operator is brought to bear upon his subject, and that sometimes too, at considerable distance; for I have found a subject affected by my influence, even when mesmerising another party, at the distance of a mile—but this may be considered an unusual case. It is a law of nature that all things should be surrounded by an effluvium or sphere which emanates from them, and is always of the peculiar nature or quality of the body from which it emanates; and these effluvia are regulated by certain definite laws. Thus the *fragrance* which surrounds the rose is the effluvium or sphere emanating from it; and this effluvium, by being dissolved in the surrounding aerial atmosphere, becomes sensible to our organs of smell, and *an idea* of its existence and quality is then transmitted to our *general sensorium*. But there are effluvia of which we should for ever remain ignorant, did we not perceive them *rationally* by their EFFECTS. Thus around magnetized and unmagnetized iron, an effluvium or sphere prevails, of which, in their *separated state* our senses give us no evidence. But we have only to bring them

into such proximity as to be *within the influence* of the *law* regulating the activity of their respective spheres, and their existence may then be instantly perceived in their mutual attraction and coherence. For it has been shown by one of the profoundest of philosophers, that these single spheres have the property of blending into one larger sphere, and that hence arises what is called magnetic attraction.

46. One of the results of the higher stages of clairvoyance, or independent internal sight, is the knowledge, that an effluvium or sphere analogous to what we have alluded to, surrounds the mental organism or spiritual body of every individual. Following the general law of nature, this sphere possesses the peculiar mental qualities of the organism from which it emanates. And hence arises the *repugnance* which is felt to the society of some persons, and the pleasure which is experienced in the company of others; and to it are referable all the remarkable instances of SYMPATHY and ANTIPATHY so frequently observed. But in these ordinary cases the active cause is latent or hidden; yet in the higher mesmeric, or rather psychic state, it often becomes sufficiently obvious even to our physical senses, for we may here see that, similar to what we have said of terrestrial magnetism, there is an actual blending of spheres. The magnet induces its state on the iron, so that it becomes magnetical; and the operator induces his sphere on his patient or subject, so that the subject becomes, as it were, *one body* with himself—the *egoism* or self-consciousness of the one being blended with the *egoism* or self-consciousness of the other.

47. Here then is the *psychological* cause for the

physiological state already mentioned. The change of state induced upon the *animus* of the subject is the *primary cause* of the change in the condition of the cerebrum; the collapse of the cerebrum closes the external consciousness, while the union of the spheres emanating from the animus of both operator and subject, causes the latter to perceive, as in himself, what really is felt in the active cerebrum of the former. And this change of state affords, I believe, the true psychological solution of the whole apparent mystery of catalepsy, phantasy, and many other curious mesmeric phenomena. As regards phreno-mesmerism, the arousing into activity one particular organ of the brain, as it would be called by one class of phrenologists, or faculty of the mind, as it would perhaps be called by another class, without the guidance, control, or balancing powers of the other organs or faculties, is a sufficient reason for the effects we see displayed.

48. But although the transfer of consciousness, and the blending of the spheres of the operator and subject, will account for many curious and otherwise inexplicable phenomena, it does not account for independent clairvoyance. Nor do I think it can be reasonably accounted for, but on the grounds already intimated—namely, the awakening of the sensational consciousness of the external of the immortal body, that is, of the psyche or animus. For I reject as purely hypothetical, altogether without evidence, and contrary to established laws, that theory which would attempt to solve it by an imaginary change of poles, or the transfer of life from the animal to the organic system. According to the latter theory, the lowest mollusk ought to possess a

more extended and spiritual perception than man; and man is to be spiritually elevated by being degraded to a level with the lowest forms of organic life.

49. The great difficulty hitherto experienced in arriving at a knowledge of the real cause of clairvoyance, has arisen from two causes; first, the *different states* of the clairvoyant subject and the observer, and the impossibility of their having the same sensational perceptions—so that the observer cannot sensationally perceive *how* the clairvoyant sees, nor can the clairvoyant adequately describe his perceptions. And, secondly, the necessity for the opening of a *higher degree of consciousness* in order fully to comprehend the lower. For instance, an animal can have no proper idea of its own nature; but man is enabled, by the possession of an internal spiritual principle, rationally and sensationally to investigate his animal body. And the mere induction of the faculty of clairvoyance does not enable the possessor of that faculty *sensationally* to perceive the *cause* of that phenomenon; this requires the awakening of a higher consciousness, though still probably belonging to the psyche, or animal part of the spiritual organism. But in this respect I have an advantage over most enquirers, in possessing a subject, who in addition to the ordinary *induced* mesmeric extasis or trance, has repeatedly been in states of spontaneous extasis of a far higher and more interior character, and the reality of these states has been proved to me by the most convincing evidence. One striking difference between these two states is, that whatever occurs to, or is seen by, the ordinary mesmeric extatic, is completely forgotten, or, more correctly, is altogether

unknown upon the return to the normal state, while the true extatic, or subject of the Superior *state*, as Davis, the American clairvoyant styles it, upon returning to the normal condition, recollects all that has been manifested to him in the abnormal condition. This singular fact receives an easy solution, if we admit the psychological doctrine, that man possesses both an *internal* and *external* memory. In the normal wakeful condition these memories act as *a one*, and hence we are only conscious of one memory. In the abnormal state of *induced* mesmerism, the *internal* memory is active while the external is dormant; and from this want of connection between the two memories arises the oblivion invariably witnessed. But in the *superior state*, or true spiritual extasis, both memories are active, but from a more interior degree than in ordinary life; and hence the extatic subject can recollect in the normal state what has transpired in the spontaneous abnormal state, and, at the same time, possesses a full consciousness of the great difference between these states, so as not to confound the perceptions and knowledges of one with those of the other.

50. A remarkable revealment of this *superior state*, or *spontaneous extasis* is, that every man while in this mortal life, is by the very laws of his being, and hence, of course, by the design of the Creator, intimately, though unconsciously, associated with the spirit-world, and this especially by what may be styled *his associate spirit*, and that in the memory of this associated spirit is, as it were, a reflection of all that exists in the memory of the associated man; so that distinctly to perceive the associated spirit is tantamount to a full per-

ception of the *character*, both mentally and physically, of the associated man, as well as of the information possessed by him. There is also a reflection of the natural organism of the man, both externally and internally, and also of the scenery perceivable by his natural senses.

51. A *true clairvoyant* is one who, by the opening of the internal consciousness, has a sensational perception of the objects of an inner or spirit-world, that is, provided the clairvoyance exists in *a sufficient degree*. If the attention of the clairvoyant is directed to any individual, the effect is to bring the clairvoyant into a *sensational* connection with the associate spirit of the person sought for; and from the normal recollections being treasured up in the *internal* memory, while the *external* memory, and all immediately connected with it is *quiescent, this associate spirit appears to the clairvoyant to be the real individual sought—* and from this source, and the *reflection of memory* above alluded to, is often obtained much of the information the clairvoyant is able to communicate respecting persons and scenery. But as man, even in this mortal life, is internally a true spiritual organism, and *as such* is, as we have already observed, a subject of the laws of the spirit-world, a clairvoyant may have a *sensational perception* of this spiritual organism, and *thence* of the natural organism, and thus of the entire man himself, however distant they may be from each other as to their natural bodies. Yet still, it is probable, that this *direct* connection is *mediately* effected by the aid of the associate spirit. Here then is the simple and rational, though deeply interesting solution of the un-

doubted fact, that by clairvoyance the actual condition of a person totally unknown to the mesmeriser and his subject, and across the broad Atlantic, has been correctly told. This I have seen extremely useful in a medicinal view—for by directing the attention of a sufficiently lucid clairvoyant to a distant patient, the disease under which the patient was laboring has been discovered, and every interior organ of the body described, both as to its actual condition and general action.

52. Most clairvoyants, strictly so called, are also LUCID, that is, they can see natural objects by an interior perception, independent of the usual visual organs, and, on this account, even when opaque substances intervene. *How* the impression of these outward objects is conveyed to the sensorium is difficult to understand; the fact that such is the case cannot be doubted by any one who has carefully examined the subject. In ordinary vision the mind does not actually contemplate the outward visible object, but the perception of that object as existing in the *imagination*. I do not use the term in the sense of *mere fancy*, as is sometimes done; but by imagination I mean *the general power of the sensorium to form images within itself of objects that are without itself*. I, therefore, consider it a true and proper faculty of the psyche, or animal mind, and thence as a sense above the ordinary senses of the body, and to which they are subservient. For it is by the outward senses, which depend on nervous influence, and their connection with this inward *image-forming* faculty, that mind and matter are brought into mutual relationship and connection.

Whether, therefore, it is by ordinary sight, by cerebral lucidity, or by the suggestions of another's mind, that the ideas of the objects are transmitted to the sensorium, they are equally *subjects* of the image-forming faculty when there, and equally real. I have partially demesmerised a lucid subject, so as to restore the normal conscious state, without demesmerising the eyes, and by that means produced *conscious lucidity*. Every thing was then stated to be seen in a most brilliant light, altogether different to common light, whether solar or artificial; and at the same time all the surrounding objects were seen *at once*, and yet a sense of their separate identity remained. Generally they seemed greatly magnified, and to have more or less of brilliancy about them; all which seems to indicate that the independent action of the sensorium produces more vivid images of the objects impressed upon it; and this might be expected from the exaltation of the senses by the opening of the perceptions of a higher ultimate.

53. We have now taken a brief survey of the principal mesmeric phenomena, and endeavored to account for them, as far as experience, observation, and reason, and necessary brevity will permit. Before concluding, I will notice two questions often proposed, though not always in the spirit of calm enquiry, but rather in that of querulous objection. It is asked, " Whether all persons are subject to mesmeric influence? and why all cannot be made clairvoyant?" In reply to the first, I answer unreservedly, that I believe all persons *are susceptible* of mesmeric influence, but in a very different degree; and this difference we might anticipate from the widely differing nervous temperaments and idiosyn-

crasies of individuals. Some will scarcely feel the influence, while others will soon fall into the "sleep." But as regards the *curative* influence of mesmerism, experience has fully proved that very great benefit may be derived without any loss of consciousness, or even any *perceptible* change of state. Yet the inducing of the *coma*, or mesmeric sleep, generally gives the operator more power over the patient. Let it be remembered, that the great use of mesmeric influence is as a *curative agent*, auxiliary or supplemental to medicine, and that the various exhibitions of catalepsy, phantasy, phreno-mesmerism, etc., are only useful as manifestations of the true nature and capabilities of the human organism. With respect to the second question I would observe, that I have been enabled to learn, that lucidity and clairvoyance can only be developed in individuals who possess a peculiar cerebral organization. This peculiar organization may be normal in some few cases, that is, it may consist with a good state of health; but in many cases it may be traced to some affection of the brain consequent on disease, and the possessor of the faculty will be delicate in health, and less fitted for the ordinary avocations of life. It is not, therefore, a faculty to be generally looked for or desired; but where it does exist, it may be most beneficially employed; and, on the other hand, it may, like all other things, be abused, though possibly, not without ultimately entailing punishment on the offender. In proper hands it may be advantageously used to ascertain the cause of disease, and the best method of effecting a cure; and it affords us a means to acquire most interesting information as to the true nature of our indwelling immortal spirit.

54. In conclusion, permit me to observe, that a calm investigation of the psychical phenomena developed by mesmerism, may become of great use in furthering the interests of religion and morality. By this means we may demonstrate that there is an *internal* way to the mind, as well as the usual external way of the outward senses. This, although admitted by believers in the authority of the Holy Scriptures, has been generally denied by an influential class of writers. It also tends to illustrate and confirm some of those striking and interesting Scripture narratives which have been so often assailed by scepticism and infidelity; and it presents man to us, both in his relation to the spirit-world and the natural world, being, even while tabernacling in mortal flesh, as to his interior, mental, or spiritual organism, in direct communication with a spiritual world, and thus capable, by the very laws of his being, of receiving influences from God and spiritual intelligences, while, by his material organism, he is constituted in direct relation with all outward things. Man is thus presented to us just in the light we might expect, considering that he is the crowning work of the Great Creator's skill. For we may see that he is really and truly that link in the great chain of creation, which God has made to join heaven to earth and earth to heaven!

APPENDIX.

MESMERIC AND PSYCHICAL EXPERIENCE.

1. E. L., the young woman who is the chief subject of the following notes, is a native of Worcestershire. She is about five feet two inches in height, rather sallow complexion, and of a nervous-bilious temperament. Her health, although at times tolerably good, is not robust, nor is she capable of much continued exertion. Before coming into my house, she had been the subject of inflammatory disease of the chest, and of fever, and not long before coming to Bolton, she had been an inmate of the General Hospital, Birmingham, on account of an injury received in the knee. The treatment there had reduced her general health, but improved the knee. She was in this state when I first saw her. Her head is well formed and fully developed. Before the time about to be referred to, she was wholly ignorant that she possessed any peculiar mesmeric susceptibilities. She has since expressed an opinion, that the extraordinary condition of her brain is the result of a very large dose of opium, which she once took by mistake, and which, for a day or two, occasioned very serious symptoms. But this may be considered as very doubtful. She completed her twenty-second year in December, 1848. She will be constantly referred to by the name of EMMA.

2. Towards the close of the autumn of 1846, my attention was directed to the action of the vapor of ether in obliterating the sense of pain—it having been recently brought into public notice for that purpose. Before this time I had seen the vapor of ether used as a substitute for the nitric oxyde, or laughing gas, and had

noticed the intoxicating and exciting effects it produced; but I was, like others, ignorant that it blunted, and in some cases, entirely removed, the sense of pain. Hearing me talk of the effects of ether, Emma said that a cousin of hers had "*mesmerised*" her and another young woman with ether, which they "*sucked*" out of a bottle—indeed, she called it "*The mesmerise.*" Being anxious to test the truth of the reports then in circulation, I asked her if she had any objection to let me see her inhale some of the vapor? She replied, "None at all, for she had no fear of its hurting her." I, therefore, fitted up a common Winchester quart bottle, merely by putting a piece of brass tubing through the cork, which went half way down the bottle, and two or three inches above it. About half an ounce of sulphuric ether was put into the bottle, and the bottle well shaken, to mix the vapor with the contained air; I then gave it her, and told her to put the pipe to her mouth and gently draw in the air in the bottle, without closing the nose, or using any of the valvular apparatus then in use. In less than five minutes I observed that her hands began to loosen their hold of the bottle, which I then removed, the pupils of her eyes became dilated, and presently the eyelids closed. I now found her insensible to pain, or rather to evince *no feeling*, which was ascertained in various ways, such as pinching and pricking various parts of the body, endeavoring to excite tittilation, and even by thrusting pins under the finger nails, but she did not evince the slightest consciousness of these experiments; on the contrary, she was soon in a merry mood, and believed herself to be among her old companions in her native place, rambling through fields, and performing, as she supposed, many rural and domestic occupations. She would laugh, dance, sing, and do many things which were suggested to her; but when awakened, she had scarcely any, if any, recollection of what had occurred. These abnormal states were continued longer than intended, on account of the difficulty experienced in arousing her; for, on one or two occasions, nearly two hours were expended in fully restoring her.

3. Other individuals were now tried, but only one was found,

at that time, at all similar to her in susceptibility to the ethereal influence, and that was a youth who had been mesmerised by Mr. Spencer Hall, when that gentleman was lecturing in Bolton. The same bottle, in like manner, with about half an ounce of ether in it, was given to him, and in five minutes he became insensible, and then exhibited similar phenomena to Emma, but not so striking. He talked and acted, and, like her, imagined himself to be in another place than where he really was. In about half an hour he spontaneously awakened.

4. The very small quantity of ether subsequently found sufficient, merely enough to scent the bottle, induced an opinion that, in Emma's case, the ether had very little to do with the strange things witnessed, but that she was, in a manner, *mesmerised*, or rather *hypnotized*, by looking at the bottle while inhaling through the tube. It was therefore resolved to try another experiment. One evening I told her to sit down, and taking a small pocket-comb desired her to look steadfastly at it. She did so, and in a few minutes fell into the simple mesmeric or hypnotic sleep. Afterwards a small magnet was used for the same purpose and with the same results. A few days further on, I mesmerised her in the usual mode, that is, by looking fixedly at her. The youth mentioned above was also submitted to a similar experiment, by causing him to gaze steadfastly on a small magnet held a few inches from his eyes. In both cases, results were obtained similar to those following the use of the ether, namely, insensibility to pain, and a sort of somnambulic wakeful dreaming. In both these cases the only difference yet perceptible between the effects of the ether and those resulting from hypnotizing or mesmerising was, that by the latter mode the limbs could be made rigid—cataleptic, as it is called—while no such rigidity could be induced after the inhalation of the ether. Up to this time, dancing, singing, and doing various things which were *audibly suggested*, as if they were real, and rigidity of the limbs, after downward passes, were the only phenomena noticed; and it was thought that the statements made by some writers, of the *personal influence*

of the operator over the subject, were merely fanciful, and not warranted by fact.

5. Some time in the summer of 1847, while experimenting with Emma, I accidently placed my hand on the part of the head marked on busts as the organ of veneration; she immediately began repeating the Apostle's creed; when my hand was removed she ceased, and when it was replaced she commenced repeating where she left off. This was the first manifestation I got of the phrenological sentiments, and interested me greatly; but it was some weeks before I succeeded in exciting the other sentiments or feelings. Afterwards benevolence, veneration, firmness, self-esteem, philoprogenitiveness, acquisitiveness, combativeness, etc., were easily excited, and often most powerfully manifested. Up to this time, no absolute proof of *personal influence* was discovered, but she became more easily and quickly mesmerised, and as easily awakened into the normal state.

6. It was now found that Emma would exhibit all the usual mesmeric phenomena, such as catalepsy, or rigidity of the limbs—for she could be fixed immovably in any position by the action of a few passes; she could be so far demesmerised as to be restored to outward consciousness, and yet be unable to move the mesmerised arm or leg. *Attraction* she could also manifest, even in the same conscious state, as I often had the opportunity of showing to friends and neighbors, who were as much surprised as amused. For example, a piece of money would be placed on a table at a distant part of the room, and it was told her she might have it for fetching it. She frequently essayed to do so, and would sometimes very nearly reach the money; but invariably, my will, and the drawing passes I made towards myself, overcame her power, and notwithstanding her determined efforts, would draw her to myself, and render all her endeavors to secure the money ineffectual. On these occasions, she described the sensations she experienced as being like cords wound round her and drawing her. The various phenomena of phantasy could also be most readily produced; but when she became clairvoyant, if she was desired to *look at* the object that

she *imagined* to be so widely different to what it really was, she would instantly perceive the *delusion*, and dash it from her; and yet, within a minute or two, she could be as easily deluded again. But the investigation of these ordinary mesmeric states was not confined to those exhibited by Emma, but their truthfulness was further confirmed in the case of several youths, who were experimented upon, both privately and publicly, and who exhibited the same phenomena, but modified in each case by the general character of the individual. Since the period referred to, Emma's susceptibility has considerably increased, and now I can fasten the arms, hands, or mouth, or fix her to the spot on which she may be standing or sitting, by a single movement or pressure of my hand, *without putting her into the mesmeric sleep.*

7. It was not long, after Emma became so fully susceptible, before opportunities occurred for proving the reality of *personal influence*, and that a highly mesmeric subject may be acted upon, even when wholly unaware of the exertion of such influence. Many experiments were tried to ascertain the truth on this point; but I will only mention three among many cases that took place spontaneously, or rather, which occurred without my mind being directed to her. Once a gentleman asked me unexpectedly, in a neighbor's house, several doors from mine, to mesmerise him. I tried, but did not succeed. On returning home, I found Emma in the mesmeric state, and, upon enquiry, found that she had gone into that state while I was endeavoring to mesmerise the gentleman. On another occasion, I was wishful to induce the mesmeric sleep on a lady, for the relief of a rheumatic affection from which she was suffering. Finding the continual *stare* very fatiguing to my eyes, and also expecting to be called away by patients, it occurred to me, that if I directed her to look steadfastly at something, it might answer the same purpose, and allow me to leave her, without interrupting the mesmeric action. I therefore arose, and took a small magnet and suspended it by a wire from a hook in the ceiling. Emma was in a room under where I was operating, and knew nothing of my movements. In a few

minutes the smell of burning linen arrested my attention, and I desired my daughter to go down stairs and ascertain the cause. She called to me quickly to come down; I did so, and found Emma *mesmerised*, and on her knees before the fire, engaged in sweeping the hearth, and her apron on fire, from contact with a burning coal that had fallen from the grate—but of this she was unconscious, and her attention was wholly directed to a point in the ceiling of the room. Having asked "What she was doing or looking at?" she replied, "*I want that magnet.*" Upon enquiry, I found that she had been engaged just under where I was sitting; the influence had passed through the floor and ceiling and affected her unconsciously in the room below, and being now clairvoyant, she immediately saw the magnet through the ceiling, etc., and pointed accurately to its situation. But from the locality of the room, and the magnet having been used without any previous intimation of my intention—in fact it did not occur to me to do so until the patient had been some time seated—she could not possibly know of its being in the situation in which I had placed it, by any *normal* means. Here then was one, among numerous spontaneous instances, of the transmission and reception of a *personal influence*, and of the reality of clairvoyance. On another occasion, I was called to see a patient residing more than a mile and a half from my residence; the case was one of *delirium tremens*, and I resolved to try the soothing influence of mesmerism, and, in this instance, succeeded in a few minutes. On returning home, I found that Emma had gone into the mesmeric state at the time I was operating on my patient; but, fortunately, she was in a situation where no harm happened to her. By way of experiment, I frequently mesmerised her when in another room, and unknown to her; but in the above-named, and other cases, I did not think of her; and the circumstance can only be explained from her known susceptibility and my being actually engaged in exerting a mesmeric influence and intention. This extreme susceptibility to my personal influence, for a considerable period, prevented my using mesmerism as a curative agent, inasmuch as I feared to exercise the power, unless I knew that Emma was in a place of safety, and would be kept from danger, in case she should become unawares mesmerised.

8. In the early part of 1847, Emma wished to have the vapor of ether administered, with the view of having an aching tooth removed without pain; but the striking effects I had seen follow upon mesmerising her, induced me to refuse the ether, and, in the evening, to mesmerise her, and thus further test the power of the mesmeric sleep to subdue pain. About 9 o'clock that evening I desired her to sit down; induced the mesmeric sleep, and then leisurely got the necessary instruments; lanced her gum; extracted the tooth; as soon as the bleeding was arrested, washed her mouth, and then aroused her. The entire time from sitting down until fully aroused, was just *fifteen minutes*. During the operation she did not evince the slightest sensibility; but as soon as the removal of the instrument gave liberty to her mouth, she began to hum a tune, even while the blood was flowing. On awakening, she knew nothing of what had taken place after going into the sleep, and could hardly be persuaded that the tooth on the table before her had been extracted from her jaw! Some time afterwards, Mr. Patrick, surgeon-dentist, of Bolton, extracted a large decayed molar tooth from her lower jaw, under similar circumstances. On the latter occasion, several friends were witnesses of the operation.

9. DISCOVERY OF LUCIDITY AND CLAIRVOYANCE.—In the autumn of 1847, it was told me, that there was a young woman in Bolton, who had travelled the country with a mesmeric lecturer, and who had been for a long time CLAIRVOYANT. Having heard much of this wonderful faculty, I was desirous to see her. She was soon afterwards introduced to me for examination. I found that she was very easily mesmerised, and in that state she knew me and others in the room; also, that she was fully susceptible of feeling; in these respects differing widely from Emma. I could not, therefore, fully satisfy myself as to *the reality* of the mesmeric state. The young woman said, that she had formerly been in the same state as Emma, but had

passed beyond it; and, from subsequent experience, I think this may be correct. She told me that she had been taken by several London physicians to examine the internal organs of patients by the faculty of clairvoyance; but when I saw her, her powers seemed to be confined to reading books with large print, with the eyes bandaged. I tried the experiment several times, but never felt satisfied with the result; as from the position in which she placed the book, the time occupied in the endeavor, and the occasional wriggling, I could never be certain that she did not see under the bandages. At other times, I was certainly much surprised at the readiness she evinced in describing a book I had in my hand. On the whole, I concluded, that her possession of the faculty of clairvoyance was, to say the least, doubtful. But it soon after occurred to me, that if she ever could see in the manner she stated, perhaps Emma could see in the same manner. At all events, I had the most positive assurance that she went into the mesmeric state, and that in that state she could not see, but that the power of vision was wholly withdrawn; the *sense of hearing* alone connecting her consciously with the external world.

10. One evening I determined to try her. But at this period she could not read, and was ignorant even of the letters of the alphabet. I therefore chose pictorial representations for the test, as being a universal language, understood alike both by the learned and the unlearned. I took a school book belonging to my daughter, which contained various wood-cuts, and opening it at one, I placed it in her hand, saying, "Emma, what is this picture?" She took the book, and as if by instinct, placed it open over her forehead and upper part of the cranium, without the least attempt to look at it in the ordinary way, and said, almost directly, "Oh yes, it is a naughty boy catching flies at the window, and his mother is looking at him." This was the subject of the picture and the story annexed. There was a figure of a boy at a window, endeavoring to catch a fly, and another figure of a female standing in the room observing him. I felt most exceedingly surprised and astonished at the correctness of the description, being assured that she could not see it

by any ordinary use of the eye, or, in fact, by the eye at all. This experiment was repeated with many different pictures, and invariably with the same result; colored pictures were also tried, and it was found that she knew the different colors accurately; but on no occasion did she attempt to use the eye—she invariably placed the object over her head.

11. It was now thought, that as mesmerism evidently rested on a psychological basis, and that a manifest connection was discoverable between the mind of the mesmeriser and the mesmerised subject, she might possibly see these pictures somehow in my memory, and not from any independent power of vision. I, therefore, requested my daughter to select the pictures, and then to put them into my hand, without telling me the subject, or letting me see them. This was repeatedly done, and the pictures as accurately described as when I knew the subject. Still it was thought that my giving her the pictures might have some effect upon her; others, therefore gave her them, or she was allowed to take them herself from a number, or to turn over the pages of a book, without any one knowing what she had taken, or had turned to, until she had described what she had selected. But it was found that it made no difference, and demonstrated, that whatever was the *power*, or wherever the *seat* of vision, *it was her own*, and independent of any one else.

12. These, and similar experiments, have been successfully performed, in private, before a select company, and also before large public audiences; and this too, with her eyes covered with plaisters, and a bandage tied over the plaisters. Not that the plaisters or bandages made any difference; but they were used for the sake of convincing sceptical people. At this time, in ascertaining the subject of a picture, she first passed the tips of the fingers of the right hand gently over it (the left hand did not seem to possess the same power), and then placed it over that part of the head, marked on phrenological busts as the organ of IMITATION. If a book with prints on the pages was given her, she would pass her right fingers gently over the page, and if it was letter-press or blank, she would say, "It

was nothing." But when she had thus found out the situation of the print, she would exclaim, " Oh yes! here it is;" or " I've got it." But whether the print was a wood-cut, or copper-plate, did not appear to make any difference.

13. A very curious phenomenon was now observed. Pictures of things did not appear to her *as pictures*, but *as the things represented*. So that *the picture* of a rose would convey as *vivid* and *real* an idea to her sensorium, as the *rose itself* would do to an individual in the ordinary state. Hence it was found, that if a picture of *thistles*, *teazels*, or other prickly plants, or of *bees*, was given into her hand, the moment the tips of her right fingers came into contact with the picture, she would exclaim that she was *pricked* or *stung*, and throw the picture from her with much violence and passion! Evidently proving, that the *representations* of things were to her *real;* and also suggesting, that she had a perception of the form of the objects, before placing the picture on her head. These experiments were performed many times, both publicly and privately. And from her invariable use of the tips of the right fingers, it was supposed that there existed some unknown but remarkable affinity, between the senses of touch and sight.

14. By the commencement of 1848, her power of internal sight had become so developed, or she had become so familiarized with her new faculty, that it was evident, from many things observed, that she could see such things *as he. mind was directed to*, without any contact. As an experiment, small pictures, and various small objects, were placed singly, first in a card box, and afterwards in a wooden box; and these she told, at times, as readily as when out of the box and in her hands. At other times, more difficulty was experienced in satisfactorily determining that she could see them. This difficulty arose from two causes: first, from the manner in which she would describe what she saw; and, secondly, from an obstinacy of temper frequently displayed, when removed by mesmeric influence from *external* habit and control. Her usual manner was to describe things *as they appeared to her in the internal state*, regardless of the names imposed upon them

by custom; sometimes she refused to call things by their accustomed name, and would always describe them in her own way, before she called them by the common name. As an instance, the following may be given. At the second public lecture, in the Temperance Hall, Bolton, on the 9th of March, 1848, a gentleman in front of the platform suggested that a picture, from among others lying on the floor, should be put into a box, and given to her—she had then been bandaged for some time. A print of a cat was selected, and put into a card box; she put the box over her head, felt it carefully with her right fingers, and then, having by a smile and ejaculation evinced that she saw the contents, she began—"It is a thing; it is a dark thing; it has four legs, a tail, a head and two eyes; things round its mouth, and it sits by the fire and says *mew*, and it's a cat."

15. One cause of difficulty in attaining clear descriptions of the things to which her attention was directed, and sometimes even in getting her to notice them, was very early perceivable. In the exalted condition of mesmerism, her mind was peculiarly susceptible of impressions from the minds of surrounding persons; hence, when environed by a knot of sceptics, as was sometimes the case, their mental influence, unconsciously to themselves, would seriously impede the faculties of the clairvoyant; and then the feeling that something was preventing the usual development of her powers, caused irritation and obstinacy. At the period alluded to, when Emma was asked "How she saw things?" she would say, that suddenly "*glasses*" came to her, and also, that she sees every thing *in light* through these "glasses;" and the situation of these "*glasses*" she always referred to the organs of imitation. When this doubting, opposing influence was brought to bear upon her, she would exclaim, "They are darkening my glasses;" or "They have taken away my glasses." I frequently found that by making *passes* from the upper part of the head, *across* the organs of imitation, I could *produce* and *increase* the clairvoyant power, which she would evince by exclaiming, "Oh, its *so* light now,;" while by making longitudinal passes, from the vortex, over the forehead

and down to the face, the sight could be immediately closed, and she would be placed in a state of darkness. Bodily fatigue, or indisposition, would, at that time, and also does at the present time, considerably impair the powers, not only of clairvoyance, but all the other mesmeric capabilities.

16. Besides the description of pictures, etc., already noticed, she frequently described persons in another room, and said what they were doing; frequently, without having her attention directed to the inquiry. At other times she would unexpectedly, and unasked, tell individuals what they had in their pockets, or what sort of food was contained in their stomach. This often afforded matter for interesting experiments; and has been witnessed by many respectable persons in the neighborhood.

17. For a considerable time after she exhibited the most distinct lucidity, with respect to objects placed near her, no trace could be found of that distant clairvoyance manifested by some mesmeric subjects: but, eventually, this faculty became as clearly developed as the other. The first time I observed this power, was in the case of some near relatives in London. She described minutely the dress and appearance of these parties; their occupation at a certain time, and many other particulars, which were subsequently found to be correct. Once I directed her attention to a female relative in London. Emma speedily found her, and began to describe her residence, etc., but suddenly her attention ceased to be directed to my relative, and she became engrossed with the description of a magnificent residence, with its elegant and costly furniture; a lady lying in a superb bed; a beautifully dressed baby; well dressed ladies in and about the room; and another room in which were older children, also beautifully dressed, and attended by ladies. From many replies to my inquiries, I considered that the only place to which her impassioned descriptions could refer, was Buckingham Palace, for the accouchment of the queen had then recently occurred. I therefore said, "Do you see any soldiers there?" "Yes," she replied, "there are soldiers at the door." I then saw that my conjecture was correct; but *why* she should have spontaneously gone there, without any request on my

part, or, indeed, any thought or desire in that respect, I could not understand. But after I had informed my relative of this occurrence, I obtained the clue to this singular transition from one subject to another. For I was informed that she had been thinking of the queen, and the interesting circumstances in which she was then placed; and had felt desirous that I should, as an experiment, try whether Emma had the power to visit and describe the interior of the palace at that time. The cause therefore, of Emma's unexpected *visit to royalty* was this: my relative had wished her to go there; when brought into mesmeric connection with her, the active sentiment of her mind, was communicated to Emma's mind; and by this means, her attention was unconsciously directed to the royal residence. But there was further confirmation that this was the true cause, and of the possibility of a mesmerised subject receiving impressions from the parties to whom their attention is directed. For when I knew, from my relative's letter, what had been the subject of her thoughts, I put Emma into the mesmeric state, and then asked her, "*How* and *why* she went to see the queen?" She directly replied, "L—— took me." But how did you get in if there were soldiers at the door? "O! I jumped over th soldiers; but L—— could not jump over them, and therefore she could not get in."

18. At this time, whenever *sent* on these *distant excursions*, she exhibited great fatigue and excitement; panting, and suffering from violent action of the heart. When asked why she panted so? she would say, "I've gone so fast,"—and "It is *such* a way!" She would also take my right hand and place it on her bosom: if I removed it, she said, "They are gone away now." But latterly she has not required any personal contact to enable her to exercise this faculty. Very many experiments were made to test this faculty: in some cases she was strikingly correct; in others only approximately so; for she would sometimes confound the recollection of *bygone* transactions existing in the minds of distant individuals, with *present* circumstances, and thus present a representation which required some explanation to unravel.

19. Having heard of clairvoyants *visiting the planets*, I determined to try the experiment with Emma. I therefore proposed *an excursion to the moon;* and not then knowing how to direct her attention to such distant objects; and she herself being, at the time alluded to, wholly ignorant of the mode by which a knowlege of distant things is obtained; and fancying that she actually traveled by some mode, I suggested the *electric telegraph* as an expeditious mode of conveyance. The suggestion answered the purpose, and she was, mentally, soon on our satelite. But on that and subsequent occasions, the great excitement produced by the strangeness of what she saw, and the *distance traveled*, caused such a palpitation of the heart, as to render it necessary to *shorten the visit*, by de-mesmerising her; being fearful that the great physical excitement might produce some serious effect on her health, if not immediate danger. Her description of what she saw was conveyed in very ejaculatory language; from the surprise and pleasure she experienced. Her statements were to the effect, that the moon is inhabited; that the inhabitants she saw were very small—dwarfs—not larger than children on our earth; their heads were large in proportion to their bodies, and the mouth *vertical* rather than *horizontal;* their voices harsh, and rough, and resembling the sound of distant thunder; and when they spoke, the speech seemed to come up from the bowels. Their "insides" were not quite like ours; the lungs especially were different. She saw some food, something that looked somewhat like bread, but they did not call it by that name. She saw only one animal, something like a very small pig. There dwellings were constructed of pieces of rocks, covered over with green stuff resembling gorse: they were very low, for she could put her hand to the top. The place did not look like what she conceived the moon to be; but a large place, and very rocky, with immense precipices, and lofty mountains. The "little folks," as she called the inhabitants, could clamber up these rocks with their hands and feet, so fast that she could not catch them. "Is there any water there?" "Yes: but it does not look like our water, but more like milk and water, and yet it is clear. (Meaning prob-

ably, that it is of greater density than our water.) It lies in the bottom of hollows, and down the steep precipices. The 'little folks' can walk upon this water and not sink; they are very light. They wear clothes; but they are very simple and all alike. They seem good sort of people. They have a curious way of jumping on the back of each other. A very little baby was seen in a sort of cradle; it died: they said what signified that, it had gone to sleep; but they did not mean sleep, but that it was dead."

20. At another time I attempted to send her to JUPITER; but the physical excitement was so great, that I thought it prudent to call off her attention, before I had obtained any definite remarks. She spoke of having been *further* than where she had before seen the "little folks;" and of seeing them as she came back.

21. Besides the power of seeing, by an internal sight, such things as were put into her hands, or to which her *attention was directed*, Emma would sometimes manifest a sort of apparently omnipresent vision. Thus she has frequently been asked to find missing or lost articles. After a few minutes consideration, she has said where they might be found; or, in other cases, got up and pointed out the place where they lay concealed. And this she has repeatedly done, when there was the most undoubted evidence, that neither herself, in the normal condition, nor the mesmeriser, nor any other individual, knew the situation of the articles she was desired to look for. Thus proving, that not only can an unusual mode of seeing be developed by mesmerism, but also an exalted degree of power, which makes all things, whatever their local position, appear directly within the sphere of vision. This power has been, on most occasions, called into exercise chiefly for the sake of experiment, and to test its reality; but it has also been applied to purposes of use. The following is a remarkable instance; and also valuable as placing the reality and powers of clairvoyance, or internal sight, beyond the reach of cavil or contradiction.

22. On Wednesday evening, December 20th, 1848, Mr. Wood, grocer, of Cheapside, Bolton, had his cash box, with its

contents, stolen from his counting house. After applying to the police, and taking other precautionary steps, and having no clue to the thief, although he suspected what was proved to be an innocent party; and having heard of Emma's powers as a clairvoyant, he applied to me, to ascertain whether, by her means, he could discover the party who had taken it, or recover his property. I felt considerable hesitation in employing Emma's powers for such a purpose; fearing that both the motive and agency might be grossly misrepresented. But the amount at stake, the opportunity for experiment, and Mr. Wood being a neighbor, induced me to comply with his request; and nine o'clock, next morning, was appointed for the trial. At that hour Mr. Wood came to my residence, and I then put Emma, by mesmerism, into the internal state, and then told her that Mr. Wood (whom I put *en rapport*, as it is called, with her) had lost his cash box, and that I wished her to tell us, if she could, where the box was taken from, what was in it, and who took it. She remained silent a few minutes, evidently mentally seeking for what she had been requested to discover. Presently she began to talk with an imaginary personage, as if present in the room with us; but as it subsequently proved, although invisible and imaginary to us, he was both *real* and *visible* to her; for she had discovered the thief, and was conversing with his mind on the robbery. She described, in the course of this apparent conversation, and afterward to us, where the box was placed; what the general nature of its contents was, particularizing some documents it contained; how he took it, and that he did not take it away to his residence at once, but hid it up an entry; and her description of his person, dress, associations, etc., was so vivid, that Mr. W. immediately recognized the purloiner of his property, in a person the last to be suspected. Feeling satisfied, from the general accuracy of her descriptions, and also from her describing the contents of the box, that she had really pointed out the delinquent, Mr. W. went directly to the house where he resided, and which she had pointed out, even to the letters on the door-plate; and insisted on his accompanying him to my house; or, in case of refusal, to the police office. When brought, and placed in connection with Emma, she started back from him, as if he had been a serpent; telling him that he was a bad man, and observing, also, that he had not the same clothes on as when he took the box; which was the fact. He denied strenuously all knowledge of the robbery, then, and up to a late hour in the afternoon; but as he was not permitted to go at large, and thus had no opportunity for destroying, or effectually concealing the box; and as Mr. Wood had promised, for the sake of his connections, not to prosecute, if confession was made, and the box and contents recovered, he, at last, admitted that he had taken it, and in the manner described by Emma; and the box and contents were found in the place where he had secreted them; broken open; but the property safe. It should be observed, that Emma had pointed out the place where the box was concealed, but we could not be certain of the place she meant, without permitting her, while in the *internal state*, to lead us to it: this the confession rendered unnecessary.

23. In other cases Emma has described articles that have been lost by parties placed *en rapport* with her, without her being asked to do so, or, indeed, anything being said respecting them. In some instances these have been most interesting experiments, affording evidence of her being able to trace a series of events, totally unknown to her in the normal state, back through a number of years.

24. Several times she has been directed to seek for persons in distant regions of the globe. Whenever she has found them, her statements of time and season, invariably coincided with the latitude and longitude of the places to which she has been directed. At present, one complete proof only has been obtained of her really having a distinct and truthful perception of such distant objects. A young man had sailed from Liverpool for New York, without apprising his parents of his intention of doing so, until the day the ship sailed. His parents immediately remitted him a sum of money by the mail steamer; but they were subsequently informed, that he had not applied for it; nor had any thing been heard of him, although the ship in which he

sailed had long arrived. In a state of anxiety the young man's mother came twenty miles to Bolton, to see whether, by Emma's means, she could learn any thing of him. After a little time, Emma found him; described his appearance correctly; and entered into so many details, as to induce his mother to rely upon her statements; and to request me to make inquiries at intervals of about a fortnight. I did so, and traced him by her means to several places; and the information thus acquired, I transmitted to his parents. On the 24th of January, in the present year, I received a note from the young man's father, informing me that a letter had arrived from his son, and that "it was a most striking confirmation of Emma's testimony from first to last"

CLAIRVOYANCE AS APPLIED TO PHYSIOLOGY AND MEDICINE.

25. For more than eighteen months, Emma has been able to see the internal organs of the human body. At first, only when placed in personal connection with the individual to be examined; but subsequently, when the parties were many miles distant. In her best state, the human body seems to her completely transparent, and might be compared to a watch, whose case and works were all of the most transparent chrystal. I discovered this power from her remarks on myself One evening she began to describe my lungs, as "*pink things*," full of holes like a sponge, with air in the holes, and thousands of little veins in all directions. She said the right lung was not so good a color as the left, and that it stuck at the middle flap. This I knew to be the case, and thought she might only be giving utterance to my own ideas. But I soon found that this was not the case; but, as in the case of the pictures, she really did see what she described. I asked her some questions about the heart, which she accurately described, as to the auricles and ventricles; the contained arterial and venous blood, etc;

but, as might be expected, in very homely language. I thought her at fault once; but found, that while I was thinking about the heart, she had wandered to the windpipe, with its rings. It was some time after the discovery of this faculty, before it could be used without inconvenience; for when her attention was directed to the internal organs of the body, the strangeness of the sight, together with the universal motion, and circulating blood, so terrified her, that she would tremble from head to foot; and, when awakened, complained of being ill and frightened, without knowing the cause. But, by degrees, she became familiarized with these investigations, and she will now calmly, and without any fear, examine and describe the internal organs. Her manner on these occasions is always serious and kind; her language soft, but, from her want of education, imperfect. Had she received an anatomical education, her gift would be more valuable, or rather, more accurate descriptions could be given; but, on the other hand, her want of education proves that she does not derive the knowledge of the internal organism of the body which she evinces, from her previously stored memory. The application of this power, appears to be one of the most legitimate uses of clairvoyance, and perhaps the most beneficial in its application. By it an accurate diagnosis may be formed of many internal diseases, which elude the ordinary mode of research. But to make a clairvoyant diagnosis, truly satisfactory, it often requires the aid of the medical practitioner, or the professed anatomist and physiologist, rightly to interpret the language of the clairvoyant. Many curious points in physiology, which, from the nature of the case, rested rather upon rational induction than positive demonstration, have, to my mind, been satisfactorily determined by the revealments of clairvoyance; especially as regards the action of the brain and nervous system, and the action of the heart; and the knowledges thus obtained have an important bearing on the mode by which diseases of these important organs may be cured.

26. On the 4th of August, 1848, a gentleman of Bolton brought a letter, written by a lady the wife of a physician in

Gloucestershire, and this lady, who had heard of other clairvoyants describing the diseases of distant people, merely by using their handwriting as a medium of communication, desired that it should be given to Emma, to ascertain whether she could discover the condition of the writer. It must be remembered that Emma could not read printing, much less writing; the subject matter of the letter was of no consequence, it was the *handwriting*, as a medium of connection. Emma put it over her head, as she used to do with pictures, and carefully felt it with her right fingers, and then said "it was a lady's *up and down strokes*," meaning by that phrase, the handwriting of a lady. She described the lady, as to her personal appearance, accurately, even to a small blemish occasioned by an accident; the internal organs of the body; an affection of the spine under which she was laboring; the situation and appearance of the place where she resided, and many more particulars. The accuracy of her descriptions was admitted by the doctor; and, subsequently, I had an opportunity, personally, to verify some of her statements. The envelope of the letter was directed by the doctor; him she described correctly, both as to his personal character, general pursuits, and literary tendencies. This was an entirely new experiment; and finding the result so unexpected and striking, it led to many more; some of which were, apparently, more remarkable. Among others, I may mention the case of a letter written by a gentleman at Cairo, which was put into her hand. She soon said it was written by a gentleman, and described him, as to the condition of his health, and the place where he was residing, together with the climate and appearance of the people there, even to the peculiar veil worn by the Egyptian ladies. The correctness of her statement, as to the gentleman's condition, was ascertained from a subsequent letter. Locks of hair have also been similarly used as a medium; but the handwriting appeared to be the easier and better mode of forming the connection.

27. On the 29th of September, 1848, an opportunity was afforded for an entirely new manifestation of Emma's powers. A highly respectable gentleman of Manchester, having, at that

time, a daughter seriously ill with a cerebral disease, which baffled the ordinary medical treatment, and which, in addition to bodily infirmity, had produced a state of insanity, had been recommended to try whether by clairvoyance a mode of cure could be discovered. He came on the previous day; but Emma then being in the state of trance, to be presently described, he could not obtain the information sought. He left with me a few pencil marks made by the lady, as a means of forming a medium of connection. On the date above, I gave this piece of paper to Emma, and asked her if she could find the person who made the marks, and tell me what was the matter with her; for at that time I had no idea of her selecting any appropriate remedies. She soon found the lady; described, accurately, the external symptoms of her complaint, and also the internal condition of her brain; to which organ she referred the whole cause of illness. After recommending various mesmeric passes, she exclaimed, pointing at the same time toward the ceiling of the room—"There is what will cure that lady, along with mesmerism; Eh! what little bottles!" These she described as containing little things like the small comfits, generally called "thousands." I said, "Is there any thing like them in my shop or surgery?" "No! you have nothing like them." "Where can they be obtained?" "There—in that big town (pointing toward Manchester), in that shop with a head in the window; they are kept there in a drawer." It would not have occurred to me what medicines she meant, but that in the previous month, when in London, I had been shown, by a lady, a case of homeopathic medicines. I do not recollect ever before seeing any; and I was quite ignorant at that time as to the mode of preparing and using them. I am certain also, that in her normal state Emma knew nothing about, nor had ever seen, any of these medicines. The shop, I subsequently found, was Mr. Turner's, homeopathic chemist, Piccadilly, Manchester, and in the shop window, there was a bust of Hahneman, the founder of homeopathy. But I was ignorant that there was such a shop in that neighborhood, having seldom occasion to go to that part of the city. I wrote to the gentleman informing him of Emma's remarks; and he directly purchased a case from Mr. Turner, and came over to Bolton to ascertain the particulars. The *sealed box* was put into Emma's hand, and as soon as she had put it over her head, she said that it contained the medicines she before saw; and pointed especially to the situation of one bottle in the case. When the case was opened, she selected a bottle from the place she had pointed out, and *tasted the globules through the glass*, without attempting to draw the cork. By way of test, the bottle was put into another part of the case, and other bottles slipped into her hand; but she invariably detected the change, by *tasting through the glass*, and putting the bottle to her forehead. From that time, the prescribed globules were daily administered, and the mesmeric passes regularly made; and the result is, the restoration of the lady to health, both in mind and body.

28. The result of this experiment opened a new field for inquiry, and led to repeated trials. A quantity of the usual medicines were mixed with sugar, and put into small vials, and given her with the homeopathic medicines, and these she would select and test in the same way; namely, by *tasting them through the bottle*. Sometimes she would select homeopathic remedies; at other times, the usual ones. She invariably calls those which she considers suitable for the disease, *nice;* the others she calls *nasty;* but I sometimes found, that the "*nice*" medicines were intensely bitter; such, for instance, as the sulphate of quinine. How she obtains this intuitive knowledge of medicines I cannot discover. The homeopathic remedies have generally been the best that could be selected according to that theory of therapeutics; and the usual medicines have been quite as judiciously prescribed, as to their *qualities;* but of the *quantity*, and mode of preparation she was unable to speak. Sometimes she was unable to point out any remedies for the disorders she described; and hence the necessity for a knowledge of the properties of medicine, in some one, in order to profit by her revealments. Her powers appear to be chiefly applicable to nervous diseases, and diseases of the lungs, liver, and heart. Many cases have been submitted to her, from different parts

of the country; and some of these, of a most serious character have been rapidly cured by an adoption of the means recommended. Since the period when this faculty for examining and prescribing for distant patients was discovered, a change has passed over her; and she can now do without any medium of connection; but requires the name and address of the party seeking relief, and that appears to be sufficient to enable her to discover them. But the handwriting of the patient, or the intervention of some friend, seems to insure greater accuracy. Upon awakening from these clairvoyant examinations, Emma has no recollection of any thing she has said or done; they being, in this respect, like all other *mesmeric* trances. But of course, the information thus obtained is available to the medical practitioner in all similar cases.

29. Her statements of the way in which some diseases are removed, and of the permeability of the solid tissues of the body, are very remarkable; but at the same time are in accordance with the suggestions of profound physiologists; and, moreover, they seem to be borne out by the facts of the case.

30. That *exalted sense*, before referred to, which enables her to see things to which her attention is directed, as apparently within the sphere of vision, whatever their locality, is also manifest, though in another mode, in her selection of medicines; for by *tasting through the bottle*, she has been enabled to identify the homeopathic globules with the tinctures from which they are prepared! This may be considered one of the strongest proofs that a medicinal virtue resides in them; for so highly attenuated are the dilutions with which they are saturated, that to the ordinary sense, they all taste alike, and merely of the sugar of milk, of which the body of the globule is composed; and I understand that they are not cognizable, even by chemical test.

SPONTANEOUS EXTASIS, OR TRANCE.

31. The foregoing notes refer to the phenomena witnessed in the state of induced extasis, or mesmeric trance; the ensuing very briefly relate states of a much higher, or more interior character, and differing, in some respects essentially, from the observed facts of ordinary mesmerism.

32. Frequently during the spring and summer, Emma would, in the mesmeric state, speak of the scenery and nature of the spirit-world, in such a way as to impress the beholder with a conviction that the descriptions she gave could not be the result of any previously acquired knowledge, or of an active imagination. She also occasionally spoke of things which had actually occurred, but which it was impossible for her to know by any ordinary means. Her ideas of religion were principally derived from the teachings of a village schoolmistress, in connection with the Church of England, and from occasional attendance at the public services of the church. She had been taught to read a little when a child, but had lost the acquirement through a fever; and, as before observed, at this time she could not read, nor even correctly tell the letters of the alphabet; and yet the ideas to which she sometimes gave utterance were of an elegant and exalted description. As she still continued to have no recollection of what she uttered when she returned to the normal state, I one day said to her, "Emma, I have heard of some persons having seen such things as you speak of, but they could recollect what they saw, and write an account of it in books." She replied, "Yes; because it was permitted them; *and she should also be permitted by and by to recollect what she saw.*" I did not tell her this when she awoke; nor did I expect then that her prediction would be verified. But subsequent events proved that she was correct in making this assertion.

33. The first of these spontaneous states of extasis, or spiritual trance, occurred on the 3rd of July, 1848, without any expectation or forewarning on her part. This did not last more than a quarter of an hour. Afterward she had several which

lasted about half an hour; and since these, some which have extended from four to ten hours. Of most of these states, she had a presentiment *while in the mesmeric state;* and in one instance foretold the occurrence nearly two months before it happened. But she knew nothing of what was forthcoming while in her ordinary wakeful state ; and for the sake of experiment, and to test the truthfulness of her predictions, she was never informed when these trances were to occur; yet she was found correct, even to the exact time. They have usually been preceded by a feeling of quietness, and a somewhat confused sensation in the head, but no pain. Several gentlemen whom I had apprised of her statements, have been witnesses of their accuracy, and of the *genuineness* of this abnormal condition.

34. In these states she preserved a recollection, at times, of the place she was actually in, and of the persons by whom she was surrounded, and, at the same time, she had a distinct and *sensational* perception of a higher and spiritual state of existence, and of a class of beings living in such a state. She would speak of these things while in the trance, and on her return to the normal state she could recollect, and would again describe what she had seen and heard. During the first trance, of four hours duration, which occurred on the 28th of September, 1848, she was so far elevated in her perceptions that she spoke of *this* world, as the *other* world, just as if she had passed from this life by death. She said, also, that the perons in the room with her appeared only like shadows, and a long way from her. Upon examination she was found, in this and other trances, insensible to pain, and her eyes upturned, as in the ordinary mesmeric state, and her limbs continued flexible. At times she would seem wholly indrawn, and then she would, as it were, return and speak of what was passing before her mental vision. But in the next trance, of six hours' duration, and subsequently, she became for a part of it quite insensible to all outward things, and perfectly cataleptic from head to foot. A gentleman from Manchester, who was present with me on this occasion, assisted me to raise her body, and we found it as stiff and inflexible as a log of wood.

35. I took the opportunity, during one of these trances, to ascertain whether she could see concealed natural substances, as in the ordinary mesmeric state. I put my hand in my pocket and withdrew it with a shilling concealed in the closed fist. I inquired, "What have I in my hand?" "Only a shilling," was the immediate reply. It must be remembered that the eyelids were closed, and the eyeballs up-turned, so as totally to prevent ordinary vision. I then put my hand into my pocket again, and withdrew it with a half-a-crown and a shilling enclosed, and asked her, "Can you see what is *now* in my hand?" she replied, "Stop a little, till I've seen these," alluding to the spiritual objects then engrossing her attention; but when I again asked her, she was about coming out of the trance, and could not then see.

36. One instance of her sight will be related, because it is a proof that there is *a reality* in her extatic perceptions, and that she then eminently possesses a super-sensual gift. On the 11th of July she told me, when in the mesmeric state, that an individual whom I well knew, but who had been dead for some years, had told her that on the following night they should come to her, and show her a book with some writing in, which she was to take and show to me. From some of her remarks, I concluded that one of three books was intended:—one, a small bible, *not then in the house.* Former experience having convinced me of the reality of her observations, and the certainty of her predictions, I got this little bible, and put it with the other books, among many more. In the night she awoke in a state of trance, similar to somnambulism, and descending two flights of stairs, selected this book from all the others, and then brought it open to me. Owing to the darkness, I inadvertently knocked the book out of her hand, while seeking a light. She speedily found the place again, by turning over the pages right and left, over her head, in her usual mesmeric manner. The passage selected was Joshua, chap. 1st, verses 8, 9. Frequently afterward, by way of test, this bible was given to her to point out this text; and this she invariably did before many persons, without attempting to look at it, but by feeling the pages and

turning them over while the book was over her head. She also told me circumstances connected with the history of that book, which I am positive she could not know by any of the usual means; for some were only known to myself. She was asked to tell by what means she found the passage, as she could not read, and was also in the dark. She replied, that the individuals alluded to, whom she said she saw in their spiritual body, had a similar book, but a larger one, open upon the left arm, and that they pointed with the right hand to the pages, and the same text; that her hands seemed guided in their movements, and when she had got the right place, she could no longer turn the pages, either to the right or to the left! Another instance of a similar kind occurred a few weeks later. After the lapse of some months, she was again tried with the small bible; but having then lost the connecting influence, she could no longer find the passage as she had previously done.

37. The subjects of these trances would afford matter for many pages; but some were of a private character, and, although highly interesting to the parties concerned, would not be interesting to others, except as illustrating the nature of the spirit's home, and some of the general laws by which spiritual associations are regulated. All that she has said tends to confirm the distinction between moral good and moral evil, and the impossibility of those who depart this life in a state of moral evil, attaining hereafter, to a state of moral goodness; in *this respect*, being strikingly dissimilar to the statements of Davis, the American clairvoyant; but who, according to his own subsequent statements, had never been in the state of true spiritual extasis, when he delivered his lectures in the mesmeric state.

38. Her general statements represent man as a spiritual being, rising from the shell of the dead body immediately after death, a perfectly organized existence, and having a complete *sensational perception* of his fellow spiritual beings, and of the beautiful scenery of the spiritual spheres; that is, provided he possessed during his natural life a moral state, in harmony with those spheres. The male and female sex retaining all the characteristcs necessary to a spiritual state of existence, and

living together in a state of angelic union. Those who have been interiorly united here, coming again into a state of union hereafter. She represents male and female spiritual beings, thus united, as appearing at a distance *as one*, and says that they are not called two, nor the married, but *the* ONE. Infants and young children, who have passed from this world by death, are stated to grow to a state of adolescence, but more speedily than in the natural world. During infancy and early childhood, they are confided to the care of good female spirits, or angels, whose delight it is to instruct them by various methods, especially *by representatives of things*. These spiritual spheres, and their spiritual inhabitants, are in close association with us, and exercise an influence over us, although we are unconscious of it. All that is wanted to have a *sensational* knowledge of their existence, is the closing of the external consciousness, and a full awakening of the internal consciousness. In the highest state of trance, she appeared to herself, to be among spiritual beings, as one of themselves; at other times she appeared to them more shadowy. The first receptacle of the departed spirit she describes as a sort of middle place or state, from which the good gradually ascend to higher and more delightful places; those that are the best having higher abodes than the others. All are welcomed by angelic spirits, on their arrival in the spirit-world; but the evil will not associate with the good, and recede of their own accord, more or less rapidly, to darker places below and to the left; but of these darker places, she had not been permitted to know so much as of the abodes of the good.

39. Being asked, in one of these long trances, if she now could explain *how* she saw distant individuals in the mesmeric state; she said, "Yes; I can see how it is now, but I could not before;" and then stated that if spirits wished to see each other, distance is no interruption; and words to the effect that spirits are not subject to our laws of space and time; and that man, *as to his spirit*, is a subject of the laws of the spirit-world, even while united to the natural body. The opening of her spiritual consciousness, gives her a *sensational* perception of the spirits

of all to whom her attention is directed; and thus, however distant the individual, he can be mentally present with her. But this she further represented, as being accomplished by the aid of intermediate associate spirits, by whom the connection is completed; and she further represented every one, as having a connection with the spirit-world *generally*; and a more *particular one*, by means of this associate spirit. Whenever Emma speaks of going into a trance, she always represents it as "*going away*," and "*going a very long way.*" Of any one that is dead, she says, "They have left their shell and gone away," and will never admit that they are dead.

40. In the mesmeric state, Emma represented the fibres of her brain as falling forward, and the hemispheres separating at the top, when she became lucid; and she further said, that a brain capable of these movements was necessary in order to attain a state of lucidity. In one of the spontaneous trances, I asked her if she could see me in the same manner as when mesmerised. She replied, that she had no recollection of the state of her brain while in the mesmeric state; but that in the state she then was, every thing seemed light, or rather was seen in light. She knew that she did not see with the eye, and yet somehow she seemed to use her eyes. She saw me plainly; yet I did not appear as I ordinarily did; she could not explain the difference, only that I appeared light. It appeared to her, that light issued from within, outward. During a subsequent long trance, I inquired whether she could see my lungs then as she had done when mesmerised. She replied in the negative, and said, "I can only see you as a cloud; yet I know it is you."

PRACTICE AND USE OF MESMERISM.

41. The induction of the mesmeric sleep, or the practice of mesmerism as a curative agent, is a very simple process. I am inclined to believe, that the result depends more on the pecu-

liar constitution of the subject, than the power of the mesmeriser. All that is required, is patience, and a proper disposition in both parties. Let the subject sit down in the easiest and most comfortable posture. The operator should be seated in front, and take both hands of his patient in his left hand, placing his right hand on the head. Then gently and slowly continue to make passes forward over the face—the operator looking steadfastly at the eyes of the subject. The room should not be too light, and every thing kept quiet. The subject should keep his eyes fixed on those of the operator, and yield himself unreservedly to his influence. If this course is persevered in for twenty or thirty minutes, some effect will generally be observed; and if the subject is susceptible, probably within five or ten minutes the sleep may be induced. If the front passes do not succeed, then it will be well to try backward passes from the forehead, over the head and partly down the spine, each party steadfastly regarding each other's eyes as before.

42. As a general rule, more striking effects may be expected, when the sleep can be produced; but it must not be forgotten that good may be done where the patient cannot go into the state of coma. Where the object is to relieve pain, first try to produce the coma; but if not practicable, or the patient objects, then simply make passes with both hands *downwards*, slowly and gently, over the parts affected, allowing the fingers lightly to touch the person of the patient, and *well shaking the hands* after each pass. This may be smiled at by the incredulous and inexperienced in these matters; but I have had proof that disease may be put into the system, and transmitted by passes from one subject to another. In cases of what are called nervous headaches, the passes should be made from the forehead over the head to the nape of the neck; and then from the forehead along the base of the brain; that is, just over, and behind the ears and a little way down the neck, and then shake the hands after each pass, as before. This will generally relieve headache in five or ten minutes, if properly performed. No fear need be felt as to the arousing of the patient. Fresh patients will generally awaken spontaneously. But by continued

back and *upward* passes, from the chest over the face and head, or by upwardly fanning the face, the patient will be aroused.

43. The curative influence of mesmerism, as it proceeds primarily from the will of the operator, though generally requiring the proper manipulations to make it susceptible, I propose to call PARAPSYCHEISM, from the Greek words *Parapsyche*, to soothe or comfort, *psyche*, the animal soul or mind.

44. The diseases to which parapsycheism, or the curative influence of mesmerism, may be most beneficially applied, are those of the brain, and nervous and functional diseases. Painful affections of the head, incipient and partial insanity, determinations of blood to the brain, giddiness and stupor, delirium tremens, and other affections of the brain may be, in most cases, speedily relieved by the application of the parapsycheic, or mesmeric influence, especially if combined with proper medical treatment, and due management. But none of the old system of treatment, bleeding and blistering, setoning and purging, must be allowed. The same remark applies to the whole range of neuralgic, and what are called rheumatic affections; and organic, as well as functional diseases of the heart, liver, and lungs. In all painful cases, it would be well to endeavor to bring this soothing influence into operation. No harm will ever be done, if the passes are made in the manner directed, and with a proper feeling and desire to do good. But while censuring the old practice of medicine, in the cases above alluded to, fairness obliges me to say that equal blame attaches to some enthusiastic mesmerists, who, from their partial knowledge are led to despise and misrepresent *all* medical treatment. The very circumstance of true clairvoyants prescribing medicines, proves that those most under its influence perceive mesmerism to be only one among other means of restoring and preserving health.

45. But the full use of mesmerism, as a curative agent, will never be thoroughly known until there are better opportunities for its practice than at present exist. It cannot be expected that medical men should generally be the actual mesmerisers, as they would not be able, except in a few cases, to bestow the

necessary time. It, therefore, requires a class of trained male and female mesmerisers to act under the superintendence of qualified medical practitioners, and perhaps it would be most successfully carried out in establishments similar to Hydropathic Institutions, but more universal in their means of cure.

46. In conclusion, I would observe to those who may read these pages doubtingly—experiment for yourselves, not confining your attention to one or two cases, but patiently investigating wherever opportunity offers; and the probability is, that you will speedily be convinced, by actual observation, of the general truths of mesmerism, and of its efficacy, as an agent for the relief of human affliction.

The following appeared in the LONDON TIMES of September 13, 1849, and has been kindly sent us by WILLIAM TURNER, M.D., of New York.

A STRANGE STORY.

[From the Bolton Chronicle.]

On Saturday, July 14, a letter was received by Messrs. C. R. Arrowsmith & Co., of this town, from Bradford, Yorkshire, containing a Bank of England note for £500, another for £50, and a bill of exchange for £100. These Mr. Arrowsmith handed over, in the regular mode of business, to Mr. William Lomax, his cashier, who took, or sent, as he supposed, the whole to the bank of Bolton, and made an entry accordingly in his cash-book. The bank-book was then at the bank, so that no memorandum of the payment was received or expected. After the expiration of about five weeks, upon comparing the bank-book with the cash-book, it was found that no entry for these sums was in the bank-book. Inquiry was then made at the bank, but nothing was known of the money, nor was there any entry existing in any book or paper there; and, after searching no trace could be found of the missing money. In fact, the parties at the bank denied ever having received the sums, or knowing any thing of the transaction. Before the discovery of the loss the bill had become due, but upon inquiring after the loss was discovered, it was found that it had not been presented for payment. It was, therefore, concluded that as the notes and bill could not be found at the bank, nor any trace or entry connected with them, the probability was that they were lost or stolen, and that the bill had been destroyed to avoid detection. Mr. Lomax had a distinct recollection of having received the notes, etc., from Mr. Arrowsmith, but from the length of time that had elapsed when the loss was discovered, he could not remember what he had done with them—whether he had taken them to the bank, or sent them by the accustomed messenger—nor could the messenger recollect any thing about them.

As might be expected, this unaccountable loss occasioned great anxiety to Mr. Lomax, and in this emergency he applied to a friend, to whom the discovery of Mr. Wood's cash-box was known, to ascertain the probability of the notes, etc., being found by the aid of clairvoyance. The friend replied that he saw no greater difficulty in this case than in Wood's, and recommended him to make the inquiry, which he said he would do, if only for his own satisfaction.

On Friday, August 24, Mr. Lomax, accompanied by Mr. N. Jones, of Ashbourne street, Bolton, called on Mr. Haddock for this purpose. The clairvoyante was put into a psychic state, and then into connection with Mr. Lomax. She directly asked for "the paper," meaning the letter in which the notes and bill were inclosed; but this Mr. Lomax did not appear to have in his possession, and she said she could not tell any thing without it. This sitting, therefore, was so far useless. The next day Mr. Lomax brought the letter, and Mr. Haddock requested that the contents might not be communicated to him, lest it should be supposed that he had suggested any thing to her. After considerable thought, the clairvoyante said that there had been three different papers for money in that letter—not post-office orders, but papers that came out of a place where people kept money in (a bank), and were to be taken to another place of a similar kind; that these papers came in the letter to another gentleman (Mr. Arrowsmith), who gave them to the one present (Mr. Lomax), who put them in a paper, and put them in a red book that wrapped round (a pocket-book). Mr. Lomax then, to the surprise of Mr. Haddock, pulled from his coat-pocket a deep, red pocket-book, made just as she had described it, and said that was the book in which he was in the habit of placing similar papers.

Mr. Lomax said the clairvoyante was right; that the letter contained two Bank of England notes and a bill of exchange; but did not say what was the value of the notes. Mr. Haddock then put a £10 Bank of England note into the clairvoyante's hand. She said that two of the papers were like that, but more valuable, and that the black and white word at the corner was longer. She further said that these notes, etc., were taken to a place where money was kept (a bank), down there (pointing toward Deansgate). Beyond this no further inquiry was made at that sitting.

On Monday, Mr. Lomax called again. The clairvoyante went over the case again, entering more minutely into particulars. She persisted in her former statements, that she could see the "marks" of the notes in the red pocket-book, and could see them in the banking-house; that they were in paper, and put along with many more papers in a part of the bank; that they were taken by a man at the bank, who put them aside without making any entry, or taking any further notice of them. She said that the people at the bank did not mean to do wrong, but that it arose from the want of due attention. Upon its being stated that she might be wrong, and requesting her to look elsewhere, she said that it was no use; that she could see they were in the bank, and no where else; that she could not say any thing else, without saying what was not true; and that if search were made at the bank, there, she said, they would be found. In the evening, Mr. Arrowsmith, Mr. Makant, and Mr. Jones came again, and she was put in a psychic state, to repeat these particulars in their presence, which was done.

Mr. Haddock then said to Mr. Arrowsmith, that he was tolerably confident that the clairvoyante was right, and that he should recommend him to go next day to the bank, and insist on a further search, stating that he felt convinced, from inquiries he had made, that his cashier had brought the money there. Mr. Makant also urged the same course on Mr. Arrowsmith.

The following morning (Tuesday, August 28), Mr. Arrowsmith went to the bank, and insisted on further search. He was told that, after such a search as had been made, it was useless, but that, to satisfy him, it should be made again. Mr. Arrowsmith left for Manchester, and after his departure a further search was made; and among a lot of papers, in an inner room of the bank, which were not likely to have been meddled with again probably for years, or which might never have been noticed again, were found the notes and bill, wrapped in paper, just as the clairvoyante had described them.

Works on Phrenology and Physiognomy,

Published by S. R. WELLS, 389 Broadway, N. Y.

"GOOD BOOKS FOR ALL."—Here are the best Works on these subjects. Each covers ground not covered by others. Copies of one or all will be sent by return post, on receipt of price. Please address as above.

American Phrenological Journal AND LIFE *Illustrated.* Devoted to Ethnology, Physiology, Phrenology, Physiognomy, Psychology, Biography, Education, Art, Literature, with Measures to Reform, Elevate and Improve Mankind Physically, Mentally and Spiritually. Edited by S. R. WELLS. Published monthly, in octavo form, at $3 a year in advance, or 30 cents a number.

Annuals of Phrenology and PHYSIOGNOMY. One yearly 12mo volume. Price 25 cents for the current year. For 1865, '66, '67, '68, '69, '70, '71. The seven containing over four hundred pages, many portraits and biographies of distinguished personages, together with articles on "How to Study Phrenology," "Bashfulness, Diffidence, Stammering," "The Marriage of Cousins," "Jealousy, Its Cause and Cure," etc. The seven bound in one volume, muslin, $1.50.

Constitution of Man. Considered in relation to External Objects. By GEORGE COMBE. The only authorized American Edition. With Twenty Engravings, and a Portrait of the Author. Muslin, $1.75.

Chart of Physiognomy Illustrated. Designed for Framing and for Lecturers. Map form. 25 cents.

Defence of Phrenology; Containing an Essay on the Nature and Value of Phrenological Evidence. A Vindication of Phrenology against the Attacks of its opponents, and a View of the Facts relied on by Phrenologists as proof that the Cerebellum is the seat of the reproductive instinct. By BOARDMAN. $1.50.

Domestic Life, Thoughts on; or, Marriage Vindicated and Free Love Exposed. By N. SIZER. 25 cents.

Education: Its elementary Principles founded on the Nature of Man. By J. G. SPURZHEIM, M.D. With an Appendix, containing the Temperaments, and a Brief Analysis of the Faculties. An excellent work. *Illustrated.* $1.50.

Education and Self-Improvement COMPLETE. Comprising Physiology—Animal and Mental; Self-Culture and Perfection of Character; including the Management of Youth; Memory and Intellectual Improvement. Complete in one large 12mo vol. Muslin, $4.00.

How to Read Character. A New Illustrated Hand-Book of Phrenology and Physiognomy, for Students and Examiners, with a Chart for recording the sizes of the different Organs of the Brain, in the Delineation of Character, with upwards of 170 Engravings. Latest and best. Paper, $1. Muslin, $1.25.

Memory and Intellectual Improvement, applied to Cultivation of Memory. Very useful. $1.50.

Lectures on Phrenology. By GEORGE COMBE. With Notes. An Essay on the Phrenological Mode of Investigation, and a Historical Sketch. By BOARDMAN, M.D. 1 vol. 12mo. $1.75.

Mental Science. Lectures on, according to the Philosophy of Phrenology. Delivered before the Anthropological Society. By G. S. WEAVER. $1.50.

Moral Philosophy. By GEORGE COMBE. Or, the Duties of Man considered in his Individual, Domestic and Social Capacities. From the Edinburgh Edition. With the Author's latest corrections. $1.75.

Natural Laws of Man. Questions with Answers. A Capital Work. By J. G. Spurzheim, M.D. Muslin, 75 cents.

New Physiognomy; or, Signs of Character, as manifested through Temperament and External Forms, and especially in the "Human Face Divine." With more than One Thousand *Illustrations.* By S. R. WELLS. In three styles of binding. Price, in one 12mo volume, 768 pp., handsomely bound in muslin, $5; in heavy calf, marbled edges, $8; turkey morocco, full gilt, $10.

Phrenology and the Scriptures. Harmony between Phrenology and Bible. By JOHN PIERPONT. 25 cents.

Phrenological Busts. Showing the latest classification, and exact locations of the Organs of the Brain, fully developed, designed for Learners. In this Bust, all the newly-discovered Organs are given. It is divided so as to show each Individual Organ on one side; and all the groups—Social, Executive, Intellectual, and Moral—properly classified, on the other side. There are two sizes, the largest is sold in box, at $2.00. The smaller, at $1.00. Sent by express.

Phrenology Proved, Illustrated and Applied. Embracing an Analysis of the Primary Mental Powers in their Various Degrees of Development, and Location of the Phrenological Organs. *Illustrated.* $1.75.

Self-Culture and Perfection of CHARACTER; Including the Training and Management of Children. $1.50.

Self-Instructor in Phrenology AND PHYSIOLOGY. With over One Hundred Engravings and a Chart for Phrenologists, for the Recording of Phrenological Developments. Paper, 50 cents. Muslin, 75 cents.

Symbolical Head and Phrenological Map, on fine tinted paper, for Framing. 25 cents.

Wells' New Descriptive Chart for Use of Examiners, giving a Delineation of Character. 25 cents.

Your Character from Your LIKENESS. For particulars, how to have pictures taken, inclose stamp for a copy of "Mirror of the Mind."

To Physicians, Lecturers, and EXAMINERS. We have a Cabinet of 40 Casts of Heads, selected from Our Museum, which are sold at $35.00. Also a set of Phrenological Drawings, on canvas, size of life, 40 in number. price $40.00. A set of six Anatomical and Physiological plates, colored and mounted, $20. Another set of twenty, in sheets, plain, $35. Colored and mounted, $60. Skeletons, from $40 to $60. Manikins, $250 to $1000. Portraits in oil from $5 upwards. Woodcuts, $3.50 to $5. Symbolical Heads, Electrotypes, $3 to $5, and $7.50, according to size.

All Works pertaining to the "SCIENCE OF MAN," including Phrenology, Physiognomy, Ethnology, Psychology, Physiology, Anatomy, Hygiene, Dietetics, etc., supplied. Enclose stamp for Wholesale Terms to Agents. Address S. R. WELLS, 389 Broadway, New York.

Works on Physiology and Hygiene.

[It has been said that, a man at Forty Years of Age, is either a "Physician or a Fool." That at this Age, he ought to know how to treat, and take care of himself. These Works are intended to give instruction on "How to Live," How to avoid Diseases and of Premature Decay. They are practical, adapted to both People and Profession.]

Anatomical and Physiological PLATES Arranged expressly for Lectures on Health, Physiology, etc. By R. T. Trall, M. D. They are six in number, representing the normal position and life-size of all the internal viscera, magnified illustrations of the organs of the special senses, and a view of the nerves, arteries, veins, muscles, etc. Fully colored, backed, and mounted on rollers. Price for the set, net $20.

Avoidable Causes of Disease, INSANITY, AND DEFORMITY, including Marriage and its Violations. By Dr. John Ellis. $2.

Children, their Management in Health and Disease. A Descriptive and Practical Work. By Dr. Shew. $1.75.

Diseases of the Throat and LUNGS. With Treatment. 25 cents.

Domestic Practice of Hydropathy, with a form of a Report for the assistance of Patients in consulting their Physicians. By E. Johnson, M. D. $2.

Family Gymnasium. Containing the most improved methods of applying Gymnastic, Calisthenic, Kinesipathic, and Vocal Exercises, to the Development of the Bodily Organs. By. Dr. Trall. Many *Illustrations.* $1.75.

Food and Diet. With observations on the Dietical Regimen suited for Disordered States of the Digestive Organs. Dietaries of the Principal Metropolitan Establishments for Lunatics, Criminals, Children, the Sick, Paupers, etc. A thorough scientific Work. By Jonathan Pereira, M. D., F. R. S. and L. S. Edited by Charles A. Lee, M. D. $1.75.

Fruits and Farinacea, the PROPER FOOD OF MAN. Vegetarian. By John Smith. With Notes and *Illustrations.* By R. T. Trall, M.D. Muslin, $1.75.

Hydropathic Cook Book. With Recipes for Cooking on Hygienic Principles. By Dr. Trall. $1.50.

Hydropathic Encyclopedia. A System of Hydropathy and Hygiene Embracing Outlines of Anatomy; Physiology of the Human Body; Hygienic Agencies, and the Preservation of Health; Theory and Practice; Special Pathology, including the Nature, Causes, Symptoms, and Treatment of all known Diseases. Designed as a Guide to Families and Students, and a Text-Book for Physicians. By R. T. Trall, M.D. $4.50. The most complete Work on the subject.

Family Physician. A Ready Prescriber and Hygienic Adviser. With Reference to the Nature, Causes, Prevention, and Treatment of Diseases, Accidents, and casualties of every kind. With a Glossary, and Copious Index. By Joel Shew, M.D. Muslin, $4.

Management of Infancy, Physiological and Moral Treatment. By Andrew Combe, M.D. With Notes and a Supplementary Chapter. Muslin, $1.50.

Midwifery and the Diseases of WOMEN. A Descriptive and Practical Work. With the general management of Child Birth, Nursery, etc. $1.75.

Movement-Cure. An Exposition of the Swedish Movement-Cure. Embracing the History and Philosophy of this System of Medical Treatment, with Examples of Movements, and Directions for their Use in Various Forms of Chronic Diseases. *Illustrated.* By George H. Taylor, M.D. Muslin, $1.75.

Notes on Beauty, Vigor and Development; or, How to Acquire Plumpness of Form, Strength of Limb, and Beauty of Complexion. 12 cents.

Physiology of Digestion. Considered with relation to the Principles of Dietetics. By Andrew Combe, D.M. *Illustrated.* 50 cents.

Philosophy of the Water-Cure. A Development of the true Principles of Health and Longevity. By John Balbirnie, M.D. 50 cents.

Practice of the Water Cure. Containing a Detailed account of the various Baiting processes. 50 cents.

Physiology, Animal and Mental: Applied to the Preservation and Restoration of Health of Body and Power of Mind. *Illustrated.* Muslin, $1.50.

Principles of Physiology applied to the Preservation of Health and to the Improvement of Physical and Mental Education. By Andrew Combe. $1.75.

Science of Human Life, Lectures on THE. By Sylvester Graham. With a copious Index and Biographical Sketch. of the Author. *Illustrated.* $3.50.

Sober and Temperate Life. The Discourses and Letters of Louis Cornaro. With a Biography of the Author, who died at 150 years of age. 50 cents.

Tea and Coffee, their Physical, Intellectual, and Moral Effects on the System. By Dr. Alcott, 25 cents.

The Alcoholic Controversy. A Review of the *Westminster Review* on the Physiological Errors of Teetotalism. By Dr. Trall. 50 cents.

The Story of a Stomach. By a Reformed Dyspeptic. Paper, 50 cents; muslin, 75 cents.

Three Hours' School a Day. A Serious Talk with Parents. By William L. Crandal. Muslin, $1.50.

Water-Cure in Chronic Diseases. An Exposition of the Causes, Progress and Terminations of Various Chronic Diseases of the Digestive Organs, Lungs, Nerves, and Skin, and of their Treatment. With engraved View of the Lungs, Heart, Stomach, and Bowels. By J. M. Gully, M.D. $2.

"A Special List" of 70 or more Private Medical, Surgical and Anatomical Works, invaluable to those who need them, sent on receipt of stamp. Address S. R. Wells, 389 Broadway, New York.

The READER will greatly oblige by exhibiting this CATALOGUE to a neighbor, who would, perhaps, be glad to procure some of the Works; or, would like to become a subscriber to the ILLUSTRATED PHRENOLOGICAL JOURNAL, or engage in the sale of these publications.

Works for Home Improvement.

This List embraces just such Works as are suited to every member of the family— old and young. These Works will serve as guides in Self-Improvement, and are almost indispensable to those who have not the advantages of a liberal education.

Aims and Aids for Girls and Young WOMEN, on the various Duties of Life, Physical, Intellectual, and Moral, Self-Culture, Improvement, Dress, Beauty, Employment, the Home Relations, Duties to Young Men, Marriage, Womanhood, and Happiness. By Rev. G. S. Weaver. Muslin, $1.50.

Æsop's Fables. The People's Pictorial Edition. Beautifully illustrated with nearly Sixty Engravings. Cloth, gilt, beveled boards. Only $1.

Benny. An Illustrated Poem. By Anna Chambers Ketchum. Published in the elegant style of Enoch Arden. A beautiful Christmas present. $1.50.

Chemistry, and its application to Physiology, Agriculture, and Commerce. By Liebig. 50 cents.

Footprints of Life; or, Faith and Nature Reconciled. A Poem in Three Parts. The Body. The Soul. The Deity. By Philip Harvey, M.D. $1.25.

Fruit Culture for the Million. A Hand-Book. Being a Guide to the Cultivation and Management of Fruit Trees. Descriptions of the Best Varieties, and How to Propagate them. *Illus.* $1.

Good Man's Legacy. A Sermon by Rev. Dr. Osgood. 25 cents. **Gospel Among the Animals;** or, Christ with the Cattle. Same. 25 cents.

Hand-Book for Home Improvement: comprising "How to Write," "How to Talk," "How to Behave," and "How to do Business," in one vol. $2.25.

How to Live; Saving and Wasting, or, Domestic Economy made plain. By Solon Robinson. $1.50.

Home for All; The Concrete, or Gravel Wall. New, Cheap, Superior Mode of Building. $1.50.

Hopes and Helps for the Young of BOTH SEXES, Relating to the Formation of Character, Choice of Avocation, Health, Conversation, Cultivation of Intellect, Moral Sentiment, Social Affection, Courtship and Marriage. By Weaver. $1.50.

Library of Mesmerism and Psychology. Comprising the Philosophy of Mesmerism, Clairvoyance, and Mental Electricity; Fascination, or the Power of Charming; The Macrocosm, or the World of Sense; Electrical Psychology, the Doctrine of Impressions; The Science of the Soul, treated Physiologically and Philosophically. One large vol. Illustrated. Muslin, $4.00.

Life at Home; or, The Family and its Members. A capital work. By William Aikman, D.D. $1.50; gilt, $2.

Life in the West; or, Stories of the Mississippi Valley. Where to buy Public Lands. By N. C. Meeker. $2.

Man, in Genesis and in Geology; or the Biblical Account of Man's Creation, tested by Scientific Theories of his Origin and Antiquity. By Joseph P. Thompson, D.D., LL.D. One vol. $1.

Pope's Essay on Man. With Notes. Beautifully Illustrated. Cloth, gilt, beveled boards. Best edition. $1.

Oratory—Sacred and Secular; or, the Extemporaneous Speaker. Including Chairman's Guide for conducting Public Meetings according to the best Parliamentary forms. By Wm. Pittenger. $1.50.

Temperance in Congress. Ten Minutes' Speeches delivered in the House of Representatives. 25 cents.

The Christian Household. Embracing the Christian Home, Husband, Wife, Father, Mother, Child, Brother, and Sister. By Rev. G. S. Weaver. $1.

The Emphatic Diaglott; or, The New Testament in Greek and English. Containing the Original Greek Text of the New Testament, with an Interlineary Word-for-Word English Translation. A work for Students in Theology, and S. S. Teachers. By Benjamin Wilson. Price, $4, extra fine binding, $5.

The Planchette Mystery; An Inquiry into the Nature, Origin, Import, and Tendencies of Modern Signs and Wonders. How to Work Planchette. 25c.

The Right Word in the Right Place. A New Pocket Dictionary and Reference Book. Embracing Synonyms, Technical Terms, Abbreviations, Foreign Phrases, Writing for the Press, Punctuation, Proof-Reading, and other Valuable Information. Cloth, 75 cents.

The Temperance Reformation. Its History from the first Temperance Society in the United States. By Rev. J. Armstrong. With Portrait. $1.50.

Ways of Life, showing the Right Way and the Wrong Way. By Rev. G. S. Weaver. Muslin, $1.

Weaver's Works for the Young. Comprising "Hopes and Helps for the Young of both Sexes," "Aims and Aids for Girls and Young Women," "Ways of Life; or, the Right Way and the Wrong Way." A great work. $3.

Wedlock; or, the Right Relations of the Sexes. Disclosing the Laws of Conjugal Selection, and showing who may and who may not Marry. For both Sexes. By S. R. Wells. Plain, $1.50; gilt, $2.

Capital Punishment; or, the Proper Treatment of Criminals. Single copies, 10 cents. **Education of the Heart.** By Hon. Schuyler Colfax. 10 cents. **Father Mathew,** the Temperance Apostle, his Portrait, Character, and Biography. 10 cents.

We have all works on Phonography and a large stock of Mechanical and Scientific Books for sale. Any book wherever published may be ordered at advertised price, and will be promptly sent, by return post, from this office. English, French, Spanish and German Works, imported to order. Agents wanted. Address, S. R. WELLS, 389 Broadway, N. Y.

CPSIA information can be obtained
at www.ICGtesting.com
Printed in the USA
LVHW061456310120
645464LV00002B/2